LENSEN

The Strange Neutrality

OTHER BOOKS BY GEORGE ALEXANDER LENSEN

Report from Hokkaido: The Remains of Russian Culture in Northern Japan

Russia's Japan Expedition of 1852 to 1855

The Russian Push Toward Japan; Russo-Japanese Relations, 1697–1875

*The World Beyond Europe: An Introduction to the History
of Africa, India, Southeast Asia, and the Far East*

Russia's Eastward Expansion (edited)

Revelations of a Russian Diplomat: The Memoirs of Dmitrii I. Abrikossow
(edited)

*Korea and Manchuria Between Russia and Japan 1895–1904:
The Observations of Sir Ernest Satow, British Minister to Japan and China*
(edited)

The Soviet Union: An Introduction

*The d'Anethan Dispatches From Japan 1894–1910. The Observations
of Baron Albert d'Anethan, Belgian Minister Plenipotentiary
and Dean of the Diplomatic Corps* (translated and edited)

The Russo-Chinese War

*Trading under Sail off Japan, 1860–99. The Recollections of Captain
John Baxter Will, Sailing-Master and Pilot* (edited)

Faces of Japan: A Photographic Study

Russian Diplomatic and Consular Officials in East Asia. A Handbook
(compiled)

Japanese Diplomatic and Consular Officials in Russia. A Handbook
(compiled)

April in Russia: A Photographic Study

*Japanese Recognition of the U.S.S.R.; Soviet-Japanese
Relations, 1921–1930*

*War and Revolution: Excerpts from the Letters and Diaries of the
Countess Olga Poutiatine* (translated and edited)

The
Strange Neutrality

Soviet-Japanese Relations during
the Second World War
1941-1945

George Alexander Lensen

THE DIPLOMATIC PRESS
TALLAHASSEE, FLORIDA

PUBLISHED BY

THE DIPLOMATIC PRESS, INC.

1102 Betton Road

Tallahassee, Florida 32303

© 1972 by George Alexander Lensen

Library of Congress Catalog Card No. 72–178091

ISBN 910512–14–0

PRINTED AND BOUND IN THE UNITED STATES

ROSE PRINTING COMPANY, INC., TALLAHASSEE

To Rumochka

Preface

The making of the Pacific War and diplomatic and political maneuvers during the conflict have been the subject of mounting interest in recent years. Spates of books have been written on American relations with Japan and China, on American relations with the U.S.S.R., and on East Asian international relations in general. Reference is made in these books to Soviet dealings with Japan, yet generally *en passant*. There are a number of studies of Soviet-Japanese relations and of German-Japanese-Soviet relations prior to the outbreak of the Pacific War and of Soviet-Japanese relations since the war. This is the first work to focus on the wartime dealings of Japan and the U.S.S.R., which maintained a strange neutrality between 1941 and 1945, while their allies were fighting each other and they themselves were at war with each other's allies.

As Japan is once again becoming Nippon, nationalist demands for the recovery of territory become louder. With the return of Okinawa by the United States, clamor for the retrocession of the Kuril Islands is on the increase. There is talk of the "illegality" of the Yalta Agreement and of the "treacherous violation" of the Neutrality Pact by the Soviet Union, whose entry into the Pacific War is likened to the appearance of "a thief at a fire."

I have tried to reconstruct the story of Soviet-Japanese relations during the Second World War as it actually unfolded at the time, rather than as it appears through the prism of later events. Warily winding my way through conflicting Japanese and Soviet sources, I have sought to tread a factual path, leaving my own reflections to a separate chapter.

Japanese and Chinese personal names have been rendered in Asian fashion, surname first. They have been Romanized in accordance with the Kenkyūsha and Wade-Giles systems respectively. Although Soviet sources limit given names to initials, I prefer full names and have supplied them, where possible, but for the sake of readability I have relegated patronymics to the index. Russian names have been transliterated in Library of Congress style. In citing place names, particularly of regions which have changed hands repeatedly, I have found the problem of spelling to be complicated by the fact that there are often two or more appellations for the same place. In making my selection, I was guided solely by the thought, which name would be most familiar to the American reader. My use of a Russian, Japanese or Chinese form, as the case may be, should not be interpreted as an endorsement on my part of any claim that the Soviet Union, Japan or China may have to a particular place.

I am indebted to Mr. Baba Akira of the Kokumin Gaikō Kaikan (The Association for [the Japanese] People's Foreign Policy) for directing my attention to the classified material pertaining to Soviet-Japanese relations during the Second World War in the Japanese Foreign Office Archives and to Mr. Suzuki Tatsurō of the Foreign Office for granting me access to the classified data. Without their kindness this book would not have been written. I am thankful also to many Japanese, Soviet, American, and English diplomats, colleagues and friends for sharing with me their diverse views on the nature of Soviet-Japanese-American relations. My prolonged stays in Japan and my visits to the Soviet Union would not have been possible without a senior fellowship from the National Endowment for the Humanities in 1967–68 and a faculty development grant and a Research Council subsidy from the Florida State University in 1968–69. *Dōmo arigatō gozaimashita!*

GEORGE ALEXANDER LENSEN

Tallahassee, Florida
January, 1972

Contents

ILLUSTRATIONS AND MAPS
(after page 84)

Japanese Concessions on North Sakhalin

Signing of the Neutrality Pact

Stalin and Matsuoka, Arm-in-Arm

"The Last Fragment of the Fascist Axis"

"Fire-Extinguishing Measures"

The Manchurian Campaign

Negotiating the Capitulation of the Kwantung Army

Signing of the Instrument of Japan's Surrender by Lieutenant General Derevianko

It is, to say the least, singular that our diplomatic vista should have been limited to that very Soviet Russia which our leaders secretly distrusted so. In the first stages of the war we vainly tried to establish a working partnership among the four powers and thereby create a common front between the Axis powers and the Soviet Union. In the middle stages we attempted a Russo-German mediation in order to avert a German defeat. In the final stages, to save our own situation we tried to curry favor with the Kremlin. Thus throughout the Pacific war our main diplomatic endeavors were concentrated upon Moscow, creating a sort of habit of mind which, I think, partly explains why we chose the Soviet government as the channel for addressing the Allied powers prior to our surrender.

—Kase Toshikazu

If Soviet-American relations during the war were called 'the Strange Alliance," Soviet-Japanese relations during the war should be termed 'the Strange Neutrality.'

—Hagiwara Tōru

1

Negotiation of the Neutrality Pact

The Manchurian Incident of 1931 impaired Japanese relations with the Soviet Union. The invasion of Manchuria brought Japanese troops within striking distance of the Soviet frontier. The Russians, from whose soil Japanese forces had withdrawn reluctantly less than a decade before, feared the repetition of a Japanese invasion. They hastened military preparations in the Soviet Far East and at the same time proposed the conclusion of a nonaggression pact between the Soviet Union and Japan. The Japanese declined, stating that there was no need for a nonaggression pact; the Basic Convention of 1925 between the U.S.S.R. and Japan and the treaty outlawing war (the Briand-Kellogg Pact to which Japan and the Soviet Union had both subscribed) were sufficient guarantee of peace between the two countries.

Japan's decision to make common cause with Nazi Germany, the virulent enemy of the U.S.S.R., in the Anti-Comintern Pact of 1936 heightened Soviet apprehensions. By the time a series of border clashes occurred, the Soviets were well prepared. On a strategic island in the Amur River just south of Blagoveshchensk in 1937, at Changkufeng near Lake Khasan in 1938, and finally at Nomonhan on the Manchurian-Mongolian frontier in the summer of 1939, where both sides committed sizeable forces supported by tanks and aircraft, the Red Army turned back the Japanese with heavy losses. At the same time the Russians put economic pressure on Japan by refusing to conclude a new, basic fishery treaty and by hindering the exploitation of the Japanese concessions on North Sakhalin.

While Japanese inroads into Manchuria in 1931 had reversed the trend toward more amicable relations between the U.S.S.R. and Japan, the bloody battles of Nomonhan paradoxically turned relations back on a more friendly course. The Soviet Union's successful defense of her frontier calmed Soviet apprehensions at the same time that it impressed on the Japanese that diplomatic measures might be less costly and more effective in resolving questions at issue between the two powers.[1]

Japan and the Soviet Union took advantage of the termination of the Nomonhan incident—a cease-fire was negotiated on September 15, 1939—to discuss the establishment of commissions for the demarcation of the frontiers between Manchukuo and the U.S.S.R. and between Manchukuo and Mongolia and for dealing with disputes that might arise; conferences were initiated also concerning fisheries, concessions and trade. The outbreak of war between Germany, France and England in September 1939 made it desirable for the Soviet Union to come to an agreement with Japan, yet the border question was complicated, and nothing came of the establishment of the border commissions even though Foreign Minister Arita Hachirō told the Soviet ambassador that "the result of the conclusion of an agreement on the boundary question with the U.S.S.R. will be analogous to the result of the conclusion of a nonaggression pact with the U.S.S.R."[2] Nor did the trade negotiations that took place in Moscow from January to April 1940 bear fruit.[3]

Meanwhile the Japanese war machine had bogged down in China in the wake of the China Incident of 1937, and Japanese relations with the United States were deteriorating rapidly. In order to improve her international position so as to be able to take advantage of the changing world order, Japan had to reach an agreement with the Soviet Union, which had shown her strength at Nomonhan. Since the traditional Japanese policy of dealing with separate issues was unsuccessful even in the relatively amicable atmosphere of post-Nomonhan negotiations, the administration of Premier Yonai Mitsumasa decided to try a new approach—to propose a general political agreement. It determined not to compromise the posture of Japanese nonintervention in the European war, lest fear of Japanese support of the Axis powers complicate relations with the United States and Great Britain; at the same time it hoped to induce the Soviet Union to discontinue her aid to Chiang Kai-shek and thus weaken Chinese resistance to Japan. But the Yonai administration was unwilling to commit Japan to a nonaggression pact, desired by the Soviet Union and recommended by Tōgō Shigenori, the Japanese ambassador in Moscow.

In Tōgō's view American policy made a Japanese-

Soviet rapproachement necessary. Not only did the United States increasingly support Chiang Kai-shek and refuse to continue vital commercial relations with Japan in an attempt to force her to withdraw her troops from China, but also was drawing closer to the Soviet Union in her anti-Japanese stance. The conclusion of a nonaggression pact and a commercial agreement with the Soviet Union, Tōgō believed, would undermine the American position and prod Chiang into making a "reasonable" settlement with Japan. (Tōgō was not motivated by friendly feelings toward the Soviet Union; he did not think of a Japanese-Soviet rapproachement as something positive so much as a step against the United States and Great Britain.) But Tōgō's recommendation had not been heeded by the administration of Premier Abe Nobuyuki any more than it was heeded by that of Yonai, even though Tōgō sent First Secretary Saitō Kiurō to Tokyo to plead with Foreign Minister Arita and with persons outside the cabinet, influential in Soviet affairs. The Yonai government instructed him to negotiate merely a neutrality pact.

On July 2, 1940, Ambassador Tōgō orally broached the conclusion of a neutrality pact for a period of five years to Viacheslav Molotov, commissar of foreign affairs. Tōgō proposed that Japan and the U.S.S.R. reaffirm the convention of 1925, whereby they had established diplomatic relations, as the basis of Soviet-Japanese dealings, that they pledge the maintenance of peaceful relations and respect for each other's territorial integrity, and that they promise to observe neutrality in the event that either of them were attacked by a third power.

Molotov's immediate reaction was that the proposal benefitted solely Japan. While such a pact would strengthen Japan's hand in China and facilitate a Japanese thrust into Southeast Asia, it would merely embarrass the Soviet Union in her relations with China and the United States. Molotov did not mean by this that the U.S.S.R. would not sign any agreement that might complicate her dealings with China and the United States—and this would have been the case with any political agreement between her and Japan—but that she would do so only for sufficient reason. If Japan was unwilling to commit herself to a nonaggression pact that would have secured the Soviet Union's eastern borders, she must give some other compensation to justify signature of a neutrality pact.

On August 14 Molotov spelled out the Russian position in writing. The Soviet Union was prepared to conclude a neutrality pact if it were made equally profitable for the U.S.S.R. She wanted the convention of 1925 modified before reaffirming it as the basis of Soviet-Japanese relations. She found several points outdated, notably its recognition of the Treaty of Portsmouth, which had ended the Russo-Japanese War of 1904–1905. The Soviet Union alleged that there had been serious violations of the terms of the Treaty of Portsmouth by the Japanese and that the extent to which its provisions should remain in effect must be reconsidered. Above all, the Soviet Union demanded the liquidation of the Japanese coal and oil concessions on North Sakhalin, contracted in December 1925, offering to pay fair compensation to the concession holders and to supply the Japanese government with 100,000 tons of North Sakhalin oil over a period of five years.[a]

[a] Molotov argued that the concessions had in fact ceased to exist; some had never been exploited at all, others had been closed down and the

Even before receipt of the written note, Ambassador Tōgō had understood from his conversation with Molotov that the surrender of the concessions would be demanded. Indeed, he had given the matter much thought and favored the liquidation of the concessions, which had cost the Japanese government a great deal of money and had been a constant source of friction between the two countries. In return, he believed, the Soviets might agree to stop aiding Chiang Kai-shek, an important consideration for Japan.[4]

Meanwhile the Yonai administration, to whose proposal Molotov replied, had been displaced by the government of Prince Konoe Fumimaro, which joined Germany and Italy in the Tripartite Pact in September.[5] In so doing, Japan shed her reluctance to complicate relations with the United States and Great Britain; at the same time she deemed it advisable now to conclude a Japanese-Soviet nonaggression pact, which she had spurned earlier. As one Japanese newspaper put it: "If Japan wants to advance in the South, she must be free of apprehensions in the North."[6,b]

During his first meeting with the Soviet ambassador, Konstantin Smetanin, on July 27, the new Japanese foreign minister, Matsuoka Yōsuke, had dwelled on the noble qualities of the Slavic soul and on the spiritual affinity of the Russians with the Ainu, the proto-white

---

Japanese had not carried out the stipulated explorations. It was evident, he asserted, that the oil and coal concessions were economically unprofitable and were merely a source of friction between the two countries. For details about the Basic Convention of 1925 and the granting of the oil and coal concessions, see George Alexander Lensen, *Japanese Recognition of the U.S.S.R.; Soviet-Japanese Relations, 1921–1930* (Tallahassee: Diplomatic Press, 1970).

[b] Diehard anti-Communists remained unalterably opposed to the conclusion of a nonaggression pact with the Soviet Union, voicing the fear, as General Araki Sadao did, that it might undermine the ideological foundations of Japan. [7]

aborigines of Japan. Receiving the ambassador in a room decorated with Russian paintings, he had spoken of his love for the Russian people and his understanding of Russian ways, reminding Smetanin that he had studied the Russian language during his service in St. Petersburg as second secretary of the Japanese embassy before the revolution (in 1913) and that he had been in the Soviet Union in 1932 and had conferred with Maksim Litvinov, then the commissar of foreign affairs, following the Soviet proposal of a nonaggression pact. A week later, on August 3, Matsuoka had again assured Smetanin of his goodwill toward Russia and had asserted that he had worked for the past thirty years to improve relations between Japan and the Soviet Union. On August 24 he had declared that he was following in the footsteps of Baron Gotō Shimpei, who had been the driving force in Japanese recognition of the U.S.S.R., and that he had appealed to his government in 1932 for plenary powers to comclude the nonaggression pact desired by the Soviet Union. Asking Smetanin to convey his feelings to Moscow, Matsuoka had alleged that he had met with Soviet ambassadors in Tokyo even when it had been physically dangerous for him to do so. "I was an advocate of a rapprochement with the U.S.S.R. even when all countries were against it," Matsuoka had insisted.[8,c]

Matsuoka had appointed Tatekawa Yoshitsugu in place of Tōgō as ambassador to Moscow. The Soviet government expressed alarm at this, for it regarded Tatekawa, a lieutenant general, as strongly anti-Soviet.

---

[c] Referring to the purge of Foreign Office personnel he had carried out as "the destruction of the Ministry of Foreign Affairs," Matsuoka called himself a "revolutionary." [9] He did not mention, of course, that the dismissed officials had been opponents of his projected alliance with Nazi Germany! [10]

But Matsuoka assured Smetanin on October 1 that Tatekawa was a close acquaintance and would speak the the same as he. Asserting that Tatekawa too was an advocate of a rapprochement with the U.S.S.R., Matsuoka declared: "I would like with the service of this ambassador to open a new page in the relations of our countries."[11,d]

On October 30 Tatekawa presented to Foreign Commissar Molotov the draft of a nonaggression pact. Its main provisions were that Japan and the Soviet Union were to pledge respect for each other's territory and not to invade each other singly or in combination with one or more powers; in the event that either of them was attacked, the other was to refrain from extending any support to the aggressors; and neither Japan nor the Soviet Union would join any coalition of powers that worked against the other directly or indirectly. The pact was to be signed for a period of ten years.[13]

Molotov responded that the Soviet government could not conclude a nonaggression pact until outstanding issues had been resolved. He told Tatekawa that this had been made clear to his predecessor.[14]

Hypocritical as the Japanese proposal for a nonaggression pact with the U.S.S.R. may sound in view of Japan's partnership in the Rome-Berlin-Tokyo Axis, which though directed primarily against the United States was also an outgrowth of the Anti-Comintern Pact, serious thought was being given at that time in Germany and Japan to the inclusion of the Soviet Union in a Rome-Berlin-Moscow-Tokyo Axis—a totalitarian front against the democracies. As a matter of

---

[d] As a token of the new spirit, the Japanese-Soviet Society, which had been disbanded in 1939, was revived in September, with Matsuoka as one of its members. [12]

fact, when the Tripartite Pact had been negotiated, Germany had promised Japan to use her good offices to improve Soviet-Japanese relations. The German Foreign Minister Joachim von Ribbentrop desired a resolution of Japanese-Soviet differences and the extrication of Japan from the China embroilment in order to permit Japanese support of Germany and Italy in the war against Great Britain.

Taking advantage of the offer of mediation, the Japanese government conveyed the text of the above-mentioned draft of a Japanese-Soviet nonaggression pact to Ribbentrop through Ambassador Kurusu Saburō prior to a visit by Molotov to Berlin in mid-November, and asked Germany not only to urge the Soviets to sign a nonaggression pact, but also to prevail upon them, singly or jointly with Germany, to advise Chiang Kai-shek to come to terms with Japan. Tokyo also asked Berlin to arrange a meeting between Kurusu and Molotov for a discussion of the Ribbentrop plan, which divided much of the world among Germany, Italy, Japan and the Soviet Union. The projected secret agreement was designed to prevent a clash between the expanding powers: it allocated to Germany, Central Africa; to Italy, North Africa; to Japan, the South Pacific; and to the Soviet Union, Iran and India.

There is no record of a meeting between Kurusu and Molotov. The Japanese government concurred with the Ribbentrop plan and was informed by Ribbentrop personally that Molotov too had reacted favorably.[15] But in point of fact, though Molotov had listened patiently to Ribbentrop's offer of German assistance in the improvement of Japanese-Soviet relations during his stay in Berlin from November 10 to 14, he had remained unconvinced by Hitler's boasts of victory and had deftly evaded committing himself or the Soviet Union.[16,e]

On his return from Berlin, Molotov received Tatekawa on November 18. Referring to his conversation with Ribbentrop, he stated that he appreciated Japan's desire to adjust relations with the U.S.S.R., but asserted that Soviet public opinion could not conceive of a nonaggression pact that did not incorporate the reversion of territory lost by Russia in the Far East, namely South Sakhalin and the Kuril Islands.[f] Since it did not expect Japan to agree to this, the Soviet government had drawn up a proposal for a neutrality pact, which, he said, would cost the Japanese merely their concessions on North Sakhalin, which they had not been exploiting for some time.

Like the neutrality pact proposed orally by Tōgō in July, the Soviet version encompassed mutual respect for each other's territory and neutrality in the event of attack by one or more other powers. Like the former it was to run for five years, but was to be renewed automatically for another half-a-decade if neither signatory gave notice of cancellation during the fifth year. Unlike the Japanese draft, the Soviet text made no mention of the convention of 1925 and was accompanied by a draft agreement for the liquidation of the oil and coal concessions on Sakhalin.

[e] As Dr. Theo Sommer has put it colorfully, Molotov "met the victory fanfares of the German Führer with skeptical irony and deftly evaded the invitation to the international *Vierer-Tanz ins Blaue* [dance of the four into the blue]."

[f] It is significant in retrospect that Molotov said "the Kuril Islands" rather than "the Northern Kuril Islands," even though only the latter had been bartered away in 1875 in exchange for South Sakhalin, which the Japanese had taken back in 1905 as the result of their victory in the Russo-Japanese War. The "return" of the entire archipelago thus was part of Soviet thinking long before the question of Soviet entry into the Pacific War, in fact before the outbreak of the war.

The Soviet Union, as Molotov had written in August, promised to pay fair compensation to the lease holders and to supply Japan with oil. At the time he had spoken in terms of 100,000 tons of Sakhalin oil over a period of five years; the draft agreement now offered 100,000 tons a year for five years on a regular commercial basis.[17]

When Foreign Minister Matsuoka was informed of the renewed Soviet demand that Japan abandon the concessions, he instructed Tatekawa to attempt to purchase North Sakhalin. In view of the strategic position of the northern part of the island vis-à-vis the estuary of the Amur river, the idea was no more acceptable to Moscow in 1940 than it had been in 1923, when advocated by Kawakami Toshitsune in his negotiations with Adolf Ioffe. As Tatekawa broached the subject on November 21, Molotov merely laughed and asked if he were joking. Asserting that Ribbentrop had told him in Berlin that Japan was prepared to give up her concessions, Molotov said that he would wait for a suitable answer.[18,g]

With Japanese-Soviet negotiations deadlocked, a liaison conference between members of the government and the chiefs of staff was held in Tokyo on February 3, 1941, to set Japanese policy toward the Soviet Union as well as toward Germany and Italy. The conferees agreed that Japan should try to convince the Soviet Union to accept the Ribbentrop plan and adjust her relations with Japan. They envisaged a Japanese-Soviet understanding along the following lines: (1) the sale of North Sakhalin to Japan (with the aid of German

---

[g] Molotov referred Tatekawa to Stalin's speech at the Sixth Session of the Supreme Soviet on March 29, 1940, "where fun was made of those who liked to buy what was not for sale."[19]

pressure on the Soviet Union) or, if this should prove impossible, the supplying of 1½ million tons of oil by the Soviet Union to Japan, even if it required the assistance of the Japanese government in boosting production; (2) Japanese recognition of the Soviet position in Sinkiang and Outer Mongolia (the Mongolian People's Republic) in return for Soviet recognition of the Japanese position in North China and Inner Mongolia, the relations between Sinkiang, Outer Mongolia and the U.S.S.R. to be decided between the latter and China; (3) the discontinuance of Soviet aid to Chiang Kai-shek; (4) the establishment of a commission representing Manchukuo, the U.S.S.R., and Outer Mongolia to delineate the frontier and cope with disputes; (5) the conclusion of a fishery agreement on the basis of Tatekawa's concession proposal or the abandonment of Japanese fishery concessions, if this were necessary to adjust diplomatic relations between the Soviet Union and Japan; and (6) Soviet provision of railway cars and freight discounts to facilitate large-scale Japanese-German trade.

In the articles of policy which it drew up, the liaison conference stated that Japan should hold a dominant position in the Greater East Asia Co-Prosperity Sphere and maintain order therein; she should preserve the independence of native states in that region and liberate the peoples in the English, French, Dutch and Portuguese colonies, granting them as much independence and self-government as they were fit to assume, ruling and leading them until such time as they could govern themselves. While retaining a preferential economic position in the Greater East Asia Co-Prosperity Sphere in the acquisition of raw materials for national defense, Japan was to grant free trade and equal commercial opportunity in other areas of commerce.

The liaison conference divided the world into four spheres, determined that this arrangement should be made permanent during the peace conference after the war: the Greater East Asia sphere, the European sphere (including Africa), the American sphere, and the Soviet sphere (including Iran and India). (Australia and New Zealand were to remain part of Great Britain, though the latter was to be treated on the same footing as Holland.)

The liaison conference agreed that it should be Japanese policy to deter the United States from becoming involved in the war. Germany, whose approval of this policy was to be secured, and Italy were to keep the Soviet Union in check. In the event that the U.S.S.R. (with whom an understanding was desired, but apparently subject to doubt) was to attack Japan, Germany and Italy were to strike the U.S.S.R. immediately. If Japan became involved in the European war, she should obtain pledges from Germany and Italy that they would not conclude a separate peace. To effect the above policies and, if necessary, to conclude appropriate pacts, the liaison conference decided to send Foreign Minister Matsuoka to Berlin, Rome and Moscow.

Another article of policy was considered, namely that Japan should immediately perfect her naval preparations while reducing her battle line in China; military preparations were to be completed with German help for which Japan would pay with raw materials and food. This objective was diluted by the conference with the general substitute statement that Japan should continue discussions with Germany concerning the promotion of complete peace in China.[20]

Stopping in Moscow en route to Berlin, Matsuoka met briefly with Molotov and then with Joseph Stalin on March 24. To the former he talked about the desirability of a nonaggression pact, but Molotov reiterated that a neutrality pact would be more appropriate. To Stalin Matsuoka lectured on the "moral Communism" of Japanese family life. Though he deemed it more suitable for Japan than the "political-economic Communism" of the Soviet state, he implied that the two ideologies were reconcilable, if not related; their greatest threat came from Anglo-Saxon liberalism, individualism and egoism.[21]

By the time that Matsuoka reached Berlin, on March 26, German-Soviet relations had deteriorated to such an extent that the friendly mediation of Germany, envisaged by the liaison conference, was impractical. But the impending break between Berlin and Moscow did not impair Japanese-Soviet relations. On the contrary, what Nazi "friendship" with the U.S.S.R. had not accomplished, Nazi hostility did. The prospect of war with Adolf Hitler persuaded Stalin, as German arguments had not, of the need for an agreement with Japan.[h] "Providence put a Russian treaty in my pocket," Matsuoka declared later.[22]

Matsuoka's attempts on April 7 and 8, following his return to Moscow from Berlin and Rome, to take advantage of the situation to exact from the U.S.S.R. a nonaggression pact plus the sale of North Sakhalin

[h] While Stalin may have underestimated the chances of a German attack, he certainly was aware of its possibility. He had been warned by this time by Great Britain and the United States of the likelihood of a German invasion, though he had probably discounted the warnings as a capitalist manuever to lure the Communist lamb to the butcher block.

met with rebuff. Neither did Molotov accept his
scaled-down proposal of a neutrality pact on the basis
of the Soviet draft of November 1940 but without the
accompanying protocol liquidating the Japanese concessions. When Matsuoka met with Molotov again on
the 11th, after a brief visit to Leningrad, Molotov not
only reiterated that the Japanese concessions must be
surrendered, but also insisted on the inclusion of a
guarantee of the territorial integrity and inviolability of
Manchukuo and Outer Mongolia in the neutrality pact.
He rejected Matsuoka's compromise suggestion that
the statement regarding Manchukuo and Outer Mongolia be made in a separate written communiqué and
that the concession question as well as fishery, commercial and boundary problems be mentioned in semi-
official letters.[23]

Matsuoka had just about given up hope of attaining
a neutrality pact and was prepared to confine himself
to the negotiation of trade and fishery agreements when
a meeting with Stalin, which he requested as a last re-
sort, unexpectedly bore fruit. In the discussion that
took place on the 12th, Stalin quickly agreed to the
use of a written communiqué and semi-official letters,
Matsuoka accepting some modification in text. In a few
minutes the Soviet dictator had removed the obstacles that had frustrated the conclusion of an agreement
for months.[24] Matsuoka boasted of this later as his
"lightning diplomacy."[25]

The following afternoon, on April 13, 1941, the
Neutrality Pact was signed by Matsuoka, Tatekawa
and Molotov. The original versions were in Russian
and in Japanese; the official translation in English. The
two treaty powers pledged to maintain peaceful and
friendly relations with each other, and to respect each

other's territorial integrity and inviolability. In the event that either of them found itself the object of hostilities by one or more third powers, the other would remain neutral throughout the entire conflict. The pact was to go into effect immediately upon ratification by the two sides and remain in force for five years. If neither power gave notice of cancellation one year prior to its expiration, it would be extended automatically for another five years.[26,1]

As agreed, a joint communiqué, signed by Matsuoka, Tatekawa and Molotov, was issued that day, stating solemnly that the Soviet Union and Japan, acting in the spirit of the Neutrality Pact, in order to guarantee peace and friendly relations between them, promised to respect the territorial integrity and inviolability of Manchukuo and the Mongolian People's Republic respectively.

The semi-official letters which were exchanged in connection with the Neutrality Pact consisted of a letter from Matsuoka to Molotov, written in English, and a Russian confirmation. The Japanese statement, approved by the Soviet side, read as follows:

Strictly Confidential

Moscow, April 13, 1941.

My dear Mr. Molotoff:

In reference to the Pact of Neutrality signed today, I have the honour to state that I expect and hope that the Commercial Agreement and the Fishery Convention will be concluded very soon and that at the earliest opportunity, we, Your Excellency and myself, shall make endeavours, in the spirit of

[1] For the full text of the Neutrality Pact, see Appendix G. A discussion of diverse views of Japanese and Soviet motives for signing the Neutrality Pact and of its ultimate significance will be found in Sandra Winterberger Thornton, "The Soviet Union and Japan, 1939–1941," MS, doctoral dissertation in government, Georgetown University, 1964, pp. 185–211.

conciliation and mutual accommodation, to solve in
a few months the question relating to liquidation of
the Concessions in Northern Saghalien under the
contracts signed at Moscow on December 14, 1925,
with a view to remove any and all questions which
are not conducive to the maintenance of cordial relations between the two countries.

In the same spirit, I should also like to point out
that it is well for our two countries as well as Man-
choukuo and Outer Mongolia to find at the earliest
date a way to instituting joint and or mixed commissions of the countries concerned with the object
of settling the boundary questions and of handling
disputes and incidents along the borders.

Very Sincerely yours,

Y. Matsuoka

His Excellency
V. M. Molotoff[27]

The Matsuoka letter deserves quotation, because it
was to become the subject of much controversy. The
inclusion of a time element— the projected liquidation
of the concessions "in a few months"—was to prove
particularly embarrassing to Japanese diplomacy later.
For the next few years questions relating to the actual
surrender of the concessions and the continued observation of the Neutrality Pact were to plague Japanese
and Soviet negotiators.[28]

The conclusion of the Neutrality Pact caused surprise in Berlin, for Hitler had hinted at the coming of
war with the Soviet Union when he had told Matsuoka, "When you return to Japan, you cannot report
to your Emperor that a conflict between Germany and
the Soviet Union is impossible."[29] Hitler's interpreter,
Dr. Paul Schmidt, wondering whether Matsuoka had

really understood the Führer's hint, reflected: "But perhaps he took this step precisely because he had realized in Berlin how critical the situation between Germany and the Soviet Union was and had wanted to secure the rear in the event of conflict."[30,j]

If Matsuoka's diplomacy raised eyebrows in Berlin, it raised tempers in Tokyo, as it became apparent that Matsuoka had made various commitments to Germany and the U.S.S.R. on his own responsibility. Premier Konoe had bypassed the Cabinet and the Privy Council to obtain imperial sanction for the signature of the Neutrality Pact,[32] and the Privy Council ratified it with "aching heart."[33]

The *Japan Times Advertiser,* which often voiced the views of the Foreign Office, gave the following appraisal of the significance of the Neutrality Pact: "Japan can now undertake either a defensive war, or an offensive-defensive one. In the latter, Japan would have to fight first to offset a threatened perilous disadvantage. She is confident that the pact with Soviet Russia assures her rear and right flank against military and naval action."[34]

The Russians, who received similar protection from the pact, regarded its conclusion as a triumph of Soviet diplomacy. They realized the fragility of any treaty, but were confident that the pact had reduced the threat of a dreaded two-front war.[35]

The signature of the Neutrality Pact had been crowned by a banquet at which the usual toasts were drunk. According to Kase Toshikazu, a Japanese diplomat who participated in the festivities, "both Stalin

---

[j] The Japanese understood that the deterioration of relations between Germany and the U.S.S.R. might drive the latter into the Anglo-Saxon camp and threaten Japan with encirclement. [31]

and Matsuoka were quite drunk by the time the latter took his leave."ᵏ When Stalin stated that diplomatic pledges must be kept regardless of differences in ideology, Matsuoka proclaimed: "The treaty has been made. I do not lie. If I lie, my head shall be yours. If you lie, be sure I will come for your head." Taken aback, Stalin replied: "My head is important to my country. So is yours to your country. Let's take care to keep both our heads on our shoulders." When Stalin toasted the Japanese officers who were present, Matsuoka quipped: "Oh, these military and naval men have concluded the Neutrality Pact from the standpoint of the general situation, but they are always thinking of how to defeat the Soviet Union." Stalin did not join in his smile, but warned drily that the U.S.S.R. was stronger than the Tsarist Russia that Japan had defeated. During the banquet Stalin told Matsuoka, "You are an Asiatic. So am I." "We're all Asiatics," Matsuoka echoed. "Let us drink to the Asiatics!"³⁶

Although Stalin was not in the habit of seeing off foreign dignitaries, he did so in the case of Matsuoka. Recalling how surprised the Axis ambassadors had been when Stalin had appeared with the Japanese on the departure platform, Kase wrote: "Stalin warmly embraced Matsuoka and even allowed photographs to be taken of the scene. In fact, he kissed rather promiscuously."³⁷

There was, of course, nothing "promiscuous" in the

ᵏ Other Japanese as well as eyewitnesses of various wartime conferences reported that Stalin did not drink alcohol, but merely a self-prepared red liquid. Japanese do not hold liquor well and, judging by his undiplomatic remarks, Matsuoka must have been intoxicated. It is less likely that Stalin was drunk, but neither is there reason to believe that the red liquid was nonalcoholic. It is well known in the Soviet Union that Stalin was fond of Khvanchkara, a red wine from his native Georgia.

traditional Russian farewell kisses, but the exuberance
of Stalin and Matsuoka was reflected in this exchange at
the railway station:

Stalin: "The European problem can be solved in a
             natural way if Japan and the Soviets coop-
             rate."
Matsuoka: "Not only the European problem! Asia
             also can be solved!"
Stalin: "The whole world can be settled!"[38]

2

The Neutrality Pact and the German-Soviet War

The Neutrality Pact between Japan and the U.S.S.R. went into effect on April 25, 1941, upon the exchange of ratifications in Tokyo. Two months had not passed when Germany, Japan's Axis partner, on June 22 invaded the Soviet Union and the latter had to ascertain Japan's intentions. But the German action had caught the Japanese by surprise, and Foreign Minister Matsuoka's answers to Soviet queries reflected the bewilderment that prevailed in Tokyo.

Matsuoka had been entertaining President Wang Ching-wei of the Nanking puppet government at a special kabuki performance of "Shuzenji Monogatari," attended by high ranking military and government officials, when news of the German strike had been rushed to him.[1] Japan had signed the Tripartite Pact with the understanding that relations with the Soviet Union would remain peaceful, in fact that Soviet adherence to the pact would be attempted. A number of Japanese statesmen, among them Premier Konoe, now called for nullification of the alliance with Germany and Italy, foreseeing that the "pact of steel," which had been intended as a diplomatic barrier to American intervention, had become a "brotherhood of the grave."[2]

When Ambassador Smetanin asked Matsuoka on June 24[a] whether Japan would abide by the Neutrality Pact, Matsuoka did not give a direct reply. He stated that the Neutrality Pact in no way affected the Tripartite Pact and that Stalin and Molotov knew that Japan would not have signed an agreement that would have done so. He confessed that he could not say anything about the attitude of his government about the situation, but promised that it would make clear its intentions after consulting with Germany and Italy, the Rome-Berlin-Tokyo Axis being the foundation of Japanese foreign policy. When Smetanin pressed Matsuoka for a specific reply whether or not Japan would observe the Neutrality Pact, Matsuoka observed that Stalin had not asked and that, therefore, he had not said anything about the relationship of the Neutrality Pact and the Axis. Personally he saw no conflict between the Japanese-Soviet pact and Japan's alliance with Germany and Italy, and Stalin must have felt the same. In response to a query from Smetanin, the foreign minister declared that Japan would abrogate the Neutrality Pact if it conflicted with her alliance with Germany and Italy. It was obvious that Japan could not side with Germany and the Soviet Union at the same time.[3]

Matsuoka stressed how unexpected the turn of events had been. Had Stalin himself not told him during the negotiation of the Neutrality Pact that the U.S.S.R. would never ally herself with the Anglo-Saxons and

[a] June 23, according to Russian sources.

would remain on the side of the Axis? Stalin had probably not dreamed of war with Germany. Matsuoka regarded the Soviet-German conflict as a tragedy and admitted that he was too astonished by its outbreak to give a clear answer to Smetanin. When he stated that his government, while as yet undecided, would give serious consideration to this important matter, Smetanin expressed the hope that Japan would be objective and fair in her attitude.[4]

Matsuoka's true feelings were revealed at the 34th liaison conference between the Japanese government and the imperial military and naval high command three days later, on June 27. He did not "do his best" to preserve friendly relations between Japan and the U.S.S.R. as he had promised Smetanin, but recommended that Japan take advantage of the German-Soviet war to invade the Soviet Union. Formerly president of the South Manchurian Railway, Matsuoka was a "continentalist" who felt that Japan's destiny lay on the Asiatic continent rather than in the South Pacific.[5] Although he had earlier gone along with the view that Japan should strike south, he now believed that Japan must first move north and then south. Not only was the southward thrust likely to involve Japan in war with the United States, an eventuality that might perhaps be avoided in a conflict with the Soviet Union, which the United States disliked; but also it would be impossible to solve the Northern Problem once the Soviet Union was defeated by Germany alone. On the basis of reports from Lieutenant General Ōshima Hiroshi, the Japanese ambassador in Berlin, Matsuoka believed that the German-Soviet war would be brief and urged prompt involvement. "Unless one enters the tiger's den, one cannot get the tiger's cub," Matsuoka declaimed.

The China war, which had drained Japan's resources, continued to dominate Japanese thinking. The alliance with Germany, the Neutrality Pact with the Soviet Union, the thrust southward, and now the invasion of the Soviet Union were all conceived or justified at least partly as measures in the struggle with Chiang Kai-shek. Thus Matsuoka bolstered his recommendation for war with the Soviet Union with the contention that the advance of Japanese armies up to Irkutsk, or even halfway, would influence Chiang to make peace with Japan. That the China war was merely a pretext was made clear when the minister of war asked Matsuoka whether the north should be attacked even if the China Incident were ended, and Matsuoka replied in the affirmative. Yet the foreign minister deemed his policy "moral"—"I insist on a moral foreign policy," he said—for the policy was faithful to the Tripartite Pact, and he repeated that Japan must act while the German-Soviet war situation was still unclear.

Those present did not disagree with Matsuoka in principle so much as in timing.

"Mr. Matsuoka, please think carefully about the present problem," Minister for Home Affairs Hiranuma Kiichirō stated. "Are you saying that we should attack the Soviet Union at once? Are you saying that as a matter of national policy we should go to war with the Soviet Union at once?"

"Just so," Matsuoka replied.

"These days one must act quickly," the home minister conceded, "but one must make full preparations. Preparations are necessary for the use of armed force and preparations must be made also for the realization of national policy. Is it not necessary first to make preparations?"

"I think I would like a decision to strike against the north first and notify Germany thereof," was all that Matsuoka replied.

"As for a moral and honorable foreign policy," Army Chief of Staff Sugiyama Gen observed in reference to Matsuoka's earlier statement, "although it is right, we are now using large forces in China. While it would be good to adhere only to righteousness, this is in fact impossible. The Supreme Command will complete preparations, but it cannot be determined now whether to strike or not." Sugiyama pointed out that even the Kwantung Army would require 40 to 50 days to make the necessary preparations. Additional time would be needed to put Japan's military forces on a wartime footing and to begin offensive action. By that time the military situation in the German-Soviet war should be clear enough to tell whether it would be to Japan's advantage to intervene.

When Matsuoka demanded that it be decided then and there that the Soviet Union be attacked, Sugiyama replied in one word: *"Ikan* [It can't be done]."[b] Navy Chief of Staff Nagano Osami agreed: "Because it is a very big problem, the Supreme Command holds the same view."[6]

As the government secretly debated how to react to the German invasion of the Soviet Union, the Japanese press gave advice from the sidelines. The *Yomiuri* advocated a Japanese attack on the U.S.S.R. It admitted that the existence of the Neutrality Pact made the situation awkward, but pointed with approval to Hitler's violation of the Russo-German Nonaggression Pact, de-

---

[b] *"Ikan"* is typically Japanese in vagueness. Professor Ike renders it as "No." H.I.H. Prince Mikasa, with whom I discussed the matter, expressed the opinion that *"ikan"* was a qualified "no," that it meant "it can't be done" in the sense of "not yet."

claring flatly that "national self-interest was the highest morality."[7]

On July 2 an imperial conference took place at which the Japanese government reexamined its policy in the light of the new situation. It reasserted its determination "no matter how the world situation changes" to adhere firmly to the policy of building the Greater East Asia Co-Prosperity Sphere; it planned to continue the war in China ("the disposition of the China Incident," as it put it euphemistically), to advance southward to lay the foundations for "self-existence and self-defense," and "depending on changes in the situation" to solve the Northern Problem. While envisioning Japanese efforts as a contribution to eventual world peace, the imperial conference was set to remove any obstacles hindering the attainment of the above objectives. The conferees agreed, therefore, to complete military preparations for war with Great Britain and the United States in case they stood in the way of Japanese occupation of French Indo-China and Thailand.

The imperial conference dealt more gingerly with the problems posed by the Soviet-German war. While affirming Japan's adherence to the spirit of the Axis alliance, it decided not to intervene until German successes created a favorable opportunity.[c] It agreed to continue diplomatic negotiations with the U.S.S.R. while making secret preparations to attack her.[9,d]

[c] Hara Yoshimichi, president of the Privy Council, felt that the war between Germany and the Soviet Union presented Japan with "the chance of a lifetime." He declared: "Since the Soviet Union is promoting Communism all over the world, we will have to attack her sooner or later. Since we are now engaged in the China Incident, I feel that we cannot attack the Soviet Union as easily as we would wish. Nevertheless, I believe that we should attack the Soviet Union when it seems opportune to do so."[8]

[d] Within a few days the Japanese army began to bolster its forces in

Willing as Japan was to fight the United States if the latter blocked her thrust south, she was reluctant to cross swords with America over Europe. In the event that the United States could not be kept out of the European conflict, Japan was obligated to come to the support of Germany and Italy, but, as in the matter of war with the Soviet Union, she was determined to make her own decision as to time and form of action.

After the conference, the very same day, Matsuoka called Smetanin to his office and told him that the Japanese government had given serious consideration to questions arising from the outbreak of war between Germany and the Soviet Union. In a prepared oral statement, Matsuoka repeated his regret that the conflict had occurred. A war between Germany and Italy, with which Japan was allied, and her Russian neighbor, with whom she wanted and had recently initiated improved relations, placed Japan in a most difficult and delicate position; he sincerely hoped, therefore, that hostilities would be terminated quickly and particularly that action would not be extended to the Far East, where Japan had vital interests. Matsuoka declared that while his government would not want its policies toward the Soviet Union to embarrass Japanese relations with Germany and Italy, it saw no reason for a change in attitude at present. The government deemed it possible to protect Japanese interests while remaining on good terms with both its allies and the U.S.S.R. Notwithstanding his personal desire to go to war with the Soviet Union,[e]

Korea and Manchuria in order to invade the Soviet Union if the Germans succeeded in overrunning European Russia. [10]

[e] Murakamy Kazuo, deputy consul general of Japan in New York and former private secretary of Foreign Minister Miki, told me that some Foreign Office officials believe that Matsuoka did not want war with the Soviet Union, but called for it as a bluff in order to embarrass and silence the military. Commenting on the conflicting views expressed by Matsuoka

Matsuoka asked that Stalin and Molotov trust him to do his best to preserve amicable relations between their countries. He did make the qualification that whether or not the Japanese government could adhere to its policy of neutrality depended on further developments in the situation.[f]

Smetanin replied that it was difficult to make an immediate comment regarding Matsuoka's statement, but he expressed thanks for Matsuoka's promise to work for good-neighborly relations with the Soviet Union.

Matsuoka stated that Japan was prepared to act as mediator between the Soviet Union and Germany. He warned that the shipment of American military aid to the U.S.S.R. via Vladivostok (i.e. past Japan) might lead to German and Italian demands that Japan cut the supply route and that Soviet-British dealings might lead to similar complications and asked, therefore, that Stalin and Molotov give serious consideration to these matters.

Within a fortnight, on July 13,[g] Smetanin was back in Matsuoka's office to inquire whether it was true that he had told the American and British ambassadors that the Soviet-Japanese Neutrality Pact had no legal validity and was not binding on Japan. Matsuoka retorted that he had stated that the Neutrality Pact did not apply to the German-Soviet war. Pressed for an explanation, Matsuoka argued that there had been no thought of such a conflict when the Neutrality Pact had been

---

to different persons, Dr. Michael Libal remarks: "It would probably never be possible to separate clearly in Matsuoka's presentations truth, self-deception and conscious misrepresentation."[11]

[f] Matsuoka told the German Ambassador General Eugen Ott of the deception, explaining that he had to mislead the Russians or at least keep them in a state of uncertainty in order to gain time for military preparations.[12]

[g] On July 12 according to Soviet sources.

signed; he felt that Japan was free to develop her own policy concerning this situation, unrestricted either by the Neutrality Pact with the Soviet Union or by the alliance with Germany and Italy. Matsuoka repeated that the Neutrality Pact did not apply to the German-Soviet war, for to have signed an agreement that contravened the Tripartite Pact would have been dishonest.

When Smetanin observed that there was discrepancy between the assertion made by Matsuoka on June 24 and again on July 2 that the Neutrality Pact and the Tripartite Pact were independent of each other and did not affect each other and the claim now advanced that Japan was restricted by neither one, Matsuoka replied that there was no contradiction. What mattered were not words but actions. Germany had not and would not ask Japan to participate in the war with the Soviet Union; on the other hand, neither should the Soviet Union allow United States military bases on Kamchatka or British officers in Siberia, a possibility reported in newspapers. In response to repeated attempts by Smetanin to obtain clarification of the views and intentions of the Japanese government concerning the Neutrality Pact and the Tripartite Pact, Matsuoka would say only that both pacts were valid and that the Neutrality Pact did not apply to the German-Soviet War.[13,h]

The enforced resignation three days later of Matsuoka, whose independent and overbearing attitude had exasperated the military, did not remove the dilemma

---

[h] According to Soviet sources, Matsuoka spelled out his contradictory views in a memorandum which he gave to Smetanin on this occasion.[14] Japanese authors admit that Matsuoka tended to be contradictory, but deny that his contradictions were deceptive in intent. "Matsuoka was a genius, dynamic and erratic," Kase recalls. "His mind worked as swiftly as lightning. People were dazzled by his brilliance . . . But he often contradicted himself. Consistency to him was, as to Emerson, 'the hobgoblin of little minds.'"[15]

facing Japan. No sooner had his successor, Foreign Minister Toyoda Teijirō, made his inaugural address, than
Smetanin appeared to ask whether he regarded the Neutrality Pact as in effect. In the conversation that took
place on July 25, Toyoda promised to give a detailed
reply after careful study of the pact. But he repeated
Matsuoka's statement that the German-Soviet war
placed Japan in a delicate position and warned that Soviet granting of military bases in the Far East to a third
power would make the situation more difficult. Smetanin
retorted that the bases should not be a matter of concern
to Japan, for despite her war with a third power, the
Soviet Union was prepared to abide by all the articles
of the Neutrality Pact. He asked whether Japan was
willing to do the same?

On August 5 Toyoda replied to Smetanin that although there might be different legal opinions about
the relationship of the German-Soviet War, the Tripartite Pact, and the Neutrality Pact, it was his personal
view that Japan would faithfully abide by all the articles of the Neutrality Pact, provided the Soviet Union
did the same in accordance with the spirit as well as the
letter of the pact. By this he meant that Soviet sale or
lease of Russian territory or the granting of military
bases in the Far East to other powers, the extension of
Soviet military alliances with other powers to the Far
East, or the conclusion by the U.S.S.R. of alliances or
pacts directed against Japan would undermine the Neutrality Pact.[1] Toyoda asked for a firm guarantee that

---

[1] The decision to observe the Neutrality Pact, for the moment at least,
had been taken at the 44th liaison conference the previous day. In warning
against the transfer of Russian territory to a third power, Toyoda referred
to the Maritime Province and Kamchatka.[16] While the question was linked
no doubt with the question of American air bases, rumors of the sale of
Kamchatka to the United States had been rife even before the war.

the U.S.S.R. would do none of these, and demanded that she promise to cease all direct and indirect aid to the Chiang Kai-shek regime. He also wanted the immediate resolution of problems outstanding between their countries, such as Soviet pressure on the Japanese concessions in North Sakhalin and Soviet declaration of maritime danger zones closed to Japanese shipping.

Smetanin expressed pleasure that Toyoda, unlike Matsuoka, had made a clear declaration of Japan's intention to observe the Neutrality Pact. He repeated that his government considered the pact as fully in effect, and agreed that the settlement of problems between the two powers was desirable. He said that he knew nothing about the relations of his government with Chiang Kai-shek, but promised to obtain a reply concerning this and other matters raised by the foreign minister.[17]

Relating the conversation with Smetanin at the 45th liaison conference the following day, Toyoda remarked that Smetanin had given the impression of feeling relieved. It was agreed at the liaison conference that while Japan should continue to perfect her defenses, she should seek to avoid war with the Soviet Union by shunning provocative actions and localizing possible disputes. Only in the event of a "frontal attack" was the Japanese army to strike back.[18]

A week later, on August 13, Smetanin transmitted Moscow's response. The Soviet government acknowledged with great satisfaction Toyoda's statement that Japan would adhere to the Neutrality Pact and reaffirmed its own intention to do the same. It declared that the problem of the North Sakhalin concessions should be solved in line with Matsuoka's letter of April 13, 1941, holding out liquidation "in a few months," and his subsequent personal message of May 31 clarifying this to mean "not later than six months from the date of his promise."[j]

The Soviet government refused to consider the question of Russian aid to Chiang, pointing out that the Neutrality Pact did not govern relations with third powers; Japan had no more right to take the U.S.S.R. to task on this matter than the U.S.S.R. would have to object to Japanese dealings with China, Germany or Italy. To allay Japanese anxiety, however, the Soviet government reaffirmed the assurance Molotov had given Tōgō, when the latter had broached the matter of a Neutrality Pact on July 2, 1940, that the problem of aid to Chiang was insignificant because of Soviet preoccupation with national defense, and added that this was even more true since the attack by Germany.[k]

Replying to Toyoda's statement about alliances with third powers, the Soviet government reminded him that Molotov had clearly stated to Tatekawa on July 15 that its agreement with Great Britain concerned Germany only and did not affect Japan. The Soviet government assured Toyoda that it had neither granted nor intended to grant military bases or territorial concessions to a third power in the Russian Far East. At the same time it wanted an explanation of large-scale Japanese troop movements in Manchukuo, which seemed inconsistent with Japanese statements concerning the observation of the Neutrality Pact.

In the conversation that ensued between Toyoda and

---

[j] See Chapter Four.

[k] Significant Soviet aid to Chiang Kai-shek, particularly in the training and equipping of the Nationalist Air Force, was given from 1937 until mid-1941, when the United States took over the task of providing China with the equipment and technical training necessary to resist the Japanese invaders. [19]

Smetanin, the Japanese foreign minister stated in regard to the Matsuoka letter, that changes in the situation since the writing of the letter necessitated a reevaluation of the problem; meanwhile, he contended, it was natural for Japan to demand and for the Soviet Union to allow unhindered use of the concessions. When Smetanin asked whether Toyoda considered the talks based on the Matsuoka letter as nullified, Toyoda reiterated that the solution of the North Sakhalin concessions problem required further study.

Toyoda justified the military build-up in Manchukuo on the grounds that Japan shared responsibility for the defense of that country and that it was natural to take precautions when a neighboring country was at war. He asserted that the preparations were not directed against the Soviet Union with whom Japan wanted to have good-neighborly relations and pledged observance of the Neutrality Pact by his country. But he warned again that the Tripartite Pact was the foundation of Japanese foreign policy and that an increase in the amount of American aid shipments via Vladivostok would place Japan in an extremely delicate situation.

On August 20 Vice Minister of Foreign Affairs Amau Eiji protested against the expected departure of an American tanker for Vladivostok, expressing concern that the oil was destined for the Chiang Kai-shek regime against which Japan was fighting. Three days later, on August 23,[1] Toyoda repeated that the continuation of the shipment of American aid to the Soviet Union via Vladivostok irritated public opinion in Japan and could arouse German and Italian reaction that would make it difficult for Japan to remain on friendly terms with the Soviet Union. Toyoda did not wish to get involved in

[1] On August 25 according to Soviet sources.

legal theories; he wanted the U.S.S.R. to look at the problem from a broad point of view.

The Soviet Union assured Japan, in a reply handed by Smetanin to Amau on August 26, that the goods purchased from the United States were for Russian consumption—to satisfy daily needs in European Russia and the southern Far East, the German attack having dislocated the economy. It stated that it saw no reason for Japan to be anxious about Soviet purchases of American goods and their transportation to Russian Far Eastern ports by normal commercial routes and made it clear that it would regard any attempt to stop ordinary Soviet-American trade by way of Russian Far Eastern ports as an unfriendly act.

Amau retorted that while trade was free in principle, consideration must be given to the sort of goods sent and to the timing of their shipment. The concentration of large Soviet forces in the Russian Far East was a threat to Japan and the transportation of military supplies to Soviet Far Eastern ports was, therefore, dangerous in the eyes of the Japanese public, and the more irritating because it was done right past Japan. He deemed it wrong for the Soviet government to regard Japanese measures to interfere with Soviet-American trade as "unfriendly," for this was no ordinary commerce but the supply of fuel for wartime use, an act that in turn seemed unfriendly to Japan. When Smetanin dismissed Amau's contention that the Soviet Far East posed a threat to Japan, since both sides had pledged to respect the Neutrality Pact, Amau warned that if the Soviet Union took advantage of the Neutrality Pact to import war materials in disregard of Japanese public opinion, doubt would be stirred up about the maintenance of the Neutrality Pact.[20]

3

The Neutrality Pact and the Outbreak of the Pacific War

On November 22, 1941, a fortnight before the Japanese attack on Pearl Harbor, Foreign Minister Tōgō sought reassurance from Ambassador Smetanin that the position of the Soviet government, expressed by Smetanin to his predecessor, Toyoda, on August 5 and 13, had not changed, that it would remain faithful to the Neutrality Pact and not enter into any agreement against Japan with a third power. Specifically Tōgō wanted to make sure that the U.S.S.R. would not make any bases available to another state. Smetanin replied that it was incumbent on both countries to adhere to the Neutrality Pact, and that the Soviet Union had done so meticulously; he reaffirmed that the U.S.S.R. would not enter into an alliance against Japan and would not provide military bases and other facilities to a third power. Queried again whether there had been any departure in Soviet thinking from his statement of August 13, he replied that he would have to reexamine

35

the records. When Tōgō on November 28 pressed him for an answer, Smetanin said that it was his personal opinion that there had been no change in the attitude of his government in regard to his statement of August 13; at least he had not been instructed to seek any modification.

Tōgō stated bluntly that Japan would regard it as a violation of the Neutrality Pact for the Soviet Union to extend a military alliance which she already had to East Asia or to conclude a new one against Japan; she would think the same of the leasing of territory or the granting of bases in the Russian Far East to a third power. When he remarked in this connection that he interpreted the ambassador's reply as an affirmation of Soviet adherence to the Neutrality Pact, Smetanin retorted that he had merely expressed his personal opinion. He offered to query the Commissariat of Foreign Affairs and to report that Tōgō would regard any deviation from the statement of August 13 as a violation of the Neutrality Pact. Tōgō eased up. He wanted to ensure Soviet neutrality, not to endanger it. He told Smetanin that he saw no need for him to question the Commissariat of Foreign Affairs; the Soviet declaration of August 13 had been clear enough and there was no ground for the misgivings he had harbored. But Smetanin now insisted that he wanted to provide the foreign minister with an authoritative answer and would contact Moscow. To this Tōgō replied that he was not concerned with the relations between the Soviet ambassador and the Commissariat of Foreign Affairs; all that interested him was that Soviet policy remain unchanged.[1]

Three days later, on December 1, Smetanin officially informed Tōgō: "The Soviet government has no intention of violating the Japanese-Soviet Neutrality Pact. It also declares that its ambassador's statement of August 13 remains in effect. This is, of course, contingent on Japan's observance of the obligations of the Neutrality Treaty."[2]

Tōgō replied that the Soviet government need not worry about Japanese observance of the Neutrality Pact. To make certain that the Soviet side had reaffirmed the commitment not to enter into any military alliance against Japan nor to lease territory or bases to a third power, Tōgō had the pertinent passages from the transcript of Smetanin's statement of August 13 read aloud. Although Smetanin repeated that these pledges were still in effect, he declined a request by Tōgō to provide written confirmation on the ground that the Japanese already had a fine record of the official statement which he had made to Foreign Minister Toyoda on August 13.

On December 6 Smetanin told Tōgō that he had been instructed by Molotov to inform him that the Soviet statement remained in full effect. Tōgō replied that he interpreted this to mean that the Soviet foreign minister personally reaffirmed the ambassador's statement of August 13.[3]

Yet only two days later, on December 8, Tōgō wanted renewed assurance of Soviet neutrality as Japan plunged into war with the United States and Great Britain, Russia's supporters in Europe.[a] Asserting that

---

[a] Japan had decided to strike the United States rather than the Soviet Union, because she was in urgent need of the raw materials in the South Pacific and the United States blocked — or at least seemed to block — her expansion in that direction. (The American attempt to bring the Japanese war machine to a halt by withholding the fuel on which it ran had had the opposite effect; unable to buy what she needed, Japan, in desperation, had determined to seize it.) Furthermore, at the time, the United States with her soft life and lack of discipline had seemed less

it was "obvious" that the conflict with the United States and Great Britain would not affect the course of Soviet-Japanese relations, he told Smetanin that the Japanese government would adhere to the Neutrality Pact, that it believed the Soviet Union would do the same, and that there should be no problem, therefore, in reaffirming the statement of August 13. When Smetanin replied that he would report to his government that Tōgō had stated that Japan's war with the United States and Great Britain would not affect Japanese-Soviet relations and that Japan would abide by the Neutrality Pact, Tōgō objected that this was only part of his statement—that Smetanin must add that Tōgō desired Soviet reaffirmation of the statement of August 13.

Similar reassurance of continued Soviet adherence to the Neutrality Pact was sought by Ambassador Tatekawa in Kuibyshev when he informed Deputy Commissar of Foreign Affairs Andrei Vyshinskii of the Japanese declaration of war against the United States and Great Britain. Irritated no doubt by the nervous demands for repeated affirmation of the same pledges, Vyshinskii retorted tartly that since the Neutrality Pact had been concluded in order to be observed, the Soviet government naturally was obliged to observe it—so long as the Japanese government did so.[4]

As the Pacific War unfolded, a number of issues

---

formidable an opponent than the U.S.S.R., particularly since the might of the Japanese navy could be brought to bear on the former more readily than on the latter.

The idea of attacking the Soviet Union was shelved rather than discarded, to be picked up at an opportune moment or if, as stated already, the Americans established themselves in the Russian Far East. Germany was asking Japan to strike the Soviet Union in the back and the Japanese suspected that the United States, whom Japan herself had made into a comrade-in-arms of the U.S.S.R. by the attack on Pearl Harbor, would seek Russian participation in the Pacific War.

threatened to break the fragile neutrality: the possible establishment of American bases in the U.S.S.R., renewed Soviet aid to China, Japanese restraint of Soviet shipping, and reciprocal harrassment.

The Question of American Bases in the U.S.S.R.

Speculation by a San Francisco news broadcast on January 19, 1942, that Walter Thurston, United States minister counselor in Moscow, had discussed the granting of American air bases in the Russian Far East with Deputy Foreign Commissar Solomon Lozovskii at Kuibyshev alarmed the Japanese, and Tōgō asked Smetanin for a denial. When Smetanin responded that he knew nothing about the matter, Tōgō vainly demanded that he deny the very possibility of such an idea.

On January 22, when Smetanin, who was returning to Moscow, paid a farewell visit to Tōgō, the latter repeated that Japan's war with the United States and England had no bearing on Japanese-Soviet relations; in fact, it was now that the Neutrality Pact really took effect. He asserted that the military agreement concluded between Japan, Germany and Italy on January 18 concerned only those countries with which all the three powers were at war,[b] and reiterated that the Soviet Union must not enter into any military alliance against Japan. Counselor Iakov Malik, who was with Smetanin and who was to succeed him as ambassador, asked if Japan would also refrain from entering into a military alliance against the U.S.S.R.; Tōgō said yes.[5]

The Soviet change of ambassadors was paralleled by a shift on the Japanese side. Dissatisfied with the re-

---

[b] For the German text of the agreement, see Bernd Martin, *Deutschland und Japan im 2. Weltkrieg,* 232–34.

ports of Ambassador Tatekawa, who had asserted as late as 1942 that the U.S.S.R. was on the verge of collapse, and eager in view of the Soviet Union's unexpected resilience and the uncertainties of the Pacific War to preserve peace with the Soviet Union, the Japanese government replaced him with Satō Naotake, a diplomat of far greater experience and stature.[6] A member of the Privy Council, Satō had served as minister to Poland (1924), minister to Belgium (1927), ambassador to France (1933) and as foreign minister (1937). Above all, he knew Russia well, having lived in St. Petersburg as attaché, third secretary and finally second secretary from 1904 through 1914, and following Japanese recognition of the U.S.S.R. as minister and chargé d'affaires in Moscow in 1925.[7]

Like their Western colleagues, the diplomats of Japan settled in the wartime capital of Kuibyshev, but on April 5 Satō and several of his subordinates, including Minister Morishima Gorō and the military and naval attachés, flew to Moscow for eleven days.[8] In a conversation with Molotov on April 6, Satō admitted that Japanese-Soviet relations were calm on the surface only; underneath, such tension had built up because of the two countries' involvement in war that the smallest incident might have grave consequences. Japan had deemed it necessary, Satō revealed, to make military preparations to repel any Soviet attack, though she hoped, he said, that the contingency would never arise. He warned gravely that the leasing of military bases to the United States or Great Britain in Kamchatka or the Maritime region would compel Japan to take up arms against the Soviet Union.

Molotov dismissed the base issue as not a matter of actuality and thus not possibly a cause of misunder-

standing. The Soviet government, he declared, regarded any promise it had made as binding and would
live up to its obligations. But there were many hotheads
in Japan who, elated with success in the south, advocated positive action in the north too, and the Soviet
Union for her part had to be vigilant. On the other
hand, he continued, it was hoped that Japan, unlike
Italy, would pursue an independent foreign policy and
not imprudently follow German direction to attack
the Soviet Union, that agreement could be reached
between Japan and the U.S.S.R. on important issues,
and that the Neutrality Pact would remain in effect in
spite of changed conditions. Satō assured Molotov that
Japan did indeed steer her own course and that Germany understood Japan's independent position.[c]

Before long Satō raised the base issue again. According to a Soviet news report, one of the American B-25's
which had raided Japan on April 18 (i.e. one of the
Doolittle raiders) had made an emergency landing in
the Maritime region, where it was detained by the authorities in accordance with international law. Satō protested to Vyshinskii that the incident suggested that
the Soviet Union had after all granted an air base to
the United States. Vyshinskii denied this, saying that
the U.S.S.R. had acted simply in accordance with the
principles of international law. The plane had not come
at the invitation of the Soviet Union; it had lost its
way and made an emergency landing. Satō replied that
even though the plane had not come at the invitation
of the Soviet Union, his government would not be able

[c] What had impressed Morishima most either on this occasion or at a
subsequent meeting on April 15 was the emotion and determination with
which Molotov had declared: "Though we are being beaten now, we shall
certainly win in the end. The Soviet Union will never compromise with
those inhuman Nazis." [9]

to regard it as an isolated incident if a similar case re-
curred. Defining an air base not merely as a place from
which planes operated, but also as one where they
could land, Satō warned again that the offer of a
base to the United States would precipitate a crisis in
Soviet-Japanese relations. Vyshinskii retorted that
whether or not similar incidents would recur did not
depend on the will of the Soviet government and
could not be interpreted as Russian granting of bases
to the United States so long as the Soviet government
followed the customary procedures of international
law in dealing with the incidents. As Molotov had already assured him, the question of American use of
Soviet bases was without foundation. Satō did not rest
satisfied. If in the future hundreds of planes, instead
of only one as in this case, landed in the Soviet Union
and were "detained," he declared, Japan would regard
this as the granting of bases notwithstanding the foreign
minister's pledge. Exasperated, Vyshinskii repeated
that the Soviet action was in compliance with international law and that there was no other way of dealing
with emergency landings.

Satō objected that Vyshinskii's explanation gave no
assurance for the future and reiterated that Japan
would regard it as a violation of the Neutrality Pact if
the Soviet Union allowed similar incidents involving an
increasing number of planes to occur. It was his suggestion that the Soviet Union insure the tranquility
of Soviet-Japanese relations by forbidding American
planes to make further emergency landings in her territory. When Vyshinskii queried on what international
law he based this idea, Satō replied that he based it on
the Neutrality Pact and his desire to maintain amicable
Soviet-Japanese relations. Vyshinskii retorted that the

Soviet Union was acting as international law required and could not do otherwise.

On April 30 Satō read to Vyshinskii a note from the Japanese government alleging that the United States had chosen the Soviet Union as an escape route for bombers returning from Japan and that Soviet action, even if within the letter of international law, was aiding and abetting the American air corps. Should similar incidents be tolerated, the United States would make systematic use of Russian territory in her raids on Japan. "Since our Empire will never be able to overlook such a situation," the note declared, "it will gravely affect the state of Japanese-Soviet relations. We fear that that is exactly what the United States wants." The note concluded with the request that the Soviet Union take steps to prevent similar emergency landings "in order to eliminate the machinations of a third country and prevent a crisis in Soviet-Japanese relations."

Reverting to the theme that the United States was trying to drive a wedge between the Soviet Union and Japan, Satō added that while his government regarded a belligerent power as guilty of violating the rights of a neutral country if it intentionally made use of the latter's territory for warfare, it regarded it as neglect of duty on the part of the neutral country, if it knowingly permitted this to occur. Vyshinskii acknowledged that a neutral country had certain obligations, but insisted that the Soviet Union strictly lived up to them. In response to Satō's suggestion that Moscow invoke article 42 of the Provisional Rules for Aerial Warfare, signed at the Hague in 1922, to exclude American planes from Soviet territory, Vyshinskii stated that the article did not specify how a neutral country could prevent such flights, particularly emergency landings, and reiterated that the Soviet Union did all that it could within the framework of international law. When Satō warned again that the recurrence of such incidents would constitute a violation of the spirit of the Neutrality Pact even if the U.S.S.R. acted in accordance with international law, Vyshinskii replied that the Neutrality Pact was part of international law and would be duly respected.

On May 4 Vyshinskii handed to Satō an official reply from his government, setting down in writing the points which he had made orally at their previous meeting. It stated unequivocally that the Soviet government had "discharged every duty laid down by international law" in dealing with the plane incident of April 18, and insisted that "it would be totally groundless for the Japanese government to conclude that Soviet territory was used as a military base by the United States for air raids on Japan if American planes and crews should be detained by Soviet authorities in the future under circumstances similar to those of April 18." The note concluded: "In reference to the Japanese government's request that the Soviet government take every necessary precaution to maintain existing relations between Japan and the Soviet Union, the Soviet government deems it necessary to declare that its handling of the incident of April 18 was in accordance with generally accepted rules of international law and that it desires to maintain the existing relations between Japan and the Soviet Union."[10]

The conclusion by Molotov of aid agreements with England and the United States on May 26 and June 11 respectively prompted Satō to make renewed inquiries about Soviet policy. Molotov assured the ambassador on June 19 that neither agreement had anything to do with Japan and that there was no change in Moscow's policy toward Tokyo. When Satō wanted to know whether this meant that the Soviet Union would not transfer, sell or lease territory or offer military bases to the United States for operations against Japan, Molotov answered that no such matters had been discussed, and remarked that rumors to this effect must have been concocted by Germany. Undaunted, Satō asked for assurance that such matters would not be discussed in the future either; Molotov replied that he was not thinking of another trip abroad or of negotiating similar agreements. When Satō once again expressed the hope of his government that the Soviet Union would not change her policy toward Japan, Molotov retorted with obvious annoyance that his country in turn expected Japan to do the same and not to listen to fabricated rumors.

As American operations against Attu Island in the Aleutians mounted, Japanese fear increased that the United States might obtain bases in Kamchatka. On May 17, 1943, Satō called on Vyshinskii. Acknowledging that the Soviet government had repeatedly promised not to lease, transfer or offer any part of its territory as a military base to a third country hostile to Japan, he declared that "while the Japanese government firmly believed that the Soviet government would not make any change in the above policy even if the Soviet Union received a request from the United States government for furnishing her with military bases, it wished the Soviet government to confirm that it would not grant such a request by the United States." Vyshinskii replied that no such request had been received and that it was inconceivable that one would be received in view of the U.S.S.R.'s strict adherence to the Neutrality Pact. In a formal written response, read by Lozovskii to Satō four days later, on May 21, the Soviet government restated its intention to abide by the Neutrality Pact so long as Japan did so, and once again blamed hostile propaganda for rumors to the contrary.[11]

On August 12 an American plane which had bombed the northern Kuril Islands made an emergency landing on Kamchatka. The plane, a B-24, based at Adak in the Aleutians and belonging to the Eleventh Air Force, had bombed Paramushiru, one of the Kuril Islands, in the first major raid on Japanese territory since the Doolittle attack on Tokyo in April 1942.[12] When Satō, who had moved back to Moscow, discussed the matter with Molotov on August 24, he reviewed and restated his warnings that repeated landings by American planes endangered not only Japanese security, but the maintenance of amicable relations between their countries.[13] Molotov retorted that the fact that only one such incident had occurred in the sixteen months since April 18, 1942, spoke for itself.[14] Yet a month later, on September 12, several American planes landed on Kamchatka after bombing the northern Kuril Islands.[15] Satō hastened back to Molotov to express the serious concern of his government and to ask that the Soviet Union make a formal protest to the United States.[16,d] Tokyo was alarmed, he pointed out, because a group of seven planes was involved this time and because a captured U.S. Army Air Corps sergeant had testified

d Such a protest was duly made by Deputy Foreign Minister Vyshinskii. Three of the American bombers had had engine trouble, four had been intercepted by Soviet pilots and forced to land. They had been part of an attack group of 19 bombers, of which only two returned to Adak undamaged. The one raid had cost the Eleventh Air Force 50 per cent of its long range fighters and over half a year was to pass before it was to be able to mount a similar offensive.

that the United States had planned all along to make use of Soviet territory for emergency landings. Molotov replied that he knew nothing about the matter, but would check with the military authorities.

On September 24 Lozovskii read to Satō a note from his government, acknowledging that seven American planes had landed on Kamchatka on September 12—three because of engine trouble, four after drawing fire from Soviet fighter planes. The planes and crews had been interned in accordance with international law. When Satō asked that Japanese officials be permitted to inspect the state of the detained American planes and crews, Lozovskii replied that this would be a violation of international law since Japan and the United States were at war. Satō then requested that the Soviet Union inform Japan of the types of planes and number of crewmen involved; this would not be contrary to international law and seemed a reasonable request in view of the premeditation of the above incident. Lozovskii countered that the disclosure of such information was not accepted practice and that the Soviet government was not obligated to provide it to Japan. As a gesture of goodwill, however, Lozovskii did inform Satō a week later, on September 30, that the seven American planes had consisted of two four-engine machines with a twelve men crew each and five twin engine machines with crews of five to six men.[17]

On June 15, 1944, two more American planes had made emergency landings in Soviet territory and on June 20 a third had done so. The machines and their crews had been interned. Dmitrii Zhukov, who had become director of the Far Eastern Section of the Commissariat of Foreign Affairs, had informed Counselor Kameyama Kazuji of this on July 8, four days after

Satō had requested information about the matter from Lozovskii.

On August 20 and on November 18 American B-29's operating out of China again made emergency landings in the Soviet Union. Although Satō sought information about the incidents, he was unable to learn anything specific. Lozovskii asserted that the planes seemed to be missing. In 1942–43 the Soviet news agency TASS had reported the landings of American planes, but this practice had been discontinued in 1944,[18] perhaps because of the Japanese inquiries that followed invariably.

The question of American bases in the Russian Far East was not a German concoction, as Molotov had suggested; it had actually been discussed by Soviet and American officials, notwithstanding Molotov's denial. The United States, which supported the U.S.S.R. in her struggle with Germany by supplying crucial war materials under the lend-lease program, expected Soviet cooperation in her conflict with Japan. In spite of the fact that Litvinov, by then the Soviet ambassador in Washington, informed Secretary of State Cordell Hull shortly after the outbreak of the Pacific War that the Soviet Union, in view of her deep involvement in the war in Europe, was not in a position to participate in hostilities against Japan, Hull sought the use of two air bases—one in Kamchatka and one in the vicinity of Vladivostok—for launching strikes against Japanese naval forces, bases and cities, warning Litvinov that it would be a "matter of great importance" if the Soviet Union refrained from cooperating with the United States in the Far East while the latter continued aiding her.[19]

General Douglas MacArthur believed that a heavy

air strike against Japanese objectives might not only destroy substantial Japanese oil supplies, but force the Japanese to pull in much of their widely dispersed air strength. Army Air Corps planners felt that the Allied position in the Far East would continue to deteriorate unless bases could be obtained for air attacks on Japan.[20] Army strategists were less enthusiastic, fearing that the facilities and resources of the Russian Far East might be inadequate for the task.[21] The Joint Staff Planners wondered whether the Soviet Union would be able to defend the Maritime Province in the event of a Japanese invasion and warned that it would be unwise for the United States to launch operations from Siberia until she was in possession of "complete information as to Soviet strengths and plans," verified by "a careful and exhaustive examination by United States officers of Soviet forces and facilities in the Siberian theater."[22]

In early 1942 Acting Secretary of State Sumner Welles proposed to Litvinov that the Soviet government allow the United States to open a new front against Japan by making bombing runs against Japanese naval bases and munitions factories from bases in Siberia.[23] In April Admiral William H. Standley, who had just been appointed United States ambassador to Moscow, asked Stalin for data concerning Soviet airfields and support facilities.[24]

As a wedge for entering the Russian Far East, the Americans proposed the opening of an Alaska-Siberian route—"Alsib"—for the shipment of lend-lease aircraft. In June 1942 President Franklin D. Roosevelt wrote to Stalin that "if the delivery of aircraft could be effected through Alaska and Siberia instead of across Africa, as is now the practice, a great deal of time would be saved" and that "the establishment of a ferry service through Siberia would permit the delivery by air of short-range aircraft to the Soviet Union instead of by sea, as is now the case." Envisaging the delivery of aircraft by American crews to Lake Baikal via Vladivostok, Roosevelt argued that "in the event of a Japanese attack on the Soviet Maritime Provinces, such a Siberian airway would permit the United States quickly to transfer American aircraft units to the latter area for the purpose of coming to the assistance of the Soviet Union." Roosevelt proposed that a United States Air Corps team, dressed in civilian clothing and posing as personnel of a commercial agency, make an exploratory flight, accompanied by one or two Soviet officials.[25]

Although the Americans were willing to exchange some military information with the Russians and to undertake a similar survey of Alaska and though Roosevelt felt that there was "practically no limit" to the aid the United States would furnish to the Soviet Union[e] if it would cooperate in opening the Alsib route and supply the Americans with information about Siberia, the Soviets were suspicious of American motives. They limited the above-mentioned American survey team to seven men and instead of attaching one or two Soviet officials to it, as Roosevelt had proposed, insisted that the Americans accompany a Soviet group on two Soviet planes. They would not let American pilots ferry planes, but demanded that Soviet pilots fly them from Alaska.[26]

When Major General Follett Bradley, who had negotiated the opening of the Alsib route in Moscow in the fall of 1942, had told Stalin that Roosevelt believed

[e] Roosevelt thought also of sending supplies to China by the Alsib route.

that a Japanese attack on the Soviet Union was forthcoming, Stalin had replied that he was keenly aware
of such a possibility, but had shown little desire for the
presence of American personnel on Russian soil even in
the event of war between the Soviet Union and Japan.[27]
The high-pressure salesmanship of American diplomacy merely stiffened Stalin's resistance. When Roosevelt proposed that Bradley be allowed to inspect Soviet military installations, Stalin fired back: "It should
be perfectly obvious that only Russians can inspect
Russian military objectives, just as U.S. military objectives can be inspected by none but Americans." He
reiterated that the Soviet Union needed help in the
way of aircraft "not in the Far East where the U.S.S.R.
is not in a state of war, but on the Soviet-German
front."[28,f]

At the Teheran Conference in November 1943 Roosevelt tried to convince Stalin of the need for combined
planning, when the latter told of the Soviet Union's intention to join the Pacific War after the defeat of
Germany.[g] A report of the Combined Staff Planners the
following month stressed the importance of bases in the
Soviet Union not merely as sites from which air strikes
and air blockades could be mounted, but from which
Japan proper could be invaded.[29]

At the Yalta Conference, at which Stalin committed
himself in writing to enter the Pacific War "within two

[f] American readers will reject the implication in Kutakov's assertion
that "the American ruling circles strove to take advantage of the threat
of an attack by the Japanese militarists on the Soviet Far East in order
to carry out military-political reconnaissance in Siberia and there establish
their military air bases," yet Russian suspicion of foreigners was so deeply
ingrained that the statement can be taken as an accurate reflection of
what Soviet leaders *thought* American motives were.

[g] For an account of American requests for Soviet participation in the
Pacific War, see Appendix E.

or three months" after the surrender of Germany and the end of the war in Europe,[30] he agreed to the establishment of American Air Force bases in the Maritime Province—at Komsomolsk or Nikolaevsk—though not on Kamchatka where there was a Japanese consul. Stalin's promise remained unfulfilled, however, as the American survey team was not allowed to visit the Russian Far East. With American forces advancing well within striking distance of Japan by the spring of 1945, the Joint Chiefs of Staff discarded the idea of bombing raids from the Maritime Province, partly because of Soviet obstruction and partly because the high logistical cost that would have been entailed was no longer justified.[31] Thus while American planes were permitted to use Soviet bases in the Ukraine for shuttle bombing runs between England and Italy on one hand and the U.S.S.R. on the other hand against German industrial targets, a matter of direct benefit to the Soviet war effort, the establishment of American bases in the Far East, which would have endangered rather than strengthened Soviet security both by inviting a Japanese attack and by acquainting foreigners with conditions and strategic installations in the Maritime Province, never materialized.[h]

The Question of Renewed Soviet Aid to China

The Soviet Union had extended significant aid to Chiang Kai-shek in the training and equipping of the Nationalist Air Force from 1937 until mid-1941.[32] In 1938–39 Soviet air units had participated directly in combat; Russian fighter pilots had defended Chung-

[h] While the Soviets refused to allow the establishment of American bases in the Russian Far East for fear of precipitating a Japanese attack, they showed their sympathy toward the United States by engineering "escapes" of the American fliers interned in the U.S.S.R. See Appendix D.

king, Lanchou, Ch'engtu, Sian and other Chinese cities. Russian bombardiers had blasted Japanese positions and staged raids deep behind Japanese lines, including, for example, an air raid on Taiwan and a flight over Japan proper.[33] When China joined the United States, Great Britain, and the Soviet Union in the Four Power Declaration on General Security at the Moscow Conference on October 30, 1943, the Japanese were worried that Soviet participation in the Pacific War had been discussed.[1] Japanese suspicions were justified, for Molotov had intimated to Harriman during the conference that the Soviet Union would join in defeating Japan after the conflict in Europe was ended, an intention conveyed unequivocally by Stalin to Secretary of State Hull on October 30.[35] But the Soviet government could not admit this intention to Japan, lest the U.S.S.R. be drawn into the dreaded two-front war.

When Satō inquired of Molotov on November 10 whether the Moscow Conference signalled any change in Russian policy toward Japan, the Soviet foreign commissar blandly assured him that it did not.[36] Molotov declared that no secret decisions had been made at the conference.[37] Molotov cut short Satō's questions about the wording of the Four Power Declaration by turning the tables on him. What was the meaning, he asked, of the reaffirmation of the Tripartite Pact between Germany, Italy and Japan on September 15? The treaty provided for mutual assistance in the establishment of their respective new orders in Europe and Asia. Considering the fact that Germany was at war with the Soviet Union, how did reaffirmation of the treaty affect

[1] For this very reason no doubt, the Soviet Union had strongly objected to the inclusion of China as a signatory of the Four Power Declaration, but the United States had insisted on it. [34]

Soviet-Japanese relations? Satō could not give a direct answer without checking with his government; he did express the belief that the Neutrality Pact remained in force since it antedated reaffirmation of the Tripartite Pact. A month passed before Satō gave an official reply to Molotov's query. The purpose of the reaffirmation of the Tripartite Pact, he informed Molotov on December 9, was to declare that it remained unaffected by the change of government in Italy, i.e. by the overthrow of Mussolini. The Tripartite Treaty, the Japanese government asserted, sought to unite Germany, Italy and Japan in common opposition to Great Britain and the United States, which were planning to conquer Europe and Asia, and did not concern the Soviet Union.[38]

At a luncheon on April 13, 1944, commemorating the third anniversary of the conclusion of the Neutrality Pact, Ambassador Malik asked Foreign Minister Shigemitsu Mamoru whether British and American news broadcasts were correct in reporting that Ambassador Ōshima would participate in a conference of Axis officials at Berchtesgaden. Shigemitsu replied that such meetings were stipulated by the Tripartite Pact; Japan had attended them in the past and would do so in the future. But he asserted that as far as Japan was concerned, Soviet-Japanese relations would not be a topic for discussion. When Malik echoed Molotov's earlier query how the Japanese-German declaration of September 15 of the previous year should be interpreted, Satō repeated that it merely stated that the Tripartite Pact would remain unaffected by the change of government in Italy and that it had nothing to do with Soviet-Japanese relations.[39]

Meanwhile, on April 8, Satō had told Molotov that rumors had reached his government to the effect that some of the American goods sent as aid to Russia by way of the Persian Gulf were being sent by rail to Ashkhabad and from there by truck to Sinkiang and eventually to Chungking. Molotov had denied that the Soviet Union was allowing the transshipment of supplies to Chiang Kai-shek. On June 24[j] Satō raised the question again, alledging that American aid to Russia was being diverted to China. He made it clear that it did not matter whether the materials were sent to the Nationalists or the Communists; in either case they would be used against Japan. Satō stated that the observance of neutrality by Japan and the Soviet Union in the Russo-German and Japanese-American wars respectively was of mutual benefit. He argued that the Japanese-American war was related to the Japanese-Chinese war and that a state which observed neutrality in regard to the former must also observe neutrality in regard to the latter.

Molotov replied that the Soviet Union would abide by the Neutrality Pact so long as Japan did so. No arms were now being supplied to China, nor was there any secret provision in his country's treaties with the United States and China or in the lend-lease agreement for doing so. But what about rumors of Japanese assistance to Germany? Such assistance would be a violation of the Neutrality Pact on the part of Japan. When Satō demanded to know on what facts the rumors were based, Molotov responded that he had not asked Satō on what facts his rumors were based.

---

[j] Kutakov states mistakenly that this exchange between Satō and Molotov and the subsequent exchange between Satō and Lozovskii took place in June and July 1943. [40] The more detailed Japanese account includes queries about the Wallace mission. Since Wallace did not arrive in the Soviet Union until May 23, 1944, [41] the conversation must have taken place in 1944.

Satō asserted that since Germany was fighting not only against the U.S.S.R., but also against the United States and Great Britain, with whom Japan and Germany both were at war, Japanese shipments to Germany could not be interpreted as anti-Soviet. For good measure he mentioned Russian shipments to the United States, and implied that they were in violation of the Neutrality Pact. Not so, responded Molotov. The Soviet Union had to pay the United States for the aid she received by sending her various materials, but though she sometimes received arms from America, she delivered none to her. Japanese aid to Germany was different, he argued, since the German war effort was directed primarily against the Soviet Union. Satō countered that he did not have any information about Japanese shipments to Germany, but the materials sent by the Soviet Union to the United States would eventually become war supplies for use against Japan. Molotov dismissed Satō's argument with the contention that if it were accepted, no trade at all would be possible. He remarked sarcastically that although he had denied clearly that the Soviet Union had furnished any aid to Chiang Kai-shek since the previous year or the year before that, he had heard no such clear denial from Satō about Japanese aid to Germany. Satō responded that he simply had no information at hand to comment on the rumor to which Molotov had referred, although his government might have the necessary facts. He reiterated that the matter of furnishing aid to Chiang differed from furnishing aid to Germany; Chiang was fighting only against Japan, while Germany was at war not solely with the U.S.S.R., but also with England and the United States. When he took issue with Molotov's assertion that Germany was fighting primarily against Russia and declared that now that the second front had been opened, this would no longer be true, Molotov broke out in laughter.[k] If such were the case, he said, Japan might indeed have to aid Germany.

Satō expressed his government's uneasiness about the prolonged stay of the American Vice President Henry A. Wallace in Soviet Asia. He wanted to know if it had anything to do with American aid to China via Russian territory. He added hastily that up to now Japan had not had any political conflict with the U.S.S.R. in China and did not desire any; on the contrary, she wished to cooperate with the Soviet Union in solving the China question.

Molotov replied that he believed that Wallace's visit had been prompted by internal conditions in the United States.[l] Wallace had wished to investigate living conditions in Russian cities and villages, a desire which the Soviet government had seen no reason to refuse. Although Wallace was touring Siberia at length, he never visited Moscow. He was accompanied by very few and relatively minor officials,[m] and there had been no discussion of American policy.[n]

[k] The second front, for which the Russians were waiting with bitter impatience, was not opened until the following month.

[l] The selection of Wallace for the mission to Soviet Asia and China was connected with domestic politics. President Roosevelt, Barbara Tuchman notes, "was considering dumping Wallace in favor of some more generally acceptable running mate, and it was a natural instinct under the circumstances to want him out of sight." [42]

[m] Wallace was accompanied by Owen Lattimore (for his expertise in "the problems involving Chinese-Russian relationships"), John Hazard (then chief liaison officer, Division of Soviet Supply, Foreign Economic Administration), and John Carter Vincent (chief of the Division of Chinese Affairs).[43]

[n] This was correct, though Wallace did exchange personal views with Russians about the Japanese menace. Noting in the account of his trip that he had been much concerned at the time "whether the Russians would be fully prepared if the Japs should strike north," he added that the step-up in American Lend-Lease shipments to Soviet Siberia after V-E day,

Satō expressed the belief that the United States was seeking to coordinate the policies of the Allied powers vis-à-vis Japan. He feared lest she use her influence in the Red Army to draw the Soviet Union into the Sino-American coalition in China. He repeated that so far there had been no great political dispute between the U.S.S.R. and Japan regarding China and hoped that there would not be any in the future. What were the views of the Soviet government on this subject? Molotov replied evasively that the Soviet Union was not in a position to comment about this. The rivalry between the Nationalist Party, the Communist Party, various self-proclaimed Communist Parties and anti-Communist parties in China was an internal matter from which the Soviet Union stayed clear; she had her hands full with her own affairs.

Satō withdrew saying that the purpose of his visit had not been to criticize the policies of the Soviet government but to exchange opinions concerning the China question. He stated that Molotov's explanations had been fully satisfactory. Molotov responded that he would still like an answer to the questions he had raised.

On July 9 Satō made an oral reply to Lozovskii. The Japanese government had indeed exchanged goods with Germany during the current war, as had the Soviet Union with the United States and England. But at no time had Japan furnished Germany with arms; she had remained neutral in the war between Germany and the Soviet Union and had taken care to restrict co-

---

"moving supplies across the North Pacific at the rate of 300,000 tons a month," helped prepare the Russians for their entry into the Pacific War. "Huge stock piles were built up like the one we saw at Magadan, to which vessels went with vital goods if the Russians felt they might be stopped by the Japs on passing through La Pérouse Strait to Vladivostok." **

operation with Germany to the conflict with the United States. Lozovskii promised to convey the Japanese reply to Molotov, but observed that there was a difference in Soviet trade with the United States and England and Japanese trade with Germany. The materials which the Soviet Union received from her allies were used in the war with Germany, while the materials which Japan supplied to Germany, notably rubber, tin and wolfram were used for war against the Soviet Union. Lozovskii and Satō agreed, however, that the general attitude of their respective governments was more important than the question of how some of the goods would be used by their recipients, and expressed belief that the continued exchange of opinions had contributed to Soviet-Japanese amity.[45]

The specter of Soviet collaboration with the United States either in the form of granting the Americans air bases or of assisting them politically in their effort to unite the various factions in China the more effectively to resist Japan continued to haunt Satō. On September 16 he queried Molotov about the Dumbarton Oaks Conference and sought renewed assurance that the Soviet Union would remain neutral in the Sino-Japanese conflict. Molotov repeated that the U.S.S.R. did not wish to get involved in the internal affairs of China.

On November 17 Satō tried to learn from Molotov what had transpired at the Quebec and Moscow conferences. Turning to Chiang Kai-shek's dismissal of General Joseph W. Stilwell as his chief of staff, Satō asserted that Japan had no territorial ambitions in China and would withdraw her troops upon the restoration of peace in East Asia. He claimed that Japan merely wished to halt English and American aggression in China and hoped to pursue a China policy agreeable to the U.S.S.R. So eager was Japan by this time to keep the Soviet Union out of the Pacific War, that Satō actually offered in the name of his government to discuss any wishes that Moscow might have about Japan's China policy. Molotov made no reply.

On January 4, 1945, Satō expressed concern about an article in *Izvestiia,* dated December 2, 1944, calling for a united front in China against the Japanese. Referring to Chungking (i.e. the Nationalist government) as "the vanguard of the United States," he blamed it for the continuing hostilities; he saw no reason, he said, why there could not be friendly relations between Japan and Communist China just as there were between Japan and the Soviet Union. Molotov retorted that the article in question did no more than provide information and reassured Satō that the Soviet government was not about to assist the United States in uniting China.[46]

Restraint of Shipping

As the Japanese plunged into the Pacific War with surprise attacks on American and British installations and shipping, a number of Soviet vessels were sunk or seized.° Soviet protests to the Foreign Office in Tokyo fell on willing ears, but it took three months to negotiate the release of the seized vessels as local Japanese customs officials, naval authorities and the military police had confiscated various equipment and the personal belongings of the Soviet crewmen and interfered

° Two merchant ships, the *Perekop* and *Maikop,* were sunk in Chinese waters. Four others were caught in the port of Hongkong—one, the *Krechet,* was sunk, another, the *Simferopol',* was severely damaged, and the remaining two, the *Svir'stroi* and the *Sergei Lazo,* were boarded and seized. [47]

with the return of the equipment, the delivery of purchased coal, and the completion of ship repairs.[48]

In April 1943 the Japanese navy seized two Soviet vessels in La Pérouse Strait.[p] The ships had allegedly been transferred to the U.S.S.R. by the United States after the outbreak of the Pacific War and that, according to articles 22 and 23 of the Japanese Code of Naval Warfare, made them subject to seizure. In repeated meetings with Vice Minister of Foreign Affairs Matsumoto Shunichi, Ambassador Malik pointed out that according to international law, particularly the London Declaration,[q] neutral ships could be seized if their transfer had been merely nominal, to conceal the true ownership of the vessels. This was not the situation in this case, however; ownership had been fully transferred to the U.S.S.R. and the United States was not in a position to use the ships against Japan.

When Malik's efforts in Tokyo went unheeded, Lozovskii handed Satō in Moscow on May 12 a strong note of protest, which warned that the failure of the Japanese government to release the Soviet vessels contradicted its professions of friendly relations with the U.S.S.R. on the basis of the Neutrality Pact and might force the Soviet Union to reexamine her policy toward Japan. In response to Satō's allegation that the Japanese Code of Maritime Warfare was in accord with the London Declaration, Lozovskii quoted article 56 of the London Declaration to show that it was not. He stated that a nation could not place its own laws above international law, and declared that it was incompre-

---

[p] La Pérouse Strait is called Soya Strait by the Japanese. The vessels were the *Kamenets-Podol'sk* and the *Ingul*.

[q] The London Declaration of the Law of Naval Warfare had been signed by the major powers, including Japan and Tsarist Russia, on February 26, 1909.

hensible that Japan should apply laws which were in conflict with international law to a neighboring neutral country. He demanded that Japan give proof of her amicable relations with the Soviet Union by action rather than words. When Satō asked whether the Soviet Union was a signatory of the London Declaration, Lozovskii retorted that the Soviet Union respected other international agreements signed by Tsarist Russia.

On May 14 Matsumoto told Malik that the matter was being delayed by the incompleteness of ships' documents and by inaccuracies in statements made by their captains, and asked for information concerning the date of transfer of title and the date of permission of navigation. This the U.S.S.R. failed to provide.[r] Meanwhile Japan refused to allow Soviet embassy officials to visit the detained crewmen. When Malik told Foreign Minister Shigemitsu on June 1 that the dispatch of embassy officials was a right, guaranteed by international law, Shigemitsu replied that the question was not a matter of international law, but of domestic procedure during wartime.

---

[r] Article 55 of the London Declaration stipulated: "The transfer of an enemy vessel to a neutral flag, effected before the outbreak of hostilities, is valid, unless it is proved that such transfer was made in order to evade the consequences to which the enemy vessel, as such, is exposed. There is, however, a presumption, if the bill of sale is not on board a vessel which has lost her belligerent nationality less than sixty days before the outbreak of hostilities, that the transfer is void. This presumption may be rebutted." Article 56 stated: "The transfer of an enemy vessel to a neutral flag, effected after the outbreak of hostilities, is void unless it is proved that such transfer was not made in order to evade the consequences to which an enemy vessel, as such, is exposed." [49] In arguing the case of the seizure of the *Kamenets Podol'sk* and *Ingul* at the War Crimes Trial in Japan, the Japanese reiterated that their seizure had been warranted, because the ships' documents had been faulty and thus had not proven valid Soviet ownership. The Soviets contended, on the other hand, that the burden of proof was on Japan and demanded what documentary evidence the Japanese had that the ships had been bought in the United States or that the ships' documents had indeed been faulty.[50]

That day, on June 1, Satō communicated to Lozovskii at Kuibyshev that investigation showed that the
Japanese government had acted properly in detaining
the vessels and that their disposition must be decided
legally by a prize court. At the same time, however,
the Japanese government was impressed by the friendly
attitude of the U.S.S.R. in reconfirming the Neutrality
Pact on May 21 and was willing to consider a political
solution of the matter for the sake of strengthening
Soviet-Japanese relations, provided Japan's rights as a
belligerent power would not be compromised. It hoped
that the Soviet government in turn would cooperate
in the solution of various outstanding problems between their countries.

Lozovskii acknowledged that a political solution
might be a way out of the legal impasse and asked
what specifically Satō had in mind. Satō replied that he
was prepared to advise his government to release the
ships immediately, if Molotov would accept the Japanese position that Japan had acted within her rights as
a belligerent in seizing them and would promise to
make every effort to solve amicably outstanding problems between the Soviet Union and Japan.

Lozovskii informed Satō the following day, on June
2, that Molotov wished to see him about the matter.
Satō proceeded to Moscow and called on the foreign
minister on June 4. Molotov handed Satō a strongly
worded note recapitulating the view that Japanese seizure of the Soviet ships was contrary to international
law. The proposal for a political solution, the note
stated, led the Soviet government to believe that the
detention of the vessels had been a political plot to
bring pressure on the U.S.S.R. to solve various un-
related problems, such as Japanese demands for oil,

and warned that the seizure and detention of the ships for over a month "must be regarded as nothing but a violation of the Neutrality Pact by the Japanese side."[51]

In the discussion that ensued, Satō expressed chagrin that the offer of a political solution had been interpreted as political pressure. But as he and Molotov restated the diametrically opposite positions of their governments, it became clear that what mattered most was not the seizure of the particular ships, but the question of future incidents. Neither side was able to compromise the principles involved—Japan could not give up the right, which she believed she had as a belligerent, to seize vessels transferred by one of her enemies to a neutral power, and the Soviet Union in turn could not agree to repeated Japanese detention of her ships.

On June 15 Satō called on Molotov and informed him of the decision of his government to release the vessels because of Moscow's intention to remain on friendly terms with Japan and to respect the Neutrality Pact. The ships were duly set free on July 28.[52]

Yet three days prior to the release of the two Soviet ships, on June 25, another Soviet merchant vessel, the *Nogin,* was detained in La Pérouse Strait on the same charge. On July 3 the Soviet government protested against this action simultaneously in Moscow and in Tokyo. Molotov told Satō that Japan had failed to give assurances that such incidents would not be repeated and branded Japanese policy toward the Soviet Union as "incomprehensible."[53] "The present state of affairs," Molotov stated, "cannot but affect Soviet-Japanese relations."[54] Satō promised that Soviet vessels would not be seized again and asserted that the Japanese navy must have acted on its own authority in the incident. He assured Molotov that the Japanese government had no intention of violating the Neutrality Pact.[55] He took the opportunity to ask again whether the Russians would remain equally faithful to the pact or whether they would grant bases to the Americans.[56]

On July 8 Molotov prodded Satō for a reply from the Japanese government concerning the release of the *Nogin.* On July 13 Malik vainly asked Matsumoto that the Soviet consul in Hakodate be permitted to visit the vessel. On July 15 Lozovskii pressed Satō for an answer. When another Soviet ship, the *Dvina,* was detained on July 20, Lozovskii summoned Satō on the 23rd and handed him a strongly worded note of protest, in which the Soviet government demanded the immediate release of the two vessels and a definite guarantee that no Soviet ships would be seized in the future; at the same time the Soviet government gave notice that it reserved the right to demand compensation for losses suffered by the Soviet Union through the detention of her vessels.

Satō replied that it was difficult for Japan to make any promises about the future, since she did not know whether the transfer of vessels to the U.S.S.R. by the United States, Japan's greatest enemy, would continue; Japan would have to extend the same treatment to other neutral states and her rights as a belligerent power would be restricted greatly. Lozovskii reiterated that the rights of belligerency were laid down by international law and that if the Soviet Union could exercise neutrality toward Japan in spite of her alliance with Germany, Japan could do the same notwithstanding Russia's alliance with the United States. The seizure of Soviet vessels was a violation of the Neutrality Pact. Satō retorted that Soviet obstruction of Japanese oil interests was a violation of the Neutrality Pact too.[57]

On August 8 Lozovskii again demanded the release of the two Soviet ships. On August 13 Satō informed him that the *Nogin* had been set free on the 9th, but that his government could make no promises about the future. It reasoned as follows: The transfer of American vessels to the Soviet Union was to the advantage of the United States in that it avoided the sinking and consequent need of replacement of vessels carrying supplies to Russia. The accumulation of large stores of American weapons and ammunition in Soviet territory near the area where Japan and the United States fought constituted a threat to Japan, because eventually these supplies might be used against her. She had no assurance that the American vessels, transferred to the U.S.S.R. and flying the Soviet flag, might not be operated by American crews, nor did she know how many vessels would be transferred in the future. There were other neutral countries, and Japan could not make an exception in the case of the Soviet Union and give up her rights of belligerency in regard to the latter only. In the all-out struggle with Great Britain and the United States, she could not afford to abandon her rights of belligerency, which, Satō insisted again, she derived from article 56 of the London Declaration.

Lozovskii retorted that the Japanese interpretation of the article was in conflict with the Neutrality Pact and that Satō had drawn erroneous conclusions, because he had begun with questionable premises. In his response, Satō left open the "political solution" of similar incidents to preserve friendly relations between the two countries, but he would make no concessions on principle.

On August 24 Molotov accused Japan of causing fluctuations in the course of Soviet-Japanese relations by the detention and release of Russian vessels and demanded a guarantee that no further incidents would take place. Satō responded that the matter was no more pleasant for the Japanese side and, though he reiterated that Japan could not give up her rights of belligerency, he expressed the opinion that now that several incidents had occurred the Japanese authorities would have more adequate instructions; the Soviet Union had no alternative but to wait and see what the future held in store. When Molotov repeated that the Japanese attitude was "incomprehensible," Satō replied that the maintenance of friendly Soviet-Japanese relations depended to a large extent on the attitude that the Soviet Union would exhibit. On this inconclusive note ended the negotiations concerning Japanese seizure of Soviet vessels obtained from the United States.[58]

Japanese restraint of Soviet shipping was not confined to the interception of vessels from America. With the outbreak of the Pacific War Japan had restricted navigation by the proclamation of maritime defense zones, which no foreign vessel could enter without prior permission from the Japanese navy. The zones embraced the regions of Tsugaru Strait (between Hokkaido and Honshu), La Pérouse Strait (between Hokkaido and Sakhalin), Tokyo Bay, Kii Channel (the strait between Honshu and Shikoku), Sasebo and Wakasa off Japan proper, Chinkai (Chinhae) Bay and Pusan Harbor off Korea, and the Pescadores (Boko) Islands, Takao (Kaohsiung) and Keelung off Taiwan.

Since article IX of the Treaty of Portsmouth prevented the closing of La Pérouse Strait,[s] a two mile wide waterway had been left open for general navigation between dawn and sunset.

The Soviet embassy objected orally on January 31, 1942, that any restriction of navigation in La Pérouse Strait was in violation of the Treaty of Portsmouth as well as of international law. To limit the passage of vessels to that strait, it added, was tantamount to stopping navigation completely for part of the year, since La Pérouse Strait froze in winter. The embassy pointed out that Tsugaru Strait connected the high seas and that any prohibition of navigation through it was a violation of international law and of Soviet interests.

Japan defended her action in a verbal note in mid-March. Insisting on the right to defend her shores now that the Pacific Ocean had become one large battlefield, she noted that restricted navigation through Tsugaru Strait was possible, subject to special permission by the Japanese navy. She argued that Japanese fishery and navigation had suffered great losses by Soviet establishment of maritime danger zones far from the scenes of battle, the closing of Tatar (Mamiya) Strait (between Sakhalin and the mainland) in violation of the Treaty of Portsmouth, drifting mines, and Soviet detention of Japanese vessels.[t]

On April 14 the Foreign Office, at the demand of the Japanese navy, informed the Soviet embassy of a number of additional zones put off limits to Soviet vessels navigating between Vladivostok and Kamchatka and

[s] Japan and Russia respectively engaged "not to take any military measures which might impede the free navigation of the Straits of La Pérouse and Tartary." [59]

[t] Reference was made here to the *Kibi Maru* Incident. For an account of the incident and the question of maritime danger zones, see Appendix C.

the American continent, lest the Japanese patrolling system be disclosed." If in a given instance entry into one of these zones was unavoidable, the Japanese navy must be duly informed; otherwise it would demand a change of course "or take other appropriate action necessitated by defense." The Soviet Union objected to the new restrictions in an oral note on April 23. She took the opportunity to justify the maritime danger zones, imposed by herself, and the laying of mines and the seizure of Japanese ships, to which the Japanese had referred in mid-March.

On October 30 Naval Attaché Mikhail Kulikov requested permission from the Japanese Ministry of the Navy for the use of Tsugaru Strait beginning in January, when drifting ice would make navigation through La Pérouse Strait dangerous. When no reply was received, Counselor Zhukov called on Kamimura, director of the Political Affairs Bureau, on December 15 and requested his assistance in obtaining the necessary permission. He renewed the request twice more in January 1943. As no response followed, Ambassador Malik declared to Vice Minister of Foreign Affairs Nishi Haruhiko on January 20 that the Japanese oral note of March 14, 1942, could be interpreted as allowing general navigation through Tsugaru Strait and that it was merely a matter of determining the manner and course of passing. Any dangers that might stem from delays in settling the matter, Malik asserted, would be the responsibility of the Japanese government. Nishi replied that the Soviet request was still under consideration and dis-

---

" The closed areas were: the northern extremity of Oki Island; the Mishima lighthouse at the northern tip of Tsushima Island; the Kamisaki lighthouse at the southern end of Tsushima Island; the southern extremity of Yakushima Island; and Torishima Island.

claimed any responsibility on the part of the Japanese government.

The following day, on January 21, Tani Masayuki, who had succeeded Tōgō as foreign minister in September, took issue with Malik's contention that Japan had agreed to general navigation of Tsugaru Strait. He said that the Japanese notes of December 8, 1941, and March 14, 1942, clearly stated that special permission was necessary and that it might be refused for military reasons. In view of the danger of drifting ice from February through April, Soviet vessels would be able to steer "any appropriate course" after passing through the route where navigation was permitted in La Pérouse Strait until entering the Onnekotan (Kuril) Strait, connecting the Sea of Okhotsk and the Pacific Ocean. They were permitted to sail close to Hokkaido and to anchor in Japanese waters in case of danger. Malik asked once again that Soviet vessels be allowed to sail through Tsugaru Strait, but Tani refused. Tani referred back to Soviet closure of Tatar Strait and the establishment of restricted zones along the Soviet shores, to Soviet mines, and the detention of Japanese vessels. On January 28, "out of Japanese consideration for the security of Soviet vessels," Kamimura presented to Zhukov a revised route that Soviet vessels were to follow in passing through Tsushima Strait.[60]

On January 30 Lozovskii handed Satō a memorandum which rejected Tani's proposal of letting Soviet vessels proceed past Hokkaido on the ground that it failed to guarantee the safety of normal shipping and thus was not a satisfactory solution to the question of Soviet navigation. The memorandum declared that the Japanese attitude contradicted the principles of international law and infringed on the legitimate rights and vital economic interests of the U.S.S.R. and warned that this would "naturally affect the progress of the fisheries talks." When Satō retorted that the fisheries treaty had nothing to do with the navigation question, Lozovskii asserted that the treaty had expired in 1936 and that its provisions had been extended by temporary agreements on an annual basis. Since the closing of Tsugaru Strait was illegal, because it was not an inland sea but a body of water connecting two high seas, and since the closure caused economic loss to the Soviet Union, it was quite natural, Lozovskii contended, that it would affect the fishery talks, which were also economic in nature. Satō considered the Soviet position unreasonable; he remonstrated that the fisheries treaty had not expired, but had been extended by the provisional agreements.

On February 3 Malik asked Tani again that Japan reconsider her closure of Tsugaru Strait. Navigation of La Pérouse Strait was absolutely impossible in winter, while the route by way of Tsushima Strait was so long as to inflict serious damage on the Soviet economy. He added that Japan's attitude regarding this matter would have a direct bearing on Russia's attitude toward various problems raised by Japan, among them the fishery question. Tani objected to the linking of navigation and fishing. Japan's fishery rights, he stated, derived from the Treaty of Portsmouth and would not be affected by the expiration of the fisheries treaty; the U.S.S.R., on the other hand, had no treaty rights for the navigation of Tsugaru Strait, and Japan was entitled to restrict passage through the strait in wartime. Tani asserted that Soviet mines made navigation through Tatar Strait impossible and that the Soviet suspension of the Tsugaru-Vladivostok shipping service had inflicted economic loss on Japan.ᵛ Japan had done all she could in arranging for navigation through La Pérouse and Tsushima Straits and hoped that the U.S.S.R. would use these two routes.

Undaunted, Malik repeated the Soviet demand for navigation through Tsugaru Strait. It had not been his intention to discuss the fishery question that day, he said, but he had felt it necessary to point out that its settlement might depend on the solution of the navigation question, since Tani himself had always related the strait matter to other problems.

Tani retorted that the Soviet side should try the two routes proposed by Japan rather than reject them out-of-hand. The U.S.S.R. had established maritime danger zones far from the fields of battle; Japan, on the other hand, was fighting in the Pacific Ocean against the United States and could not allow Soviet nagivation through Tsugaru Strait.

The next day, on February 4, Malik sent a note to Tani informing him that six Soviet vessels were ice-bound in La Pérouse Strait and that the U.S.S.R. would hold Japan responsible for any damage to the vessels. He renewed the request for permission to sail through Tsugaru Strait. In a reply delivered on the 5th, Tani disclaimed any Japanese responsibility and repeated that passage through Tsugaru Strait could not be allowed for military reasons.

An attempt by First Deputy Foreign Commissar Vyshinskii to put pressure on Tokyo by delaying issuance of a transit visa to the Japanese ambassador to Italy, Hidaka Shinrokurō, and staff until Tsugaru Strait was opened was checkmated by Ambassador Satō, who re-

ᵛ With the outbreak of the Pacific War the Soviet Union had closed Vladivostok to foreign vessels.

minded him that the release of the detained Soviet seamen had been made conditional on the issuance of the transit visa.ʷ On February 10 Satō reaffirmed the determination of his government to keep Tsugaru Strait closed.[61]

Reciprocal Harassment

The outbreak of the Pacific War had reduced border conflicts between Japan and the U.S.S.R., as both powers were preoccupied with other regions and sought to avoid a two-front war. Not only were border incidents less frequent—half as many in 1942 as in 1941—but they were also less serious. No military engagements occurred and although a number of military and civilian trespassers were arrested and some killed, both sides exercised restraint.ˣ

Incidents at sea were more difficult to control. The problem of drifting Soviet mines, concerning which Japan had protested strongly in late 1941, remained un-

---

ʷ After the outbreak of war with Germany, the Soviet Union had made it increasingly difficult for Japanese officials to pass through her territory. In the fall of 1942 she issued transit visas to diplomatic and consular representatives en route to posts in Italy, Switzerland, Bulgaria and France in exchange for Japanese repatriation of Soviet sailors detained in Hongkong and Singapore. Agreement was reached readily for the passage of diplomatic couriers back and forth, since this was of equal interest to both sides.

ˣ A tabulation by the Japanese Foreign Office of alleged Soviet violations of Japanese territory — the Foreign Office did not make a similar tabulation of alleged Japanese violations of Soviet territory—showed a decrease in total number of incidents from 195 in 1939 to 58 in 1942. The breakdown of incidents was as follows: Violation of the boundary, shooting, kidnaping and detention: 133 in 1938; 148 in 1939; 94 in 1940; 44 in 1941; 19 in 1942. Violation of air territory: 27 in 1938; 42 in 1939; 17 in 1940; 47 in 1941; 38 in 1942. Interference with river navigation: 3 in 1939; 1 in 1939; 8 in 1940; 3 in 1941; 1 in 1942. Seizure of boundary marks and detention of rafts: 0 in 1938; 0 in 1939; 28 in 1940; 3 in 1941; 0 in 1942. Others: 3 in 1938; 4 in 1939; 4 in 1940; 1 in 1941; 0 in 1942. Grand total: 166 in 1938; 195 in 1939; 151 in 1940; 98 in 1941; 58 in 1942.

solved. In 1942 and in 1943 Japan protested repeatedly, pointing to the loss of lives and property and reserving the right to demand damages. Yet when a number of Soviet vessels were sunk in Japanese waters by submarine and air attacks and Moscow protested to Tokyo, the Japanese government disclaimed responsibility and contended that the ships must have been sunk by American or British submarines and planes.[62]

The Japanese conflict with the United States had a direct bearing on Soviet-Japanese relations in other ways. American freezing of Japanese funds in July 1941 affected Soviet-Japanese relations, since various Japanese payments to the U.S.S.R. had been made until then via New York. In October 1941 the Japanese government proposed that Gosbank, the Soviet state bank, open a special account with the (Japanese) Bank of Korea in Tokyo and that transactions in either direction be made through this account. The Bank of Korea would be willing, at Soviet request, to make payments in the currency of a third country, except one which had seized Japanese funds, with Japan meeting any balance in gold. Details concerning various rates of exchange, including a special exchange rate for diplomats, were to be worked out between Gosbank and the Bank of Korea. In mid-January 1942 the Soviet Union accepted the Japanese proposal with the proviso that in the event of gold payments the gold was to be delivered to the Vladivostok branch of Gosbank, with a 6 per cent charge added to meet the cost of transporting the gold to the world markets. Japan regarded the surcharge as unreasonable, and considerable debate ensued over this issue.[y]

Meanwhile, with the outbreak of the Pacific War, the Japanese had taken possession of foreign banks, among

[y] See Chapter Five.

them the American Chase Bank in Hongkong. The Soviet Union, which had an account with the bank, demanded a full refund, insisting that international law entitled her to it. But the bank gave full refunds to Japanese depositors only; Axis accounts were settled at 50 per cent of deposit, those of neutrals at merely 20 per cent.

As the Soviet Union and Japan were at war with each other's allies, they tried to restrict the movements of each other's representatives. The Japanese diplomats in the U.S.S.R. had been evacuated to Kuibyshev along with the representatives of the other powers in the winter of 1941. As noted, visits to Moscow for conferences with top Soviet officials were arranged, but Japanese requests in 1942 to inspect the state of the embassy property in Moscow and of the consular building in Petropavlovsk were turned down; the Japanese in turn denied Russian petitions to check the condition of the Soviet consular building in Nagasaki.[z]

In August 1942 the Japanese broke up an alleged Allied espionage ring in Shanghai, arresting a total of 45 persons, among them 13 citizens of the U.S.S.R.[aa] Twenty of the 45 were prosecuted before a military tribunal. Nine of those convicted were Soviet citizens. They included officials of Intourist (the Soviet travel agency), commercial agents and a newspaperman, and were accused of having gathered and transmitted information about Japanese military forces and their plans.

[z] The "reciprocity" to which both sides resorted in granting or refusing visas, internal travel requests, assignments of doctors, issuance of permits, etc. extended even to the issuance of driver licences, a Soviet driver continuing to fail his tests until his Japanese counterpart in the U.S.S.R. passed his.

[aa] The other foreigners, arrested as spies, were 13 White Russians, 3 Latvians, 2 Austrians, 2 Luxemburgers, 2 Englishmen, 2 Americans, 5 Chinese, 1 Jew, and 1 Iranian.

Six of the Soviet defendants received sentences ranging from 3 to 10 years imprisonment; three were given suspended sentences of 2 years and were put on probation for five years. Protests by the government of the U.S.S.R. were of no avail.

The suspicions and passions of wartime led to the harassment of foreigners. Two minor incidents will serve to illustrate how individual Russians and Japanese became victims of the strained state of Soviet-Japanese relations.

On January 30, 1942, a Japanese inspector in plain clothes demanded to see the identification papers of a correspondent of the TASS news agency in Tokyo by the name of Kozlov, who was on his way back to the Soviet Union through Korea. Kozlov refused and in the argument which ensued allegedly used rude and threatening language and, when he got off the train, refused to stay at the hotel suggested by the Korean police authorities. Kozlov was arrested on charges of interfering with the execution of official duties. A lady's gold watch was found in his pocket and though he insisted that he had bought it in Tokyo, he was charged also with trying to carry it out without the necessary permission. In response to Soviet protests it was hinted that charges would be dropped if Kozlov apologized. On the advice of the Soviet embassy, Kozlov refused, and was sentenced to six months imprisonment; he also had to pay a fine and his watch was confiscated. Kozlov made two legal appeals. Both were turned down and he was not permitted to leave until he had served his sentence.

The Soviets in turn sentenced Kohara Shozo, the chauffeur of the Japanese military attaché in Moscow, to eight months in jail for assaulting a Russian fellow driver, even though the latter had received no physical injuries and the two had been quickly reconciled. The severe sentence appeared to be partly a reprisal for the sentencing of Kozlov, partly the result of a dispute between the Soviet government and the Japanese embassy as to whether the Russians had the right to summon the Japanese employee, who lived in the embassy, directly or whether the Japanese embassy had the right to forbid his appearance in court. As in the case of Kozlov, the individual involved became a pawn in a diplomatic confrontation over matters of diplomatic "principle" and lost.[63]

4

Liquidation of the North Sakhalin Concessions

One manner of harassment on the part of the Soviet Union was interference with the operation of the oil and coal concessions on North Sakhalin. As will be recalled, Japan had agreed at the time of the signing of the Neutrality Pact that the question of their liquidation was to be solved in several months, but upon Germany's invasion of the Soviet Union she had begun to backtrack on her commitment. The U.S.S.R. could not revoke the protocols of 1925, but she could hamstring the operation of the concessions in such a way as to make them so unprofitable that the Japanese companies would stop using them; then they might be induced to return them "voluntarily" or be deprived of them for not living up to the concession agreements.

Soviet interference with the operation of the concessions took various forms. Some Japanese workers and supervisors were denied entrance or exit visas, others were shadowed and occasionally arrested on one charge or another. Approval was withheld of plans of operation which the oil and coal companies presented to the Soviet authorities. Access was limited or not given at all to regions where the Japanese wanted to prospect for oil and guards were not provided to protect Japanese property when the Japanese were absent; Japanese vessels were forbidden from unloading their supplies, or the supplies were confiscated if there was any violation of the letter of the law. Duties and fines were imposed if the Japanese sold more than the authorized amount of goods to their own employees or sold to Soviet organizations in violation (or alleged violation) of Soviet customs laws. Payment was delayed for electricity furnished by Japanese companies to neighboring villages, and Soviet enterprises trespassed on concession property.[a]

The approach of the Pacific War had brought additional problems for the beleagured concessionaires, as the aforementioned freezing of Japanese assets by the United States made it impossible for them to continue reimbursing the Soviet Union for various expenses in dollars via New York, as had been done until then. Nor could they, after the outbreak of hostilities, obtain from the United States issues of the American magazine *National Petroleum News,* on the basis of which Japanese compensation to the Soviet Union for the use of the oil concessions had been calculated.

There is no need to reconstruct the countless arguments and discussions that developed around every is-

[a] It is impossible to tell when delays were merely bureaucratic and denials a legitimate means of safeguarding Russian interests and when certain measures were taken, or not taken, as intentional harassment. Yet if one looks at the total picture, Soviet interference with the operation of the concessions seems to have been deliberate—and justified from the Soviet point of view.

sue. Taken singly, the questions were usually of little importance and often remained unresolved. Though Ambassador Satō argued at one point that a small problem might grow big, Deputy Foreign Commissar Lozovskii retorted that to say so, was merely to use big words. But while Satō may have exaggerated the significance of a particular issue, piled together, the many little problems did form a "heap of a problem," because Soviet restrictions crippled the Japanese enterprises to such an extent[b] that the Japanese government had to step in with subsidies to keep them operating.

The Soviet Union and Japan both linked the question of the oil and coal concessions with other issues—the Neutrality Pact, the fisheries concessions and trade. In the letter which Matsuoka had given to Molotov at the time of the signing of the Neutrality Pact, he had expressed the expectation and hope that the commercial agreement and the fisheries convention would be concluded very soon and the question of the liquidation of the North Sakhalin concessions solved in a few months. This was construed by the Japanese to mean that the liquidation of the concessions was contingent on the conclusion of satisfactory commercial and fishery agreements. To Molotov's assurances in May 1941 that the setting of a firm date for the liquidation of the concessions would contribute to a quick solution of the commercial and fisheries question, Tatekawa responded that a quick settlement of the commercial and fisheries problems would lead to the prompt liquidation of the con-

[b] Crude oil production decreased in round figures from over 180,000 kilotons in 1936 to 150,000 in 1937 and 127,000 in 1938; by 1939 crude oil production had declined to under 85,000 kilotons and by 1943 to 17,000. Bituminous coal production suffered a similar fate, dropping from about 178,000 kilotons in 1936 to less than 47,000 in 1937 and to between 5 and 7,000 a year thereafter.

cessions.[1] Matsuoka reiterated to Smetanin on May 29 that the solution of the fisheries question and the conclusion of a treaty of commerce must precede the surrender of the concessions. Declaring that this was the only way of furthering Japanese-Soviet amity, he asserted that otherwise there would be failure and he personally would have to resign or commit hara-kiri.[2]

As the Soviet side persevered in its insistence on a definite date for the liquidation of the concessions, Matsuoka on May 31 conveyed a personal message through Tatekawa, in which he pledged that the problem would be solved not later than six months from the date of his original promise, but renewed the plea that the trade and fisheries questions be settled before that in order to strengthen his domestic position, the abrogation of the concessions being a delicate political issue in Japan.[3]

Upon the German invasion of the Soviet Union, the Japanese renewed their procrastination. On August 13, 1941, Foreign Minister Toyoda parried Smetanin's demand that the liquidation of the concessions be carried out on the basis of Matsuoka's letter and personal message with the assertion that the unexpected changes in the situation required further discussion. When Smetanin asked pointblank whether the promise to liquidate the concessions was still valid or not, Toyoda retorted evasively that Japan wanted to solve the problem basically after sufficient study. Vice Minister Nishi, to whom Smetanin posed the same question on December 12, responded that since the outbreak of the German-Soviet War had prevented the signature of the commercial agreement and since the uncompromising attitude of the U.S.S.R. had blocked the conclusion of a fisheries agreement, Japan found it difficult to solve the concessions question. Nishi asserted that Matsuoka's pledge had not lost its effect, but that changes in the situation made it impossible to carry it out.

For a number of months the Soviet Union did not belabor the issue for fear of provoking a Japanese attack. With the containment of the German onslaught and Japanese involvement in the Pacific War, however, she felt secure enough to renew her demand for the liquidation of the concessions. On April 6 and 14, 1942, Molotov told Ambassador Satō that inasmuch as the Soviet Union was living up to her commitments, Japan must do the same. When Satō asserted that the concessions question should be reexamined, because Japan had consented to it originally in payment for the Neutrality Pact which now, due to changed circumstances, benefitted primarily the Soviet Union, Molotov pointed out that the present situation was as difficult for Japan as for the U.S.S.R. and warned that if the commitments were not met, the validity of the Neutrality Pact would be in question. Satō responded that Japan did not mean to negate the Matsuoka letter; it was just that changes in the government could greatly influence policy. To this Molotov replied with a forced laugh, that if that was so, the problem would never be settled.

On June 4, 1943, Molotov took advantage of Japanese detention of two Soviet vessels to file a protest in which he linked the detention of the vessels and the delay in the liquidation of the concessions as a violation of the Neutrality Pact, and insisted that Japan live up to her commitments. He asked Satō, to whom he handed the note, why Japan did not give up the concessions; their surrender had been a condition for the conclusion of the Neutrality Pact and Matsuoka had twice promised in writing that they would be returned.

Satō's response that the liquidation of the concessions

had been promised in expectation of the prompt conclusion of fisheries and trade agreements and that these had not materialized did not satisfy Molotov, and on June 15 he pressed the ambassador for a more acceptable explanation. Satō now elaborated that the delay in the surrender of the concessions had been occasioned by a change in the government and a change in popular feeling due to the outbreak of the Pacific War. He admitted that the liquidation of the concessions was necessary, but said that it would take considerable time and patience. When Molotov persisted that the Japanese must live up to their commitments, Satō asserted that while Japan had never negated Matsuoka's letter and merely delayed its application, the letter had been merely a personal note and not, as the foreign commissar contended, a condition for the Neutrality Pact, which had gone into effect unconditionally upon ratification.

Molotov disagreed. He insisted that the Neutrality Pact would not have been signed without Matsuoka's letter, and again demanded a prompt resolution of this matter.[4]

It was not Molotov's argument, but the continued deterioration in Japan's military position and the desire to deprive the Soviet Union of incentives for entering the war that persuaded the Japanese to liquidate the concessions without further delay. The decision was reached at a liaison conference between the government and the Imperial Headquarters on June 19, 1943, and at a conference between the army, navy, and Foreign Office on June 26. The liaison conference agreed to preserve peace with the Soviet Union and to induce the latter to remain faithful to the Neutrality Pact with Japan. "In order to solve positively outstanding questions between Japan and the Soviet Union," the conferees specifically resolved "to transfer to the Soviet Union for countervalue the North Sakhalin oil and coal concessions."[5,c] On July 3 Ambassador Satō informed Molotov that the declarations made by the Japanese and Soviet governments on May 21 regarding their intention to abide by the Neutrality Pact paved the way for the liquidation of the concessions and that he was prepared to discuss the necessary procedures.

The procedure problem was essentially a question of whether the amount of compensation should be settled before or after the signing of an agreement to liquidate the concessions. The Soviet side wanted the details of compensation worked out afterwards; Satō proposed first an informal agreement in Moscow to surrender the concessions, to be followed by the negotiation of appropriate compensation in Tokyo, and only then the conclusion of a formal agreement. The problem was complicated by Satō's attempt to link the liquidation of the concessions with the signature of a fishery treaty. (This was not a tactic to delay matters. Satō had felt for some time that the concessions had to be surrendered; he simply regarded the fishery rights as a matter of life and death for Japanese fishermen and deemed it expedient to take advantage of the liquidation of the oil and coal concessions to extend the fishery concessions.)

When Satō requested of Molotov on July 8 that the signing of the concessions liquidation agreement be accompanied by a Soviet reaffirmation of the Neutrality Pact and by the initialling of a fishery agreement, Molotov reiterated that the surrender of the concessions had been a prerequisite for the conclusion of the Neutrality

---

[c] The Japanese agreed also, somewhat more vaguely, "to grasp the trend of American-Soviet relations and of German-Soviet relations and then cope with changes in the world situation."

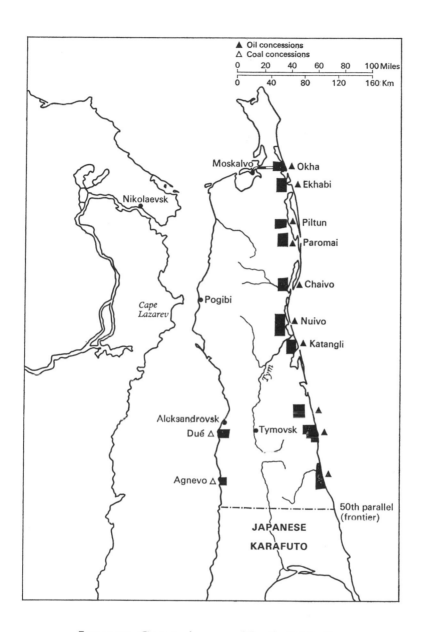

Japanese Concessions on North Sakhalin.
(Source: John J. Stephan, *Sakhalin. A History* [Oxford: Clarendon Press, 1971], p. 110. Reprinted with permission of the publisher.)

Signing of the Neutrality Pact.

Seated: Molotov. Standing, from left to right: Pavlov, Kozyrev, Tsarapkin, Fujii, Miyakawa, Tatekawa, Sakamoto, Lozovskii, Stalin, Matsuoka, Vyshinskii, Kase, Yamaoka, Yamaguchi. (From *Izvestiia*)

Stalin and Matsuoka, Arm-in-Arm.

"The Last Fragment of the Fascist Axis."

(From *Izvestiia*)

"Fire Extinguishing Measures."

(From *Izvestiia*)

THE MANCHURIAN CAMPAIGN

Negotiating the Cap-tulation of the Kwantung Army.

Signing of the Instrument of Japan's Surrender by Lieutenant General Derevianko.

Pact and that it was merely a matter of Japan carrying out her obligations. He did not object to parallel consideration of the fishery and concessions questions, but said that Satō should discuss these matters with his deputy, Lozovskii; he personally had lost confidence in a quick solution of the concession question and was preoccupied with the Soviet-German War.

Satō conveyed to Molotov at this time Japan's terms for the liquidation of the concessions: (1) compensation for the equipment of the oil and coal companies as well as for expenses connected with the dissolution of the companies; (2) compensation for loss of revenue from the concessions, from the date of their surrender to the original date of expiration in 1970; (3) payment for the above compensation in commodities desired by Japan; and (4) sale to Japan at a fair price of a certain amount of North Sakhalin oil for a certain number of years. Molotov remarked that he deemed compensation for rights until 1970 unreasonable and that, like Matsuoka, he wanted to put a time limit for the liquidation of the compensations. Satō replied that it would take two to three months to work out the compensations; while Japan was prepared to surrender the concessions at the same time as the signing of the treaty, she would not sign until the compensation issue had been resolved.

The Soviet Union was in no hurry to settle the problem. Her attitude, which seemed "negative" to the Japanese Foreign Office, may have been due not only to preoccupation with the war with Germany, but to the realization that time was on the side of Russia—that sooner or later Japan would have to modify her terms to obtain an extension of the coveted fishery rights. In July and August Lozovskii and Molotov repeatedly sidestepped Satō's offer to discuss compensation, while complaining that Japan was not living up to her commitment to liquidate the concessions.

In November Satō requested the reopening of the fisheries and concessions talks and this was done on an alternating basis, the first fisheries conference being held on November 19, the first concessions conference on November 26. At the concessions conference Satō modified the terms for liquidation, conveyed by him to Molotov on July 8. Rather than demand full compensation for the equipment and cost of dissolution of the companies, Japan now asked merely that they be permitted to dissolve without loss or gain. Lozovskii replied that it was not the responsibility of the Soviet government to share the losses of Japanese companies, losses which were due to mismanagement. Nor was it reasonable for Japan to expect compensation for the unused portion of the original concessions, as their liquidation had been promised in exchange for the Neutrality Pact (which, by implication, constituted compensation). Without replying directly to Satō's repeated objections that while Matsuoka had agreed to the liquidation of the concessions he had not agreed to do so without compensation, Lozovskii asked what commodities Japan wanted. He also wished to know whether, if the Soviet Union made payments to Japan in goods in compensation for the liquidation of the concessions, she could receive payments from Japan in goods for the fishery rights.

The expression of Soviet interest in receiving commodities from Japan opened a new vista for bargaining. Satō replied that it had been decided that the fishery payments be made in gold and the supplying of special commodities was a political question, but that he was willing to refer the matter to his government.

At the second fisheries conference on December 3, Lozovskii stated that the liquidation of the oil and coal concessions must precede the signing of a new fisheries treaty. When Satō reverted to the question of terms, Lozovskii produced the preface of the Soviet memorandum of May 31, 1941, which stated that the liquidation of the concessions was a prerequisite for the conclusion of a fisheries agreement, to prove that the Soviet demand was reasonable. What with Lozovskii insisting that the liquidation of the concessions precede the fishery treaty and Satō demanding that a compensation agreement precede the liquidation of the concessions, specific figures were discussed at last.

On December 7 Counselor Kameyama informed Nikolai Generalov of the Far Eastern Section of the Foreign Commissariat that the cost of dissolving the coal and oil concession companies would amount to almost 100 million yen.[d] This prompted Lozovskii to remark at the second concessions conference on December 17 that the companies must have existed for the purpose of being in debt, a charge which Satō denied. Satō stated that compensation figures for the renunciation of the unused portion of the concessions—what the Japanese called "future concessions"—would be reported shortly, but that their computation was closely related to the amount of oil and coal the Soviet Union would agree to supply Japan. Satō expressed Japan's desire for 200,-000 tons of oil a year and 100,000 tons of coal a year for five years. While Lozovskii again rejected Japanese claims of compensation for "future concessions," he raised the question of the mutual supply of strategic goods; specifically, the Soviet Union wanted to receive

[d] 99,060,000 yen minus 2,950,000 in cash and securities on hand and payments made in commodities.

crude rubber in exchange for the oil and coal demanded by Japan.[e]

Satō lost no time in pointing out that this was a basic change in Soviet attitude; there was no connection between the demand for strategic goods and the supplying of oil and coal, which had been discussed as a prerequisite for the liquidation of the concessions for the past two years. Now it was Lozovskii's turn to justify a shift in position by pointing to changes in the war situation. When Satō retorted that the outbreak of the Pacific War had no connection with the concessions problem and in no way obligated Japan to supply the Soviet Union with such products as crude rubber, Lozovskii remarked that he understood the Japanese view, but that the supplying of strategic goods must be on a reciprocal basis.

On December 31, at the third concessions conference, Satō communicated the amount of compensation that Japan desired for the renunciation of the unused portion of the concessions: just over 42½ million yen.[f] Lozovskii rejected the demand again on the grounds that Japan had agreed to liquidate the concessions for political reasons rather than as an economic deal and that there was no special agreement nor stipulation in the original concession contracts for the purchase of the concession rights. He added that no compensation had

---

[e] On his return to Japan Morishima proposed to the Foreign Office that Japan supply the desired rubber in exchange for platinum, which she needed badly. Nothing came of this and other proposals for the exchange of commodities, because of disagreement in army, navy and Foreign Office circles in Japan. [e]

[f] The Japanese calculated that the Soviet Union might be able to obtain 1 million tons of oil a year from the concessions. They would have liked to have received 10 per cent of the amount, or 100,000 tons, a year for 27 years as compensation and, as Satō told Lozovskii at the above meeting, had come up with the 42½ million yen figure on the basis of this estimate.

been paid by the Japanese to the Russians for unused "future concessions," when they had bought (through Manchukuo) the Chinese Eastern Railway. In fact, the total compensation that the Japanese had paid for the Chinese Eastern Railway and the concessions that went with it had been smaller than the amount now demanded, even though the C.E.R. complex had been far more extensive than the North Sakhalin concessions.[g] Lozovskii repeated that there was no reason why the Soviet Union should share in the losses of the Japanese companies, particularly since the latter, while losing money, had paid dividends.

Satō responded that it was normal for a business company to pay dividends. While there was no obligation in the contracts that the companies show a profit, they had indeed planned to make a profit during the entire period of operation. They had invested heavily and had been forced to cease operations before realizing the expected return on their investment. It was only reasonable, Satō argued, for those responsible for the unexpected liquidation of the concessions to bear the losses. Satō repeated that although it was true that Japan had agreed to the liquidation of the concessions for political reasons, it had been understood by both sides from the very beginning that there would be due compensation.

Lozovskii did not object to compensation, but it was the view of his government, as he stated repeatedly, that compensation be paid not for might-have-beens but for actual value, i.e. for the equipment and machinery on North Sakhalin.[7] On January 7, 1944, he conveyed a

[g] For a detailed account of the negotiations leading to the sale of the Russian-built Chinese Eastern Railway or the North Manchurian Railway, as it was called by the Japanese, see George Alexander Lensen, *The Soviet Union and the Manchurian Crises* (Tallahassee: Diplomatic Press, 1973).

counter-offer. The Soviet Union was prepared to supply Japan on normal commercial terms with 50,000 tons of oil a year for five years *after* the war. To this Satō responded on January 11 with a demand for 150,000 tons of oil a year for five years beginning from the moment of the liquidation of the concessions.[h]

The Soviets did not agree and on January 21 levied fines on the Japanese companies for not living up to the contracts by not exploiting the concessions. The fines were larger than the compensation for "future concessions" demanded by Japan and thus threatened to deprive the latter of any oil whatsoever.[i] Realizing that further bargaining was futile, the Japanese accepted in principle a compromise offer made by Lozovskii on January 26: the Soviet Union would pay Japan five million rubles (4⅓ million yen) at once in addition to selling her 50,000 tons of oil a year for five years upon the termination of the war.

A Japanese draft agreement was presented on February 7 and a Soviet draft on February 19. The Soviets wanted the concessions restored at the time of the signing of the protocol; the Japanese objected that domestic methods of procedure made this impossible. They agreed, therefore, first merely to initial the protocol, Japan to begin taking steps for the liquidation of the concessions from that moment. The surrender of the concessions would be completed with the final signing of the protocol; simultaneously fishery rights were to be extended for another five years.

On March 10 the concessions protocol was initialled;

[h] According to Soviet calculations this was twice what the Japanese themselves were producing on North Sakhalin at the time.

[i] Soviet sources do not mention this important ploy; they attribute Japanese capitulation to Russian demands solely to Japan's desire to obtain Soviet consent to the fishery convention before the opening of spring navigation.

on March 30 it was signed along with the fisheries proto-col.[J] Supplementary articles stipulated that evacuation of the concessions was to take place with the beginning of navigation in 1944. The Soviet side pledged not to levy taxes or fees on returning Japanese; severance pay for Soviet workers was to be given by the Soviet gov-ernment, severance pay for Japanese workers by the Japanese government. The five million rubles were to be paid by the Soviet government within one week af-ter the protocol went into effect to a special account of the Japanese government in the Soviet State Bank in Moscow and were convertible, at Japanese request, into gold, to be conveyed to the representative of the Japa-nese government at Manchuli Station. Japanese vessels would be allowed to enter Okha, Nabil, Aleksandrovsk and Due to carry away the Japanese stores of coal and oil, the operation to be completed with the assistance of Soviet labor within four months from the beginning of navigation.[8]

Ratification by the Emperor was required before the protocols could go into effect, and ratification by the Emperor depended on prior approval by the Privy Coun-cil. Although Satō had signed the protocol liquidating the concessions, he was worried whether the Privy Council would go along with it. He felt that the Privy Council was very cold toward the Foreign Office and tended to delay important treaties with trivial questions; he had doubts whether it would accept the liquidation of the concessions. To Satō's relief, the Privy Council spoke well of the protocol in view of the world situa-tion, and Ishii Kikujirō actually called it a "hit" and praised Satō highly in front of the Emperor.[9]

[J] For the text of the protocol, transferring the oil and coal concessions, see Appendix G.

The Russians were equally satisfied. They regarded the liquidation of the Japanese concessions on North Sakhalin 26 years ahead of their scheduled expiration as a triumph of Soviet diplomacy.[10]

5

Extension of the Fisheries Protocol

The fisheries negotiations, like the oil and coal concessions talks, followed the vagueries of the world situation. Japanese and Russian demands increased or declined in direct relationship to the international position of Japan and the Soviet Union.

Japanese fishing in Russian water was regulated by the Fisheries Convention of 1928,[a] which had been concluded for a period of eight years and had been extended subsequently by a series of provisional agreements in May and December 1936, December 1937, April and December 1939 and January 1941. A modified fisheries convention had been negotiated in 1936, but the Soviet Union had withheld signature upon Japan's adherence to the Anti-Comintern Pact in November of that year. The agreement of January 1941, which was the sixth provisional agreement, was to run till the end of the year, at which time it was to be replaced by a new fisheries treaty.

[a] For the full text of the fishery convention and attached protocols, see Lensen, *Japanese Recognition of the U.S.S.R.*, 217–316.

A committee, consisting of Counselor Nishi and four Japanese colleagues plus Deputy Foreign Commissar Lozovskii and four Soviet colleagues, was formed to hammer out the new treaty, but by mid-February the arrangement was found to be too cumbersome and the negotiations were left in the hands of Nishi and Lozovskii alone.

Nishi proposed the conclusion of a new fisheries treaty, identical in provision with the old one, for a period of five years, and wished to extend Japanese leases for the duration of the treaty. Fees and fines due to the Soviet Union were to be computed at the average rate over the past three years and were to be paid in a lump sum in yen; Soviet state enterprises were to be limited, as in the past, to fishing grounds with a production of up to five million poods.[b]

In the discussions which ensued in February and March, Lozovskii expressed willingness to accept a five year treaty, but objected to an automatic five year extension of the fishing leases. He argued that an automatic extension would be in violation of the auction system, and remarked that national and strategic considerations might necessitate the closing of fishing grounds.[1] Lozovskii pointed out that due to natural phenomena rivers changed their course; since fishing was not allowed in waters approaching river inlets, the shifts in rivers might put some fishing grounds into the forbidden region. He added that fishing grounds where the supply of fish had become exhausted should be closed also. "There are changes in the economic value of the grounds, there are changes in the world market, and there are changes in the entire situation," Lozovskii remarked in support of the argument that the auction system be preserved,

[b] One pood equals about 36 pounds avoirdupois.

for at auctions all these circumstances were taken into consideration.

The Soviet Union did not reject the idea of a lump sum payment in yen as such, but would not consider it unless compensation would be made for changes in the exchange rate. The cost of changing rubles into yen, as then applied in the payment of lease fees, was 20 per cent higher than in January, when the lease fees had been determined. Unless the lease fees were raised to make up for the difference, Lozovskii argued, the Soviet Union stood to lose almost one million yen out of the four million yen due her from Japan.[3,e]

The Soviet Union backed her demand for higher lease fees with the argument that the Nichi-Ro Fisheries Company, a Japanese concern, had shown an increase in profits, as reported by the economic journal *Diamond*. The Japanese countered that this was true only of the company's operations outside of Soviet territory; the rate of profit in Russian waters remained small.

When Lozovskii persisted in his demand for increased fees, Nishi offered on March 17 to make a lump sum payment 25 per cent higher than the average amount for the past three years on condition that the U.S.S.R. would promise to keep the fishing grounds open. Japan would not object, he stated, to the cancellation of the contracts for 19 out of the 39 fishing grounds, which

[e] In 1931–1936 the Japanese had an average of 368 fishing grounds in which they annually caught some 60½ million salmons and produced an average of 990,000 cases of canned salmon. In 1937–1941 their fishing grounds declined in number to an average of 329, yet their productivity increased; they caught an average of over 65 million salmons, producing an average of over 1 million cases of salmon. A similar increase occurred in the crab industry, production advancing from an average of about 37,000 cases of canned crabmeat in 1932–1936 to an average of 63,000 cases in 1937–1941. Under the circumstances, Kutakov argues, the Soviet government could not but object to the Japanese attempt to lower the rental fee while keeping the number of fishing grounds the same. [4]

had not been exploited in the past.[4] Japan would be willing also to consider an increase in the number of bays and river inlets where Japanese were forbidden to fish, provided this did not prejudice their efforts to begin fishing in areas previously requested. Nishi expressed willingness to continue the discussion of pending questions concerning the management of fishing grounds, but reiterated the demand that the operation of Soviet state enterprises be limited to five million poods.

Lozovskii rejected a lump sum settlement that would be lower than the amount paid for the current year. He insisted that the auction system was fundamental to the treaty and that payment must be made on the basis of the official rate. Nor did he accept any limitation on the operation of Soviet state enterprises; he argued that this was an internal matter and could not be made subject to an agreement with a foreign power. As for the closing of additional fishing grounds, this was necessary for national and strategic reasons: Japan herself had many closed and fortified areas far outside her territorial waters.[5]

On April 5 Lozovskii made a counterproposal, in which the factories, fishing grounds, bays and river inlets that were to be closed were specified. If all further payments were made in yen at the exchange rate set by the Soviet State Bank on January 2, 1940,[d] Moscow would lower the lease fees, calculated in rubles, by 22 per cent.[6] The auction system must remain in effect, however, and no treaty limitations could be imposed on the operations of Soviet state enterprises.

While the Japanese took issue with practically every point in the Soviet proposal, their main objection was

[d] According to that exchange rate, 100 yen equaled 124 rubles and 28 kopecks.

to Soviet insistence on the retention of the auction system, for the results of previous auctions had been disappointing. The crux of the problem, the Japanese felt, lay in the fact that the political and economic systems of the U.S.S.R. made any real auction impossible. They were quite willing to leave the auction stipulation in the treaty, but wanted the allotment of fishing grounds done in fact by agreement between the two governments.[7]

The two sides were separated by a basic difference in attitude. The Japanese felt that they had a right to fish in Soviet waters and that this right had economic and monetary value. But the Russians maintained, as Lozovskii put it, "that the rights of the Japanese in the Far Eastern waters of the U.S.S.R. derive from the convention and the concessions contracts; if there will be a fisheries convention and concessions contracts, Japanese subjects will have specific rights, if there will be no convention, neither will there be rights."[8]

As the controversy was reduced to a few basic issues, Ambassador Tatekawa took them up directly with the foreign commissar. In mid-May he informed Molotov that Japan was willing to withdraw her proposal for a lump sum settlement and to make individual payments at the official rate in yen, convertible upon demand into gold.[9,e] She was prepared also to give up her demand that the operation of Soviet state enterprises be restricted by treaty and to accept the closing of additional river inlets and bays. But she refused to recognize any restrictions on the open seas and requested that some fishing grounds which had been closed since 1940

---

[e] But Japan sought a decrease in lease fees of 53 per cent on two of the grounds, of 43 per cent on grounds received during the auctions in April 1939 and March 1940, and of 39 per cent on the other ones.[10]

be reopened. Tatekawa made it clear that the Japanese government was interested above all in the extent to which the Soviet Union would meet its demand for the stabilization of the fishing grounds—for the renewal of the leases currently in Japanese hands.

The Soviet government was not willing to guarantee Japanese retention of all fishing grounds. Yet while insisting on the closing of fishing grounds that the Japanese had not exploited for the past two years and while clinging to the retention of the auction system, it made an important concession. As Molotov conveyed to Tatekawa on May 31, the Soviet government was prepared to allay Japanese fears by stipulating that so long as the treaty was in force, Russian fishery enterprises would receive not more than 10 per cent of the Japanese fishing grounds; it was willing to make the oral promise, furthermore, that this 10 per cent would not include any of the fishing grounds where the Japanese had canning factories. The Soviet government was willing to extend the effectiveness of the special contracts for the exploitation by Japanese subjects of all twenty canneries and the 29 fishing grounds attached to them for the entire duration of the new convention.[10] Molotov agreed that the exclusion of foreign fishermen from bays and inlets stipulated in the first article of the protocol would not extend to the open seas; on the other hand, certain regions—Pos'et Bay, Peter the Great Bay, the area between Olga Bay and Vladimir Bay, Sovetskaya Gavan', De Kastri Bay and Avacha Bay—would be closed for strategic reasons.[11]

On June 10 Tatekawa once again rejected the auction system. "The Imperial Government cannot understand," the Foreign Office wrote in the note which he transmitted, "why the Soviet Government so stubbornly insists on the retention of the auction system, which has caused so much harm in the relations between the two countries."[12] Tatekawa challenged the closing of the above regions in so far as they encompassed the open seas. It was Japan's position that the distinction between territorial waters and open seas was governed by international law and not subject to bilateral alteration.

The Soviet government was still studying the Japanese objections, when the German invasion of the U.S.S.R. brought the fisheries talks to an abrupt halt.[13] When they were resumed on December 17, because the provisional agreement, concluded in January, neared expiration, Japan, flushed with victories in the Pacific, renewed such demands as the limitation of the operation of Soviet state enterprises. The old method of payment, involving dollars sent via the United States, was no longer possible, of course, and Japan proposed payment in yen, only half of which were to be freely convertible into foreign currency or gold; the remainder were to be used by the Russians for the purchase of commodities and consumer goods in Japan. But the Soviet Union persisted in her refusal to restrict the production of her state enterprises and demanded that Japan pay the entire amount of lease fees in convertible yen. When the Japanese government remarked that it would have thought the Soviet government would be pleased with the offer in view of the shortage of commodities in Russia, Moscow replied testily that Japan too was short of commodities; if it needed to import anything from Japan, it would do so directly, through the Commissariat of Trade.

On January 10, 1942, Japan agreed to make the full payments in yen, but controversy continued as to the date for determining the rate of exchange of yen for gold and as to which side was to bear the expense of transporting the gold to the world markets from Vladivostok, where it would be paid by the Bank of Korea. On this and other issues both sides were willing to compromise, because they were equally interested at the time to preserve amicable relations with each other. Thus the Soviet Union and Japan split the cost of transporting the gold to the world markets; Japan agreed to a charge of 4 per cent instead of the 6 per cent demanded by the U.S.S.R. They also found a formula to modify the auction system: Japan promised not to bid on certain fishing lots, while the Soviet government made a declaration to the effect that Japan should have no difficulty in regaining by auction desired grounds whose lease had expired at the end of the year.

On March 20 the seventh provisional agreement was signed, with the hope expressed once again that a new "permanent" treaty would be concluded during the year. The provisional agreement extended various contracts and leases at somewhat increased fees, payment to be made in convertible yen or in foreign currency to a special Gosbank account in the Bank of Korea in Tokyo or, at the demand of the Soviet government, in gold to the Vladivostok branch of the Soviet State Bank. The Soviet Union pledged to make no difficulties in issuing visas to Japanese fishery workers and to allow managers easy access by extending to them group visas. She undertook not to levy duty on food supplies brought in excess of the stipulated amount and yielded on other points, necessary for the operation of the Japanese concessions. She agreed to limit the operation of the Soviet state enterprises to five million pood of fish in 1942.

On December 7, 1942, Ambassador Satō, who had

replaced Tatekawa, presented to the Soviet government a new draft of a fisheries treaty. It proposed an eight-year extension, without auction, of the leases then held by both sides and the continued limitation during that period of the production of Soviet state fisheries to five million pood of salmon and trout. It stipulated that in the future, leases be divided equally between the Soviet Union and Japan, grounds to be chosen by lot. Substitute grounds of equivalent economic value were to be provided in the event that some of the areas had to be closed for natural reasons. The Japanese draft expressed the desire for a reduction in lease fees and provided for the study of this and other problems by experts from both countries.

The Soviets replied on December 18 that the Japanese draft was a step backwards, that it revived demands made before the German invasion of Russia, but abandoned in more recent negotiations.

With neither side willing to make major concessions, the negotiation of a new fisheries treaty was shelved and attention given once more to the conclusion of a slightly modified provisional agreement. As it was, it took again until spring to conclude an agreement valid only until the end of the year, the negotiators seeming unable to gain ground in their perpetual race with time. The eighth provisional agreement, which was signed by Satō and Lozovskii on March 25, 1943, reflected a weakening in the Japanese bargaining position. It raised the transportation of gold to the world markets from 4 to 5 per cent and somewhat reduced the number of fishing grounds allocated to Japan.

When discussion of a new fisheries treaty was resumed in the fall, the auction question remained the central issue. In view of the Pacific War the Soviet side demanded, furthermore, that the Japanese refrain from entering not only the bays and river inlets heretofore closed, but that they forego managing any fishing grounds off the east coast of Kamchatka and Oliutorskii Bay for the duration of the conflict. This region, the Soviets felt, was too close to the zone of military operations and the presence of Japanese vessels could precipitate hostilities. Besides, they pointed out, in 1942 the Japanese had exploited only 15 out of 149 fishing grounds in this area, in 1943 none.

The annual dickering about provisional agreements was beyond the patience of both governments at this juncture of history, and they agreed on a five year protocol, initialled on March 19, 1944, and signed on March 30 of that year together with the oil and coal concessions protocol, extending the series of provisional agreements that had annually prolonged the fisheries convention of 1928 since its expiration in 1936 until December 31, 1948. Both sides made significant, if temporary, concessions. The auction system was modified. It was recognized as applying to some but not all fishing grounds: the Japanese were guaranteed the retention of 52 fishing grounds where they had erected factories; the Soviets were limited to a possible increase of 10 per cent in fishing grounds which they could win from the Japanese at auction. Japan agreed to the extension of the limits of the closed areas[f] to the open seas. While she dropped her objection that this was contrary to international law and accepted the Soviet contention that these areas corresponded roughly to the maritime danger zones, proclaimed by the U.S.S.R. in 1941, she made it clear that this must not be construed as an acceptance of the So-

---

[f] Pos'et Bay, Peter the Great Bay, Olga Bay, the Vladimir Bay region, Sovetskaia Gavan', De-Kastri Bay, and Avacha Bay.

viet position in principle; she went along with the limitation as an exceptional wartime measure. Japan consented temporarily to interrupt fishing operations along the east coast of Kamchatka and Oliutorskii Bay, with the U.S.S.R. assuming the obligation to protect the unattended Japanese property in this region.[*] By this time Japan's military position had markedly deteriorated and the price which Japan had to pay for the five-year extension of fishery rights in Soviet territory included, as related in the preceding chapter, the liquidation of her oil and coal concessions on North Sakhalin.[14]

As American submarines began to decimate Japanese shipping, it became necessary for Japan to arm her fishing and merchant vessels. On May 19, 1944, Satō asked Lozovskii that Soviet consuls be empowered to allow the visit of vessels armed for self-defense and that local authorities be appraised of the permission. When Lozovskii replied that the matter required careful study because armed ships differed in nature from mere fishing or merchant vessels, Satō declared that steps could be taken to seal their guns in Soviet waters.

The answer which Lozovskii eventually gave on June 3, after being prodded by Satō on May 30, was negative. The Soviet Union would not admit armed vessels into her waters. When Satō appealed to Lozovskii in the name of Russian goodwill to appreciate the need of Japan to arm her fishing and merchant vessels, the latter replied coldly that whether or not Japan had to arm vessels was an internal matter of no concern to the Soviet Union. Her strict observance of neutrality in the war between Japan and the United States and England dictated that she exclude all armed vessels from her wa-

[*] For the full text of the fisheries protocol and related notes, see Appendix G.

ters, a fact which, he noted pointedly, was not disadvantageous to Japan at this juncture.

When a Japanese vessel was sunk that month by a submarine in broad daylight while lying off the Soviet coast, Japan informed the U.S.S.R. that she expected her to demand of Washington that the United States respect her territorial waters, and asked to be informed of the American reply. The Russians answered that the matter of a Soviet demand to the United States was not a topic that they could discuss with Japan. They stated that they shared Tokyo's concern, for they themselves had lost vessels to unidentified submarines. But while they did their best to guard Soviet waters, they remarked, it was physically impossible for them to guarantee the safety of every vessel.[15]

6

The Agony of the Japanese Embassy

When Satō had proceeded to the Soviet Union as ambassador in March 1942, he had taken with him the
China specialist Morishima Gorō as minister because of
his expertise in general affairs. An outspoken opponent
of the alliance with Germany, Morishima had been
swept away by the "Matsuoka Tornado," as Matsuoka's purge of Foreign Service officials unsympathetic
to the Axis was popularly called; he had been reinstated
after Matsuoka's fall, following Hitler's unilateral decision to invade the Soviet Union. In his memoirs of
his service in Moscow, entitled "The Embassy in the
Soviet Union in Agony," he relates the persistent attempts of Satō and himself to persuade the Japanese
government to adopt a more realistic policy toward
the U.S.S.R.

Before their departure for the Soviet Union Satō and
Morishima had several sessions with the makers of Japanese policy. Satō met once with Prime Minister Tōjō

Hideki, once with Navy Minister Shimada Shigetarō, and twice with Foreign Minister Tōgō Shigenori; Morishima attended the second conference with Tōgō and had a meeting of his own with Major General Satō Kenryō, chief of the Military Affairs Bureau of the War Ministry.

There was considerable public feeling at this time that Japan should make an effort to end the conflict between Germany and the U.S.S.R. so that the war against the United States and Great Britain could be pursued with greater vigor, but neither Tōjō nor Tōgō nor Shimada expressed a desire for Japanese mediation. The chief of the Military Affairs Bureau stated outright that the army did not want the embassy to take up the matter of peace between Germany and the Soviet Union, nor did it wish it to raise any new questions between Japan and the latter, but to confine itself to the conduct of routine business.[1]

The course of the Russo-German war was uppermost in the minds of Morishima and Satō in the months following their arrival in Kuibyshev. Reading through the dispatches which Satō's predecessor had sent to Tokyo, Morishima was amazed at the simple assurance with which Tatekawa, a lieutenant general, had asserted that the Germans would win a decisive victory in the summer offensive of the second year, i.e. in the coming months. Neither Satō, nor Colonel Yabe Chūta, the military attaché, nor Morishima shared this optimism. Satō doubted that the Germans had sufficient reserves, and the officers of the military attaché section repeatedly warned that the Soviet military forces must not be underestimated.

As the German offensive, when it came, dragged on until autumn without succeeding to capture the major oilfields in the Caucasus or to force the surrender of Stalingrad, and the overextended German lines did not pull back to secure winter positions, the Japanese military experts foresaw catastrophe. Even so, they were surprised, when the expected Russian counterattack occurred, at the excellence with which the Soviet drive was executed.

The annihilation of General Friedrich Paulus's divisions in January 1943 seemed to crush all hopes for a German victory in the East, and as a large Anglo-American force had landed in North Africa in November 1942, Satō realized that Germany herself might be threatened soon. "This is the first step of the advance of the Allied armies into Europe," he said. But the embassy was in the dark about Japan's own misfortunes in the Pacific. Though newscasts of the British Broadcasting Corporation made it wonder about the stream of victory reports which it received from Tokyo, it did not appreciate the extent of misinformation supplied by the Foreign Office. As Morishima noted in his diary on the evening of May 18, 1942: "Invited to the celebration of the great victories in the Coral Sea and in Burma, jointly sponsored by the military and naval attachés."[2]

Misinformed though Satō was of the situation in the Pacific, it was obvious to him that Allied successes elsewhere dictated some sort of diplomatic measures. When the Foreign Office failed to respond to his detailed reports on the war in Russia and to his reflections on the implications of German reverses there and in North Africa on Japan's international position, he concluded that Tokyo still overestimated Axis strength and sent Morishima, who shared his views, to deliver to the government a lengthy note, written in his own hand, and supplement it with a detailed personal report. So

critical was the situation, Satō felt, that he instructed
Morishima to convey his views not only to the Foreign
Office or to officials in other branches of the govern-
ment, but to influential friends in private life.

Though it was toward the beginning of December
that Satō requested permission for Morishima's return,
over a month passed before the necessary approval arrived from Japan, and it was not until February 24,
1943, after a long and arduous journey through Siberia and the Russian Far East, that he was able
to see Foreign Minister Tani.

Tani had invited his staff to listen to Morishima's report. Present were the Vice Minister of Foreign Affairs and the directors of the various departments. The
gist of Satō's lengthy note, which Morishima conveyed,
was that (1) Germany must abandon her reckless policy
toward the Soviet Union and withdraw her forces to
a defensible position along the frontier; she must similarly tighten, if not curtail, German-Italian operations
in North Africa; (2) Japan must concentrate all her
efforts on gaining that year an invincible position in her
struggle with England and the United States; she must
avoid any incident with the Soviet Union, lest the latter be tempted, when her military position improved,
to abandon the neutrality which Japanese success required; (3) If Japan remained on good terms with the
U.S.S.R. while gaining a clear upper hand in the Pacific, she might yet find an opportunity for making
peace with England and the United States or at least
for attaining a cease-fire.

Morishima spoke for more than two hours. Several
questions were asked, but no one took issue with
what he said. Suddenly somebody laughed. Baffled,
Morishima asked why. Because, the minister and his

staff replied in unison, the views of the embassy coincided so much with their own that it was funny. Relieved that his mission to Tokyo might prove less difficult than expected, Morishima joined in the laughter.[3]

Several days later two top-secret telegrams arrived from Moscow. Detailing further German reverses, Satō insisted that concrete steps must be taken at once to improve Soviet-Japanese relations. Satō recommended that Japan carry out the surrender of the North Sakhalin concessions, promised by Matsuoka in 1941 but shelved following the German invasion of Russia, and make reasonable modifications in her position to facilitate the conclusion of a new fisheries treaty, pending already for eight years. Satō also favored reinforcing the general Neutrality Pact with specific agreements, such as, for example, a guarantee on the part of Japan not to furnish bases to Germany and Italy in East Asia in exchange for a guarantee on the part of the Soviet Union not to furnish bases to England and the United States in Siberia and the Russian Far East. In a separate telegram Satō instructed Morishima to act in support of these recommendations, but though the latter daily asked to see Foreign Minister Tani, he could not get an appointment until March 11.

Morishima did talk to Premier Tōjō on March 8 and after many requests once again on April 17. During the first meeting Morishima conveyed to Tōjō only Satō's general note and not the specific recommendations made in the telegrams, believing that he should first discuss them with the foreign minister. After listening to Satō's plea for bettering relations with the U.S.S.R. because of German reverses, Tōjō raised a disconcerting question: Might such an improvement in Japanese-Soviet relations not alienate Germany and prompt her to make peace with England and the United States, leaving Japan to continue the conflict single-handedly?

During the second conference with Tōjō, Morishima presented a lengthy memorandum in which he outlined his own views on the world situation. For an hour and twenty minutes the premier listened quietly as Morishima pointed out that Japan could not win the war. The best for which she could hope would be a draw and that could be obtained only by denying Soviet bases and assistance to England and the United States and by convincing the American public that the high cost of war did not justify its continuation. Referring to mounting dissatisfaction in the United States with the burdens of war, Morishima asserted that the dissatisfaction could be fanned sufficiently by a Japanese agreement with the Soviet Union and the concentration of Japanese military efforts against the United States and England to bring about a Republican victory in the national elections of 1944, and the Republicans, he believed, would be likely to modify American policy to assuage popular dissatisfaction. Going back to the question raised by Tōjō during their first meeting, Morishima expressed the belief that the provisions of the projected agreement with the U.S.S.R. could be explained to the satisfaction of Hitler, and that at any rate things had gone too far for Germany to sever her ties with Japan. Furthermore, whatever risk there might be of damaging Japanese relations with Germany would be outweighed by the possibility of alienating the United States and England from the Soviet Union.

At the conclusion of Morishima's presentation Tōjō said "I understand very well," asked a few questions, and told Morishima to stand by for possible consultation.[4]

Shortly thereafter Tani was replaced by Shigemitsu as foreign minister. When Morishima called on the latter on April 26 to present him with a copy of the memorandum he had handed to Tōjō, Shigemitsu told him abruptly to return to his post. His outspoken "defeatist" views had obviously embarrassed, if not angered, some of his colleagues, and the complaint had been lodged that his presence in Tokyo was troublesome. Morishima replied that the prime minister had told him to stand by. But the next day Shigemitsu informed Morishima that he had talked to Tōjō, and repeated the demand that he return to Moscow. He told him briefly that Satō's recommendations had been accepted in principle and that appropriate instructions would be sent directly to the embassy.[5]

The vital negotiations about the liquidation of the oil and coal concessions and the extension of the fisheries protocol, which Satō began with Molotov in June, were interrupted by the imperial navy's seizure of Soviet vessels laden with American lend-lease supplies. Whatever justification there might have been for the Japanese action, it was obvious not only to Satō and Morishima but also to Tōjō and Shigemitsu that the incident must not be allowed to obstruct the discussion of the far more important issues before them. Yet this is what happened as the imperial navy for a long time resisted the demands of the Japanese government for the release of the vessels, while the Soviet Union refused to deal with anything else until this was done. Not until November was Satō able to announce the release of the ships and the consent of the Japanese navy to refrain vis-à-vis the Soviet Union from exercising such rights of belligerency.

By this time Italy had been knocked out of the war

and plans had been completed for the opening of a second front in Europe; Japan's bargaining position had declined further. Yet when the fisheries and concessions talks were resumed on November 15, the Soviets made no particular difficulties. The Japanese abandoned efforts to attain elaboration of the Neutrality Pact partly because they could not agree among themselves whether it was appropriate to put in writing their denial of bases to their allies. The negotiations could probably have been concluded by the end of January 1944. That they took until March 30, Morishima complains in his memoirs, had been due to the fact that "minor officials and experts in Japan in their usual way wasted time paying scrupulous attention to minor details of no importance."[6] While there was public satisfaction in Japan at the signing of the fisheries and concessions protocols, the Japanese negotiators were not elated. They realized that the time had passed for using the agreements as stepping stones for a Soviet-Japanese rapprochement.[7]

7

Denunciation of the Neutrality Pact

As the German war machine bogged down in Europe and the wind went out of the sails of her own advance in the Pacific, Japan sought to secure her back by improving her relations with the U.S.S.R. For this purpose the Foreign Office wished to send an important dignitary to the Soviet Union and to Europe, and instructed its ambassador in Moscow to secure the necessary assent. Ambassador Satō cabled back that the Soviet government would never agree to receive a special envoy who was slated to visit Europe also, and recommended that the proposal be modified to limit the mission to Moscow only, but was ordered to act as instructed.

On September 10, 1943, Satō informed Foreign Commissar Molotov that his government would like to send a special envoy to Moscow to lay bare its thoughts. After an exchange of views with Molotov he would proceed to western Europe to study conditions there and confer with leading officials, then would return to

Moscow for further talks before heading back to Japan.

As predicted by Satō, Molotov was not satisfied with his vague statement that the purpose of the dispatch of a special envoy to the Soviet Union and central Europe was to hasten the promotion of friendly relations between Japan and the U.S.S.R. He asked for a more specific explanation of the concrete purpose of the mission and wanted to know what the exact position of the special envoy would be. Would he visit also the states with which the Soviet Union was at war and what would be the scope of negotiations in Moscow?

Satō was unable to assure Molotov that his government had a particular plan in mind. He speculated that the special envoy's views would be similar to his own but that he would be able to contribute to a Soviet-Japanese rapproachement by his visits to other countries. Though it was likely that he would visit the states with which Russia was at war, for they were Japan's allies, Satō declared, such a journey would be in the interest of the Soviet Union as well as of Japan, since it would have the improvement of Soviet-Japanese relations as its major purpose.[1]

On September 13 Molotov read the Soviet reply to Satō. It stated that although his government found the Japanese proposal very unclear, it believed, in view of the projected round trip between Moscow and Europe, that it was the objective of the special mission to halt hostilities between the U.S.S.R. and the countries with which she was at war. "The government [of the Soviet Union] appreciates the peace efforts of the Japanese government and would welcome the proposal under different circumstances," the note continued; "but at present we are at war and the [Soviet] government cannot halt the hostilities with Germany and her allies in Europe, and there is no possibility of making peace."[2,a] Although Moscow rejected the Japanese proposal, it assured Tokyo that it was "in agreement with the intention of the Japanese government to maintain and promote friendly relations between Japan and the Soviet Union."

Satō expressed regret that the good offices of the Japanese government had not been accepted. He stated that to the best of his knowledge the Japanese proposal had not been discussed in advance with other countries (i.e. that it had not been a German peace feeler); it was purely Japanese in origin. Yet the restoration of peace between the Soviet Union and Germany was vital, he said and predicted the likelihood of another proposal by his government.[4,b]

Seven months passed before the Japanese renewed the idea. They did so on April 8, 1944, when congratulating the U.S.S.R. on the signing of the fisheries and concessions protocols. At this time fighting had not yet been resumed between the German and Russian armies after the winter lull and Foreign Minister Shigemitsu believed that the Soviets might agree to a truce after they had recovered their prewar territory.[6,c] In a message to Molotov, conveyed by Satō, Shigemitsu reiterated Japan's

[a] Morishima quotes a slightly different wording: "But since the Soviet Union thinks that there exists absolutely no possibility for peace between the Soviet Union and Germany, though it appreciates greatly the peace efforts of the Japanese government, it has no choice but to decline the proposal concerning this matter." [3]

[b] The Soviet government informed Washington of the Japanese proposal on September 16. [5]

[c] Yet Shigemitsu cannot have been optimistic. In his memoirs he derides army advocacy of an end to the German-Soviet war: "It is not easy to employ impractical military arguments in practical foreign policy. It is childish to fancy of manipulating other countries by toying with foreign policy measures and to be able to bring about one morning peace or war between one country and another." [7]

sincere desire to develop friendly and neighborly relations with the Soviet Union, and asserted that the proposal to send a special envoy, made in September of the
previous year, had been advanced in recognition of the
special role that Japan and the U.S.S.R. should play in
bringing about world peace. The conclusion of the fisheries and concessions protocols, he wrote, presented a
favorable opportunity for improving Soviet-Japanese relations further by settling the trade and boundary questions mentioned in Matsuoka's letter of April 13, 1941.

Molotov told Satō that he would give a formal reply
after studying Shigemitsu's message in detail. His immediate reaction was that although the conclusion of the
fisheries and concessions protocols was of mutual benefit in that it removed sources of discord, the situation
had changed greatly since Matsuoka's letter, when neither country had been at war, and that the significance
of the boundary and commerce issues raised by him
must be reexamined in the light of current events. Molotov did request elaboration as to what benefits could be
derived from closer relations between the two countries.

Satō was unable to be specific; he had no instructions
to broaden the scope of the negotiations. He did repeat, however, that the proposed dispatch of a special
envoy would be in the interest of world peace, specifically of peace between the Soviet Union and Germany.
Molotov wanted to know whether new developments
had prompted the repetition of the proposal which had
been rejected in the fall. Had Germany asked Japan to
act as mediator? Satō replied that he did not think so. He
added, perhaps as a feeler, that he did not think that
the Soviet Union would desire the unconditional surrender of Germany, publicly demanded by the Allies,
that she would want an "honorable" peace. Molotov

retorted curtly that at present he thought only of the war, not of making peace.

On April 12 Molotov read to Satō the formal reply of his government to Shigemitsu's proposal:

> The Soviet Union acknowledges Mr. Shigemitsu's message, conveyed to V. Molotov by Ambassador Satō on April 8, and states that the Soviet government fully respects the efforts of the Japanese government to improve the situation; yet considering [the fact] that the proposal of Minister Shigemitsu is still the same as [that made] in September of last year and that there has been no change in the situation since the Soviet government promptly replied to that proposal, there is nothing to add now.[8]

When repeated attempts on his part to discuss the exchange of commodities, even on a small scale, and to deal with matters concerning the boundary between the U.S.S.R. and Manchukuo were side-stepped by the Russians as "too complicated" for wartime deliberation,[9] Satō was not surprised. He had vainly advised Tokyo that it was the belief of the Japanese embassy in Moscow that the proposal to discuss the boundary and trade issues at this time would only arouse laughter on the part of the Soviet side. Morishima, who was called home for consultation, reiterated to Shigemitsu on September 3 that conditions were unfavorable for negotiating with the Russians.[10]

Yet the following afternoon, on September 4, Shigemitsu showed Morishima the hand-written draft of a telegram to Satō informing the latter that the Japanese government had decided to send a special envoy to Moscow to negotiate with the Soviets in cooperation with him. Shigemitsu cabled that Hirota Kōki, former premier and one-time ambassador to the Soviet Union, would be the envoy,[d] but instructed Satō not to disclose who would be dispatched when he sought Russian assent for the mission. Surprised, Morishima asked what the special envoy would be negotiating. "That we are going to decide now," Shigemitsu replied and squelched any opposition on Morishima's part by announcing that the decision had been reached at the meeting of the Supreme Council that day and had already been reported to the Emperor.

Morishima gained the impression that the foreign minister had no choice, that Shigemitsu and Satō both would have been forced to resign had they opposed the decision to dispatch a special envoy to the U.S.S.R. Although he deemed such a mission pointless, if not harmful, Morishima felt that Shigemitsu and Satō were the right men for their jobs and must not be forced out at this critical time. To make sure that Satō realized the seriousness of the situation, Morishima, with Shigemitsu's permission, amended the telegram and sent one of his own, alerting the ambassador to the fact that the dispatching of a special envoy had been the decision of the Supreme Council and had already been reported to the Emperor. To indicate his own approval, he added that he himself had had a part in drafting the foreign minister's telegram.[11]

When Ambassador Malik on September 8 paid a courtesy call on Shigemitsu prior to a trip home, the foreign minister told him that he had been considering calling Satō back to Tokyo for consultation, but that he would prefer instead to send a high-ranking personage, familiar with internal conditions in Japan, to Moscow as a special envoy. The envoy and two or three companions would be selected from among persons known to be

---

[d] Matsuoka, who had negotiated the Neutrality Pact, was rumored to have been one of the candidates for the mission.

sympathetic to the Soviet Union and most suitable for the task of improving Russo-Japanese relations. They would assist the Japanese ambassador in Moscow and make a full presentation of the intentions of the Japanese government.

The proposal was formally conveyed to Molotov by Satō a week later, on September 16. Satō pointed out that it did not entail visits to other countries; it had nothing to do with the earlier proposals of sending a special envoy. When Molotov desired more specific information, Satō replied merely that while Soviet-Japanese relations were friendly, there were many problems that required discussion, problems that concerned their two countries directly as well as broader ones, resulting from the war in Europe and in Asia. He himself had been away from Japan for two and a half years; he agreed with Shigemitsu that it would be important for Molotov to confer with someone more familiar with the internal situation in Japan.

Molotov declared that the Neutrality Pact had normalized Soviet-Japanese relations and that although there had been misunderstandings in the past, there were none now. He was pleased that friendly relations had been preserved. Since the day-to-day problems had been solved by normal means, Molotov remarked, he could not but wonder what purpose there would be in sending a special envoy. More important, others too, in the Soviet Union and abroad, would speculate about such a mission, even if it would visit only Moscow. It would be interpreted as a move for ending hostilities with Germany, but it was too early for that. When Satō hastened to assure him that this was not the objective of the mission now proposed, Molotov remarked that he then saw nothing new that required discussion with a special envoy. Although Ambassador Malik was young, the Soviet government was satisfied with him and it was also satisfied with Satō. It would be glad to deal with any problems through regular diplomatic channels. When Satō asked Molotov to give the matter of sending a special envoy further thought, Molotov retorted that he had already done so, adding jokingly that although a Greek philosopher had once said that the universe is changing, the position of the Soviet government remained unchanged.[12]

Morishima recalls in his memoirs:

> When I saw the telegram of the meeting between Satō and Molotov on the 16th, I thought: "Molotov's divine wind has blown."[e] The Supreme Council had decided to send a special envoy against its will because of internal conditions. Although we [Satō and Morishima] had not vetoed it, we had realized fully that such a mission would at the very least arouse Soviet ridicule and expose our shame throughout the world. All that was left for us to do was to try to lessen the shame as much as possible. But because the Soviet side decided not to accept a special envoy, the decision of the Supreme Council became as worthless as shit.[13,f]

When Shigemitsu asked Morishima on September 20 what steps Japan should take in the wake of the new rejection of her proposal, he replied, none. He reiterated the view that Japan was not in a position at the moment to carry on fruitful discussions with the Soviet Union and that to persist in asking the Russians for new talks would only lay bare Japan's weakness. But Shigemitsu angrily objected that the domestic situation did not

[e] "Morotofu no kamikaze ga fuita."
[f] "Saikōkaigi no kettei mo kuso mo atta mono de wa nakunatta shimatta."

allow such a do-nothing policy and that the Supreme Council demanded active negotiations with the Soviet Union, if need be by the ambassador.

The next day, on September 21, Morishima challenged Shigemitsu's assertion that the Supreme Council insisted on an active policy vis-à-vis Russia. He had discussed the matter with the minister of the navy, the army chief of staff and other high-ranking officers and had come to the conclusion that it was only the Office of the Chief of the General Staff and not the Supreme Council as a whole which continued to insist on active negotiations with the Russians in the belief that Soviet sympathy, if not support, might yet be enlisted on the ground that the U.S.S.R. would need an unweakened Japan on her side in the confrontation that she was bound to have eventually with the United States and England.

Shigemitsu reconsidered the question with Navy Minister Yonai Mitsumasa and others and finally decided to go along with Morishima's "stand-still" theory. To appease Army Chief of Staff General Umezu Yoshijirō and to end discussions in the Supreme Council, however, it was agreed to send to Satō through Morishima instructions which seemed to call for increased activity but, in fact, because of their vagueness, required nothing new. Satō was requested merely "to make efforts" to explore further the real intentions of the Soviet Union toward Japan and, in the event that Germany surrendered or made peace, "to make efforts" to attain Russia's friendly disposition toward Japan.[14]

The above instructions were approved by the Supreme Council at its regular session on September 28. When Morishima in his final meeting with Shigemitsu remarked that the instructions coincided with his stand-still theory, the latter disagreed.

> Your so-called stand-still theory might be justifiable under normal circumstances [the Foreign Minister declared]. But the present state of affairs is not normal. To tell the truth, we have already passed the decisive stage of fighting. War thereafter is unreasonable. Japan is now engaged in an unreasonable war. Diplomacy too is [no longer] ordinary diplomacy; we must pursue unreasonable diplomacy. This is not a time when we are allowed the luxury of saying, as you do, that to try to approach the Soviet Union under the present circumstances is merely to exhibit our weakness or that such an approach may have unfavorable results for us. This is a time when we must try to take all possible measures without asking what the results might be and to trust to a lucky chance, however slim it might be.[13]

Shigemitsu told Morishima to convey to Satō that he wanted him to do his utmost to find some means of conferring with the Russians and, if possible, to have a heart-to-heart talk with Molotov about such general topics as the China question, the Pacific question, and future relations between Japan, the Soviet Union, the United States and England. Shigemitsu asked whether it would not be possible to have talks with the English side in Moscow. When Morishima uttered that that would be useless, Shigemitsu exploded: "Don't say only, 'It is useless, it is useless!' "[16,g]

Delayed by transportation difficulties, Morishima did not return to Moscow until November 9. He immediately went into a huddle with the ambassador and though he had arrived at midnight and was no doubt exhausted from the long wartime trip, conferred with

g *"Dame da dame da to bakari yuu na."*

him until 3 A.M. and again, after a brief sleep, during
most of the day and on the morning of the eleventh.
Satō shared Morishima's pessimism, but agreed to act in
accordance with the wishes of his government.

One issue that might provide the opportunity for a
discussion of international relations in general was the
question of the extension of the Neutrality Pact, and
Satō wired Tokyo for appropriate instructions at the
earliest possible time.[17] As he was to explain to his government in a dispatch in mid-December, there were
two roads open to Japan in connection with the extension of the Neutrality Pact: (1) to raise the question of
its extension; (2) to do nothing in the hope that the
deadline for its cancellation would be allowed to pass
and it would automatically be in effect for another five
years. He appreciated the fact that it would be very
important for Japan to know as soon as possible
whether or not the Soviet Union intended to abrogate
the Neutrality Pact and acknowledged the argument
that she would not extend the agreement without a
price. But he was sure that once the question was
raised, the U.S.S.R. would demand more compensation
than the extension of the Neutrality Pact was worth
and personally favored, therefore, a course of inaction.
If Tokyo wanted him to take the initiative, he must
know what price it was prepared to pay for continued
Soviet neutrality.[18]

Whatever hopes there might have been of letting
the Soviets forget about the deadline for cancelling the
Neutrality Pact and thus attain its automatic extension
were dashed by the appearance of an article on the
subject in a Swiss newspaper and its reprinting in the
Soviet press. But while the Japanese government instructed Satō to go ahead and open talks on the exten-

sion of the Neutrality Pact, the cabinet had not been
able to agree on the matter of compensation and
wished Satō to ascertain the attitude of the Soviet
Union before adopting a definite policy of its own.[19]

There was a great deal of truth in Molotov's remark
that the position of the Soviet government remained unchanged. The warning of Vladimir Lenin that Japan
was Soviet Russia's most dangerous enemy, reinforced
by the Japanese Intervention in the Russian Far East
and by the bloody border clashes of the 1930's, had
never been forgotten by the Soviet government. Sincere as its desire was to improve relations with Japan, it
did so with serious mental reservations, ever distrustful
of the Japanese militarists. That the Japanese did not
appreciate the extent of Soviet hostility is evident from
the hope they placed repeatedly on Soviet assistance
in ending the Pacific War. It seemed possible to the
Japanese, who did not know of the Soviet pledge to
enter the conflict, that the U.S.S.R. might be willing
to assist Japan not only in order to obtain various concessions from her, but "by earning prestige as the mediator of peace, [to] secure a dominant influence in the
postwar international situation."[20] They did not appreciate sufficiently that while it had been in the interest of President Theodore Roosevelt to bring the
Russo-Japanese War to an end before the balance of
power was destroyed in East Asia, the preservation of
the *status quo* was undesirable for Stalin. The destruction of Japanese power was advantageous for the Soviet
Union as was the continuation of the war until her
forces could intervene and occupy Manchuria. The
Japanese were shocked, therefore, when Stalin voiced
what he no doubt had felt all along, namely that Japan
was an aggressor on a par with her German ally.

Stalin's remarks were made on November 6, 1944, in a speech celebrating the twenty-seventh anniversary of the October Revolution. Focussing on Germany, by which Russia had been despoiled twice in a generation, Stalin warned that her defeat of itself could not ensure peace. He predicted that Germany would recover her strength "in such a brief period as twenty or thirty years," and insisted that "peace-loving countries" must protect themselves from renewed aggression by totally disarming the defeated states and by setting up an international organization with the minimum military power necessary for the preservation of peace and the guarantee of security. It was in his analysis of the better military preparedness of the "aggressor countries" that Stalin mentioned Japan and equated the Pearl Harbor attack with the German invasion of the U.S.S.R., a link which the Japanese Foreign Office regarded as "unprecedented slander of Japanese conduct."

When Satō protested against Stalin's remarks to Molotov the following day and asked how it was possible for Molotov to have stated in September that Soviet-Japanese relations were normal and improving and then for Stalin to assert a month and a half later that Japan was an "aggressor country," Molotov replied diplomatically that Stalin's criticism had been theoretical and confined to events of the past; besides, statements made in a speech should not be regarded as of consequence.[21]

Satō had another conference with Molotov on November 17. Although the Democratic landslide in the United States had further disheartened him, he remained true to his instructions and did all he could to woo the Soviet Union, but to no avail. Molotov passed over in silence Satō's references to the threat of American and British capitalist imperialism and refused to be dragged into a discussion of United States policy in China or of the Chinese Communist Party, alleging that these were internal matters of no concern to the Soviet Union. Molotov sought refuge in generalities and repeated that if Japan would abide by the Neutrality Pact so would his country, though he was careful to qualify almost every sentence with the words "at the present time."[22] When Satō declared that it was assumed that the question of Siberian bases had been discussed at the Moscow conference and that his government wished confirmation that no change in Soviet attitude had occurred, Molotov replied that there was nothing new about the Siberian base question—he admitted that it had been discussed before—and that Stalin in his speech of November 6 had indicated no change in Soviet policy toward Japan.[23]

An attempt by Satō the following month to discuss the situation in French Indo-China, where Japan had surrendered administrative power to an "independent" government, was also parried by the Soviet side with the assertion that it was a local problem. Nor did Satō succeed during a conference with Molotov on January 4, 1945, in the wake of Turkey's rupture of diplomatic relations with Japan, to entice him into a discussion of any problem not directly connected with Soviet-Japanese relations.[24]

With the onset of 1945, Japanese statesmen began to wonder whether the Soviet Union would renew the Neutrality Pact for another five years or give notice of its denunciation in April. The Japanese were eager to ascertain Soviet intentions as soon as possible, but had to approach the subject gingerly.

On February 22, 1945, Satō asked Molotov, who had

just returned from the Crimea, whether the Yalta Conference had dealt with the Far East. Molotov replied that it had been concerned primarily with European affairs, consideration of the Far East being excluded except for some reference to the problem of creating a peace machinery after the war. When Satō pressed for details, Molotov replied evasively that Soviet-Japanese relations were confined to relations between the U.S.S.R. and Japan and that these were neutral.

Satō declared that he inferred from Molotov's statement that Soviet policy remained unchanged.[h] He reiterated that the Japanese government definitely wished to continue the Neutrality Pact and wanted to know the attitude of the Soviet side. Molotov asserted that he had been too busy to study the matter, but promised to give a reply as soon as possible. When a month passed without an answer, Satō asked to see Molotov. He was told that Molotov had many visitors scheduled and would not be able to receive him for some time. On March 24 Satō met with Lozovskii, who repeated that Molotov would not be able to meet him for several days, though he would see him, of course, regardless of how the Neutrality Pact question was decided. Satō reiterated that his government definitely wished to continue the pact and expected the Soviet government to concur; it would like to know its decision.[27]

On April 5 Molotov received Satō and read to him the following declaration:

The Neutrality Pact between the Soviet Union and Japan was concluded on April 13, 1941, i.e. be-

[h] The Japanese embassy in Moscow did not suspect that the Soviet Union had agreed to enter the Pacific War outright. Although Morishima did not exclude the possibility of Soviet military action, he expected political intervention backed by the threat of force. [26]

fore the attack of Germany on the Soviet Union and
before the outbreak of war between Japan on the one
side and England and the United States of America
on the other side.

Since that time the situation has changed cardi-
nally. Germany has attacked the U.S.S.R., while Japan, an ally of Germany, is helping the latter in her
war against the U.S.S.R. Besides this, Japan is waging
war against the United States and England, who are
allies of the Soviet Union.

Under these circumstances the Neutrality Pact between the Soviet Union and Japan has lost its
meaning and a prolongation of this Pact has become
impossible.

On the basis of the aforesaid and in accordance
with article III of the said pact, which provides for
the right of denunciation one year prior to the expiration of the five-year period of effectiveness of the
Pact, the Soviet Government hereby declares to the
Japanese Government its wish to denounce the Pact
of April 13, 1941.[28,1]

In response to Satō's query what the attitude of the
Soviet Union would be toward Japan until the expiration of the Neutrality Pact a year hence, Molotov replied that it would be the same as before the signing of
the pact. When Satō pointed out that it was the view
of his government that although the treaty powers had
the right to announce the abrogation of the pact one
year before its expiration, it was to remain in effect the
full five years, Molotov agreed, even though the Soviet
Union had already committed herself at Yalta two
months before to enter the Pacific War within 90 days
of the surrender of Germany.[j] When Satō expressed

[1] This was translated directly from the official Russian text. Slightly
different versions will be found elsewhere. [29]

[j] Kase writes that Japan had reason to be wary of the Soviet Union's
intentions, because she had not waited until April 13 to denounce the

regret at the decision of the Soviet government, Molotov retorted that it had acted fully in accordance with the provisions of the pact and repeated that the U.S.S.R. would honor it as long as it was in effect. As for the future of Soviet-Japanese relations, he would give no assurances, saying only that current international affairs in East Asia and Western Europe were very complicated.[30]

Neutrality Pact. [29] Japan was justified in expecting a Soviet attack (she herself had planned to attack the U.S.S.R.), but not because of the early cancellation of the pact. Molotov merely reacted to the persistent urgings of the Japanese that the Soviet government declare as soon as possible whether or not it intended to continue the pact.

8

Attempts at a Rapprochement

At a diplomatic reception in April 1945, following the formation of the Suzuki cabinet, Foreign Minister Tōgō impressed on Ambassador Malik the Soviet Union's obligation to remain neutral. When Ambassador Satō duly echoed the reminder in Moscow, Foreign Commissar Molotov responded on April 27 that there had been no change in the attitude of his government on this matter.[1] Yet Tōgō's concern was not allayed, for he knew that the Soviet Union had been moving large numbers of troops to the east since the end of February. With the defeat of Germany in May, the situation became critical for Japan. Tōgō, who had served as ambassador to Moscow and was familiar with Russian feelings, realized that in view of Japan's inability to continue the war successfully, it was too late for a basic revision of Soviet-Japanese relations, but he deemed it imperative to begin negotiations to keep the U.S.S.R. out of the war and, if possible, to secure her good offices in concluding peace on better terms than the unconditional surrender demanded by the Allies.[2]

The idea of settling the Pacific War through the good offices of the Soviet Union had been broached to Tōgō by the Lord Keeper of the Privy Seal Marquis Kido Kōichi as early as July 1943, upon the fall of Benito Mussolini. Kido had reverted to the question of a Soviet-Japanese rapprochement the following year, placing hope in Russia's Oriental heritage as a common bond.[3] Another reason why Kido sought to make peace via Moscow was that the so-called pro-Soviet faction in the imperial army favored such a move and he hoped that the rest of the army might be induced to go along with peace talks in general. Realizing that the Soviet Union with her important Far Eastern interests was bound to be involved in any peace negotiations, he felt Japan had nothing to lose and everything to gain by getting on her good side, for she alone among the powers with whom Japan retained diplomatic relations was influential enough to be of assistance.[4]

Some informal Japanese attempts to promote a Soviet initiative in ending the Second World War had taken place already. On February 15, 1945, Miyakawa Funao, who had served in Russia for many years before and after the Revolution[5] and now was consul general at Harbin, had called on Ambassador Malik in Tokyo as on an old acquaintance and in his conversation with him twice had suggested that the war had reached a stage when one of the more prominent world leaders with the necessary prestige, authority and persuasive power should come forth in the role of peacemaker and demand of all the countries that they halt the fighting. If Stalin were to do so, Miyakawa had argued, "Hitler would end the war and Roosevelt and Churchill would not dare to object to such a proposal by the Soviet government."[6] A similar suggestion had been made by Tanakamaru, the representative of the Nichi-Ro Fisheries Company, to Malik on March 4 and again on March 21; he had asked whether Foreign Minister Shigemitsu had not broached the question of a Soviet peace move and had offered his services in negotiations with Shigemitsu's successor, Tōgō. Malik had replied that he saw no reason for a go-between; the foreign ministers and ambassadors of a power could readily arrange meetings without resorting to private individuals. On April 20 Tōgō himself had told Malik that the amicable relations between their countries were "the only bright spot" on the world scene and that he hoped that this bright spot would scatter the war clouds and become the nucleus around which peace could be restored. He had expressed his "unofficial" and "strictly personal" desire to meet with Molotov upon the latter's return from the San Francisco conference, but had never extended an official invitation.[7]

At the time of the Russo-Japanese War, Japan had induced the American president to come forward "on his own initiative" to appeal to the belligerents to lay down arms. She now wanted the Russian head of state to do the same and by his "initiative" provide an honorable way to end the war.

At a series of meetings in mid-May the Supreme Council for the Conduct of the War, consisting of the prime minister, the foreign minister and the four military chiefs and thus popularly known as the Big Six, agreed unanimously to enter into negotiations with the U.S.S.R. It set as the objectives: (1) prevention of Soviet entry into the Pacific War, (2) enticement of the Kremlin into an attitude of friendliness, and (3) Soviet mediation of an end to the conflict. But as Foreign Minister Tōgō and War Minister General

Anami Korechika could not agree on Japan's remaining war capabilities and on the possible peace terms, the third point was shelved temporarily—"not for the sake of compromise," as Professor Butow notes, "but for the benefit of those who were eager to negotiate a rapprochement with the Soviet Union that would permit Japan to continue the war in the Pacific."[8] When Admiral Yonai proposed at the meeting on May 12 that Japan turn to the Soviet Union for help, Tōgō cautioned that the time for a Soviet-Japanese rapprochement had passed, but Army Chief of Staff General Umezu saw the Soviet Union as the natural go-between. General Anami expressed the view that the Russians would not want to see Japan crushed by the Americans and might wish to keep her relatively strong as a buffer between their possessions and the United States. Premier Suzuki Kantarō likened Marshal Stalin unto Saigo Takamori, the celebrated chief of staff of the imperial forces during the battle of the Meiji Restoration who had negotiated with the commander-in-chief of the Shogunate forces the surrender of Edo castle without fighting so that the capital city had been spared destruction, and expressed belief that he would make every effort on their behalf if asked.[a] And Navy Minister Yonai dreamed of obtaining Soviet oil and aircraft in exchange for Japanese warships![10]

On May 14 Tōgō brought to the meeting of the Su-

---

[a] Tōgō was to reiterate the conviction that the Soviet Union would neither supply Japan with war materials nor become her ally at another Supreme Council meeting on June 6. But, as before, this "whisper of actuality in a wilderness of make-believe" was not heard by the majority.[8] Ironically leftist Japanese historians have castigated the wartime government for turning to Moscow. "The plan of the ruling circles [of Japan] to make use of the Soviet Union in their attempt to conclude peace was an impertinent plot of persons who had forgotten their numerous treacherous acts in regard to the Soviet Union."[9]

preme Council a draft memorandum outlining the policy to be adopted. It advanced an amazing line of argument, playing on Soviet gratitude and self-interest. The Japanese negotiators were to try to convince the Russians that they owed their victory over Germany to Japan's abstention from the conflict and that it was to their advantage in view of the forthcoming struggle between the Soviet Union and the United States to preserve an adequate international position for Japan. They were to propose an alliance between the U.S.S.R., China and Japan against the United States and Great Britain!

The Supreme Council realized that the Soviet Union would be conscious of the rise in her prestige due to the collapse of Germany and the sharp decline in Japanese power and that her demands, if she agreed to some arrangement with Japan, would be great. So desperate was Japan's position, however, that the Supreme Council (over the objections of the war minister) was prepared to purchase Soviet assistance—even neutrality—by the return to Russia of South Sakhalin and the leases of Port Arthur and Dairen (Dalny), taken from her in the Russo-Japanese War, by the abrogation of Japan's fishery concessions, the opening of Tsugaru Strait, the surrender of the Japanese railways in North Manchuria, and the conversion of Inner Mongolia into a sphere of influence of the Soviet Union. If necessary, the Supreme Council was willing to give up even the Northern Kuril Islands, obtained from Russia in 1875 in exchange for Japanese recognition of Russian title to all of Sakhalin.[11,b] "If a ship is doomed, what matters

[b] The concession of territory to the Soviet Union as a means of insuring Soviet neutrality, if not of gaining her aid, had been considered as early as September 1944 by the Japanese Foreign Office under Tōgō's predecessor Shigemitsu Mamoru in a draft document entitled "Diplomatic

its cargo, however precious?" a Japanese diplomat commented later. "Jettison the cargo as fast as possible, if only doing so may save the ship."[13,c]

The man chosen for the delicate task of wooing the Soviet Union from the Allied camp was Hirota Kōki, whom Shigemitsu had wanted to send to Moscow and who had once told Tōgō that he would be glad to be of assistance in efforts to improve relations with the Soviet Union. On the evening of June 3 he strolled into the Hotel Gōra in the Hakone mountains, where Ambassador Malik was staying, and dropped in for a visit. Hirota told Malik that it was fortunate indeed that the Soviet Union and Japan had not crossed swords in World War II. He expressed pleasure that the U.S.S.R., in spite of heavy losses, had emerged victorious in the struggle with Germany, and asserted that the future safety of Asia lay in the hands of the Soviet Union, whose territory embraced a large part of Asia. Malik replied that he too was happy that the performance of his duties had not been marred by war between their states, but he expressed concern about the role of Japanese militarists and of statesmen influenced by "other countries" (i.e. Nazi Germany). Hirota answered that the Japanese were united around the imperial family and desired good-neighborly relations with the Soviet Union and China. He assured him that many influential persons whom he knew favored cooperation with Rus-

Measures to be taken vis-à-vis the Soviet Union." Thought was given to recognition of a Soviet sphere of interest in Manchuria and Outer Mongolia, surrender of the North Manchurian Railway, and retrocession of South Sakhalin and the Northern Kuril Islands; the abrogation of Japanese fishery rights in Soviet waters; unrestricted passage of Soviet vessels through Tsugaru Strait; revision of the Neutrality Pact; cancellation of the Anti-Comintern Pact and the Tripartite Pact; etc.[12]

[c] A month later, on June 15, Privy Seal Kido was to go so far as to tell Tōgō that Japan must seek to obtain an honorable peace through Soviet mediation "regardless of the price."[14]

sia, just as men like Prince Itō Hirobumi and Count Gotō Shimpei had done in the past. He counted himself among those who advocated Russo-Japanese friendship.

Malik invited Hirota for dinner at his hotel the following day. As they continued the conversation during the meal, Malik asked what specifically Hirota had in mind in regard to the relations between the Soviet Union, China and Japan. When Hirota merely repeated general assurances of Japan's goodwill, Malik stated that the peaceful policies of the Soviet Union had not prevented either war with Germany or hostile manifestations on the part of Japan. This had left a bad taste in Russian mouths; he himself lacked a feeling of trust and safety. What concrete steps were the Japanese prepared to take to reassure the U.S.S.R.?

Hirota declared that since the number of persons in Japan who understood the attitude of the Soviet Union had increased, he would like to arrive at a basic, long-term improvement in Soviet-Japanese relations, whether by a treaty, a pact or any other form of agreement. Japan was prepared to consider and discuss the Soviet Union's views on this matter. In response to a query by Malik, Hirota assured him that he was speaking not only for himself but for the Japanese government.[d] Although Hirota pressed for a speedy answer, Malik replied that the question required careful study and that he would not be able to reply until the following week.[16]

Meanwhile Tanakamaru called on Malik again at the

[d] Yet Malik, according to Kutakov, continued to regard Hirota as a private person.[15] To a Soviet diplomat the idea of a private go-between may have been more difficult to accept than to a representative of a Western country, where private individuals may wield greater influence than civil servants.

Soviet embassy and intimated that Japan would like to obtain surplus airplanes from the U.S.S.R. When he reverted to the question of Stalin calling upon the United States and Japan to conclude peace, Malik asked what specifically Tanakamaru had in mind in view of the American demand for unconditional surrender. Tanakamaru replied that Japan might agree to the restoration of the *status quo ante bellum;* she could not go along with the surrender of Taiwan and other demands made by the Americans. As Tanakamaru had stated before, his views were personal. Yet they were not purely his own; they reflected the feelings of a number of influential Japanese.[17]

When the week in which Malik's reply was due came and passed without word from the Soviet embassy, Hirota on June 17 tried to invite Malik for dinner, but Malik declined on the grounds that he was busy.[18]

On June 20 and again on June 22, the Emperor urged Tōgō to expedite the negotiation of peace and Tōgō in turn, on June 23, prodded Hirota to resume his conversations with Malik. Hirota hesitated to show undue haste lest Japan's desperation be exposed, but Tōgō had insisted that speed was of the essence; if the Soviet Union was unwilling to become involved, Japan must turn elsewhere without delay.[19,e] When Hirota duly contacted Malik the following day and persisted in his demand for a reply to his overture of June 4, he was shocked to learn that Malik had not communicated his proposal to Moscow. Malik asserted that it had been too abstract and that he needed something more concrete before he could make a report.

---

e Yet after the war Hirota blamed the government for "dillydallying" too much. "We acted too late. We should have begun negotiations earlier . . ."[20]

In spite of the imperial desire to terminate the war as soon as possible, Hirota did not turn to the question of Soviet mediation. Instead he proposed the conclusion of a Soviet-Japanese agreement to take the place of the Neutrality Pact, whose denunciation Moscow had announced. Hirota stated that Japan was prepared to give full consideration to Soviet demands regarding economic and political relations between the U.S.S.R. and Manchukuo and to Soviet economic wishes in Southeast Asia. He asserted that Japan's stand on China corresponded (or could be made to correspond) to that of the Soviet Union. It was Japan's sincere desire to establish such relations as would be of mutual benefit to the position of their countries in Asia in the future.

Malik insisted that he could not take the initiative in regard to problems that might arise in the realm of Soviet-Japanese relations, but must act in response to instructions from Moscow. As for the other matters, he could not report about them until they were formulated more concretely. Exasperated, Hirota pleaded that if Malik would only look at the implications of what he had said, he would realize that there was nothing that could not be solved by discussion—that Japan was ready to settle any problem.

When Malik again required him to be specific, Hirota declared that Japan had the "passionate desire" to improve relations with the Soviet Union if only the latter was willing to do so. The reason he kept asking for a general statement of Soviet intent was that there were still groups in Japan which had doubts about the future attitude of the U.S.S.R. toward their country. He wanted to clarify whether or not the Soviet Union was willing to conclude an agreement with Japan that would be more substantial than the Neutrality Pact and whether or not she was prepared to consider more than merely friendly relations in the near future. But Malik rejected such a broad approach. Nor was it enough, he said, to list the problems to be discussed; he wanted to know concretely how the Japanese proposed to solve them. As Malik continued to demand something "concrete," Hirota asked whether he meant details of proposed solutions or a draft treaty. Malik replied that either would be concrete.

During dinner Hirota alluded to the potential might of a Soviet-Japanese alliance. "If the Japanese navy were strengthened and joined forces with the Red Army," he proclaimed, "they would form the strongest combination in the world." Hirota stated that Japan would like to receive oil from the Soviet Union, providing in payment such tropical products as rubber, tin, lead and tungsten, if the Soviet Union did the transporting. Malik questioned whether the Japanese army would go along with the plan, which obviously reflected naval thinking. He remarked that his own country had a shortage of oil and that conditions were too dangerous to receive the products from the south.[21,f]

One of the most incredible aspects of the Hirota-Malik talks was that Ambassador Satō had not been appraised of their occurrence at once and that Minister Morishima, whom Satō had sent to Tokyo to learn specifically what concessions his government was prepared to make to purchase Soviet nonintervention and who had been back in the capital since March 31, had been

---

f Kase asserts that Hirota's suggestion that the Japanese navy and the Red Army would produce an invincible combination had been made in jest; Butow feels (and I concur) that Hirota had been in "dead earnest." Kutakov appraises Hirota's proposals as "provoking," and notes that Malik's response to his request for Soviet oil—"This is a complicated and delicate question"—was identical with that made by Satō, when the latter had rebuffed Lozovskii's attempt to obtain Japanese rubber.

informed only of their existence and not of their content.[g] This may have been due in part to the irritation that the Foreign Office had felt at the "negative" attitude of Satō and Morishima; the very fact that it had solicited the assistance of Hirota had shown that it had lost faith in the efficacy of its embassy. When Tōgō had told Morishima in April that every effort must be made to influence the Soviet Union in favor of Japan, Morishima had replied: "There is no hand left to play. Both Mr. Satō and I are in the last desperate stage of a battle with our swords broken and no arrow [left] to shoot." Undoubtedly such back talk, however justified, had frayed the nerves of the harassed Foreign Office officials.[23]

When Morishima had seen Tōgō two months later, on June 22,[22,h] Tōgō had reiterated that the Japanese government must use all means to improve relations with the Soviet Union. As Morishima had objected that there were none, Tōgō had scolded him (as Shigemitsu had) that this was no time to argue whether or not there were means; Japan had reached a stage when she *had* to do something. "We may *have* to do something extraordinary," Tōgō had added and had revealed to the flabbergasted Morishima that negotiations had been under way between Hirota and Malik.

"If you and Mr. Hirota have successfully racked your brains and have thought of a brilliant idea to attract the Soviet Union," Morishima had stated with bitter sarcasm, "Mr. Satō will, of course, work very hard. But is there such a brilliant idea? What is it?"

[g] Even the Emperor did not learn of the three-point plan of negotiations and of Hirota's talks until June 20. [22]

[h] The destruction of the Foreign Office complex and of Morishima's own house in the big American air raid of May 25 was responsible for the great time gap.

"I can't tell you now," Tōgō had replied, and when Morishima had persisetd, he had said: "Why don't you see Mr. Hirota and ask about it?"

"Has Mr. Satō been informed about this matter?" Morishima had inquired.

"He has not yet been informed," Tōgō had replied.

"Sore wa komaru [That's too bad]," Morishima had remarked heatedly. "Unless Mr. Satō is fully informed of important negotiations with the Soviet side in Tokyo, a great hitch may occur."

Tōgō had finally promised to inform Satō—after the talks had reached a certain stage.[24,1]

The secrecy surrounding the talks was due also to the fear of a military coup d'état by diehard nationalists if they learned of them. As Admiral Okada Keisuke confided to Morishima on June 24, the senior statesmen tried to be as secretive and circumspect as possible in all peace maneuvers, lest the young military extremists spoiled everything by seizing the Emperor and abducting him to Manchukuo.[26]

Morishima was on his way back to Moscow when Hirota called on Malik at the Soviet embassy on June 29 with a concrete proposal. By this time the position of Japan had deteriorated further and it had been decided at the imperial conference on June 22 to try to make peace through the U.S.S.R.[27] When General Umezu had sought to apply the brakes again by urging "utmost caution" in view of the political repercussions that a peace offer might entail, the Emperor had reprimanded him, "It is all very well to be cautious, but if we are too cautious we shall miss our opportunity."[28]

After telling Malik that the Japanese government wished to conclude an agreement with the Soviet

¹ He did so in a telegram on July 10. [25]

Union that would guarantee permanent peace between them and provide for cooperation on their part in the maintenance of peace throughout East Asia, Hirota handed him the following proposal:

> To conclude a nonaggression pact between Japan and Russia covering a long period of years (say 20 or 30 years) with an aim to mutually aid each other for the maintenance of peace in the East, with the following conditions as its basis:
>
> (1) Neutrality of Manchukuo. Concretely speaking, Japan shall withdraw her forces from Manchukuo after the Great East Asia War.
> (2) If Soviet Russia will supply Japan with petroleum, Japan shall give up her rights of fishing stipulated in the Treaty of Portsmouth.
> (3) Japan is ready to consider any other proposals which Russia may desire to negotiate with Japan.
> (4) Japan has no intention to keep possession after the war of the lands which she has occupied during the Greater East Asia War.[29]

When Hirota requested a speedy reply, Malik stated that he would first need additional details: What was the extent of the area that the Japanese had in mind when they spoke of "East Asia"? When would they end the war? What was the relationship between the fisheries concessions and oil? Malik also wanted to know whether there was any truth to reports that peace talks were taking place between Japan and the United States through Sweden. Impossible, Hirota retorted; Japan wanted to discuss everything first with the Soviet Union.[1]

---

[1] Shigemitsu and Tōgō both had considered Swedish mediation, as the King of Sweden would have been sympathetic to the Japanese desire to retain the monarchy and as the United States had added Japan experts to her Scandinavian legations, but had not pursued the matter vigorously,

In the days that followed, Hirota tried repeatedly to see Malik again, but was told every time that he was ill. The last attempt made by Hirota to call on Malik— "to inquire after his health," as he put it—was on July 14. Malik would not receive him.[k] Someone else at the Soviet embassy meanwhile informed Andō Yoshimitsu, the director of the Political Affairs Bureau of the Foreign Office, that the reply was taking so long because Hirota's proposal had been dispatched to Moscow by courier.[31] This bit of news was a bitter blow to the Foreign Office, which had assumed that the proposal had been forwarded by cable.[32,l]

Efforts by Ambassador Satō to elicit a response from Deputy Foreign Commissar Lozovskii on July 10 and directly from Foreign Commissar Molotov on July 11 were unsuccessful. Molotov stated that he had received only a brief telegram on the subject and could not reply until he had seen the detailed proposal which, he affirmed, was being sent by courier. Though Sato promptly repeated the full content of Hirota's proposal, Molotov reiterated that he could not reply until he had studied Malik's report. Molotov showed no enthusiasm, and it was evident that no answer to this proposal could be expected soon. Molotov did not react to Satō's declaration that Japan, for the sake of peace, renounced

---

doubting apparently Sweden's ability to modify the Allied demand for unconditional surrender. No peace talks with or through Sweden were under way when Japan turned to the Soviet Union for assistance.

[k] In the words of Kase: "The whole episode was like angling in waters where no fish lived."[30]

[l] Although Butow comments that the use of the slower method of communication "inevitably forced the assumption that the Soviet Union was not sincerely interested in furthering the negotiations," the use of a courier may have been a justified precaution; after all, the Americans had cracked the Japanese code and there was no way of telling whether they might not also be intercepting the Soviet messages from Japan.

any intention of annexing or possessing the regions occupied by her during the war.[33]

During the meeting with Molotov Satō had inquired about the purpose of T. V. Soong's visit to Moscow, for talks between Soong, president of the Executive Yüan of the Chungking government and Chiang Kaishek's brother-in-law, and Stalin and Molotov had given rise to speculation that the Soviet Union might be planning to enter the war against Japan. Molotov had replied that Soong's visit had nothing to do with the Hirota-Malik talks.[34,m]

Meanwhile rumors of a forthcoming conference between American, English and Soviet leaders had prompted the Emperor to prod Premier Suzuki to make haste. Tōgō had warned on June 22 that a special envoy must be sent to Moscow before the Russian statesmen left for the conference,[35] and the Emperor had impressed on Suzuki on July 7: "We may miss a precious opportunity while we are trying to ascertain the attitude of the Soviet Union. It would be better to ask outright the good offices of the Soviet government for the restoration of peace. . . ." Suzuki had conveyed the imperial feelings to the Supreme Council on July 10 and it had been agreed, in line with the Emperor's expressed wish, to send an emissary to Moscow. So pressed was Japan for time, as word of the imminence of the departure of Stalin and Molotov from Moscow for Potsdam reached her, that Tōgō, on Suzuki's insistence, did not wait for a report from Satō about his meeting with Molotov on July 11, but cabled to him the very next day, on July 12, that though he felt "like one marching out troops without sufficient reconnais-

---

[m] Soong discussed the implementation of the Yalta Agreement as it applied to Chinese territory.

sance," acting as he did before the receipt of word from the ambassador, "it is considered proper to convey to the Soviet Union, prior to the commencement of the Three Power Conference, the imperial wish to end the war."[36]

His Majesty, the Emperor [the imperial wish read], grieved by the fact that the current war is increasing the suffering and sacrifice of the people throughout the belligerent nations day after day, wishes the quick termination of the war. But so long as the United States and England insist on unconditional surrender [on the part of Japan] in the Greater East Asia War, Japan cannot but fight to the last with everyone joining hands [in a common effort] for the sake of honor and the existence of the fatherland. Since it is truly against his desire that the shedding of the blood of the people of the belligerent nations on both sides be increased further, he wishes that peace be restored as quickly as possible for the benefit of the human race.[37]

The statement was telegraphed in Japanese; Satō had to have it translated into Russian. He was instructed that the translation be exact and be rendered as the words of the Emperor.

Attached to the document was a letter in Satō's name to Molotov, conveying the Emperor's desire to send Prince Konoe Fumimarō to Moscow with a personal letter expressing the imperial wish. The letter from Satō stressed that this mission was completely different in nature from those proposed in the past, since it was due to the personal wish of the Emperor, and sought an answer, in principle at least, before Molotov's departure for the Big Three Conference. Konoe could not reach Moscow before then, but would like to meet with the Soviet leaders as soon as possible after their return. It was requested that a Soviet plane be dispatched to Manchuli or Tsitsihar to fetch the prince.[38,n]

On July 13 Satō made a vain effort to see Molotov. While he had been distressed by the Hirota-Malik conversations, he welcomed the imperial wish and the idea of sending Prince Konoe, for this was in line with his own thinking.[40] But he was told that Molotov had no time to receive him and that he should talk to Lozovskii. He met the deputy foreign commissar at 5 P.M. that afternoon and handed him a Russian translation of the imperial wish to end the war and the top secret letter from himself to Molotov, stating the Emperor's desire to send Konoe to Japan with the original copy of the imperial declaration. Satō stressed that the proposed dispatch of the prince by the Emperor differed in character from earlier proposals of special missions and asked that the Soviet government reply before Molotov left town at least whether it agreed to it in principle. In answer to Lozovskii's query to whom the imperial message was addressed, Satō declared that the imperial wish, by its nature, was not addressed to anyone in particular, but that he would like it to be transmitted to Mikhail Kalinin, chairman of the Supreme Soviet of the U.S.S.R., to Stalin, and to Molotov.

Lozovskii responded that he fully appreciated the Japanese government's desire for a prompt reply, but since some of the Soviet leaders were scheduled to leave that very night, it was truly impossible to give any answer prior to Molotov's departure. He did promise, however, to deliver Satō's letter to Molotov at once. Satō asked that Lozovskii telephone Berlin (Pots-

---

[n] Konoe and his suite, including Vice Minister of Foreign Affairs Matsumoto Shunichi, Shigemitsu, Kase, as well as one general and one admiral, were to fly away in great secrecy, lest the ultranationalists thwarted their departure. [39]

dam), where Molotov was headed, and obtain a reply. Lozovskii said he would try to do so. In the middle of the night Nikolai Generalov, head of the Japan Desk in the Foreign Commissariat, telephoned the Japanese embassy and left a message for Satō from Lozovskii to the effect that there would be a delay in the Soviet reply because of the departure of Stalin and Molotov.[41]

Satō informed the Foreign Office of his conversation with Lozovskii and of the telephone message. He cabled Tōgō that while it was uncertain how the Soviet Union would react to the question of sending Konoe, the proposal as now stated was too vague to be attractive.[42,o]

Satō's surmise was correct. On July 18 he received a confidential letter from Lozovskii, acknowledging receipt of his letter to Molotov and of the text of the imperial wish.

> By order of the Soviet government [Lozovskii wrote] I have the honor to call your attention to the fact that the imperial wish stated in the message of the Emperor of Japan is very general in form and contains no concrete proposal. The mission of Special Envoy Prince Konoe is also unclear to the Government of the U.S.S.R.
>
> The Government of the U.S.S.R., accordingly, is unable to give any definite reply as to either the message of the Emperor of Japan or the dispatch of Special Envoy Prince Konoe mentioned in your letter of July 13.[44]

Undaunted by the new rebuff, Tōgō instructed Satō on July 21 to elaborate on the objectives of the Konoe mission and to state outright (as the telegram of July

---

o "I thought it very strange that, on the ground of being occupied with preparations for a trip, the high Russian authorities should refuse to receive our Ambassador and should delay their reply to an address so portentous," Tōgō recalled after the war. "Stupidly, I failed to imagine the truth . . . ."[43]

12 had not) that its main purpose was to secure Soviet mediation in ending the war on terms better than the unconditional surrender demanded by the Allies.[p] Tōgō telegraphed:

We cannot accept unconditional surrender under any circumstances. . . . It is obvious that, if the war be protracted, more blood will be shed by both sides, yet the Japanese nation will rise as one man against the enemy if he persistently demands unconditional surrender. But we intend, in conformity with the imperial wish, to bring about through the good offices of the Soviet Union a peace which is not the so-called unconditional surrender in order to avert the coming about of such a situation. It is necessary to make all possible efforts to cause Britain and the United States clearly to understand the above-mentioned intention of Japan. We cannot, therefore, ask the Soviet Union to use her good offices without attaching any condition; at the same time, it would also be impossible as well as disadvantageous, in view of the domestic situation as well as of external relations, to set forth concrete terms of peace immediately now.[q] Under such delicate circumstances, Prince Konoe shall convey to the Soviet Government the concrete intentions of Japan based upon the imperial wish, and after giving full consideration to the Russian demands in East Asia, he shall request the Soviet Government after consultation to negotiate with Great Britain and the United States.[47]

On July 25—Tōgō's telegram had been delayed somewhere[r]—Satō clarified to Lozovskii orally that Konoe's

[p] Although Japanese peace feelers had been made toward the Soviet Union as early as February 1945, they had not been requests for mediation. The cable of July 21 constituted the first direct effort to obtain mediation. [45]

[q] The Japanese government could not come to an agreement on peace terms as the military still insisted that Japan was not beaten! [46]

[r] Such delays were frequent. In winter they could be attributed to weather conditions in Siberia; yet they persisted in summer. Repeated

mission would be "to request the Soviet government to use its good offices to bring the war to an end and to disclose to the Soviet government the concrete plans of the Japanese government concerning this and at the same time to discuss items concerning the establishment of Japanese-Soviet cooperation, which must be the foundation of the foreign policy of the Japanese empire during and after the war."[49] Asked whether the concrete plans which he mentioned referred to the ending of the war or to the strengthening and promoting of closer Soviet-Japanese relations, Satō replied that Konoe had concrete proposals regarding both. He noted that Konoe enjoyed the full confidence of the imperial family and held an eminent position in government circles; the scope of his mission and his powers thus would be broad. When Lozovskii stated that he wished to have Satō's clarification in writing, Satō agreed to draw up a document, even though he exceeded his instructions in doing so. He deemed it justified, however, particularly because of the absence of the Soviet leaders in Potsdam.

Reports that the Potsdam Conference was to be recessed and that Winston Churchill and Clement Attlee were to return to England on July 26 to be at home when the election results would be announced prompted Tōgō to instruct Satō on July 25 to seek to meet Molotov at any place designated by the Soviet side and, laying bare Japanese peace plans, to request Soviet mediation. Satō was to tell Molotov that it was the purpose of the special envoy to invest Stalin with the role of advocate of world peace and that Japan was prepared to accept Soviet demands concerning East Asia.

---

attempts by Morishima to trace the source of delay ended in failure: the Japanese Telegraph Service always blamed the Soviet Telegraph Service and vice versa. [48]

He was to prod the Russians into action by warning that if they did not show any interest in the Japanese request for mediation, Japan would have to turn elsewhere. On July 28 Tōgō repeated the instructions that Satō meet with Molotov as soon as possible concerning the above, adding that he should also endeavor to learn Molotov's attitude concerning the Potsdam Declaration.[50]

The Potsdam Declaration of July 26, calling for the unconditional surrender of the armed forces of Japan, had been issued in the name of the United States, Great Britain and China only, but Satō had cabled Tōgō, upon learning of it through a B.B.C. broadcast, that he presumed that the Soviet Union had participated in its formulation and that it constituted in effect her answer to the Japanese proposal of dispatching a special envoy.[51] Upon receipt of Tōgō's instructions, he tried to verify his assumption and went to see Lozovskii on the afternoon of July 30. He told him that the unconditional surrender demanded in the Potsdam Declaration was "quite out of the question for the Japanese Government," but that Japan was prepared to make extensive concessions to bring the war to an end, if only such a form could be avoided and her honor and existence guaranteed. He pressed for a Soviet reply to the imperial wish and his own letter of clarification, and begged that Stalin give serious consideration to the Japanese request for Soviet mediation. In asking Lozovskii to convey everything that he had said to Molotov, Satō added meaningfully: "It is expected that the Soviet government may have various requests and directions to make with regard to its services and I understand that Prince Konoe will be invested with broad authority in negotiating with the Soviet government."[52] Lozovskii replied that the Soviet government could not give a final reply in view of the absence of the head of state and the foreign minister from Moscow.[53]

On August 2 Tōgō once again impressed on Satō the urgency of obtaining Soviet consent to Konoe's visit and, should this prove impossible, Satō himself was to seek an immediate audience with Molotov to set forth the Japanese position. The government was desperate to end the war before an invasion was launched by the Allies. On August 4, in advance of Molotov's return, Satō informed the private secretary of Lozovskii that he must see the foreign commissar as soon as possible. The moment that he learned of Molotov's arrival, on August 6, he renewed his request for a meeting. The following day he was informed that Molotov would see him in the Kremlin on August 8 at 8 P.M.[54]

On the morning of August 8 Satō was asked to come to the Kremlin earlier, at 5 P.M. When he stood before Molotov at last, however, he did not get a chance to expound the proposals of his government. As he began to congratulate him on his safe return, Molotov interrupted him, bade him take a seat, sat down himself, then read the following declaration:

> After the defeat and surrender of Hitlerite Germany, Japan became the only great power that still stood for the continuation of the war.
>
> The demand of the three powers, the United States, Great Britain and China, on July 26 for the unconditional surrender of the Japanese armed forces was rejected by Japan, and thus the proposal of the Japanese Government to the Soviet Union for mediation in the war in the Far East loses all basis.
>
> Taking into consideration the refusal of Japan to capitulate, the Allies submitted to the Soviet Government a proposal to join the war against Japanese

aggression and thus shorten the duration of the war, reduce the number of victims and facilitate the speedy restoration of universal peace.

Loyal to its Allied duty, the Soviet Government accepted the proposal of the Allies and has joined in the declaration of the Allied Powers of July 26.

The Soviet Government considers that this policy is the only means able to bring peace nearer, free the people from further sacrifice and suffering and give the Japanese people the possibility of avoiding those dangers and destruction suffered by Germany after her refusal to capitulate unconditionally.

In view of the above, the Soviet Government declares that from tomorrow, that is August 9, the Soviet Government will consider itself to be at war with Japan.[56]

The sudden declaration of war shocked the ambassador, even though he had been prepared for the worst for some time. Yet he kept his composure, "feeling that what was to come had come at last." Satō expressed his regret at the decision of the Soviet government and remarked bitterly that he could not understand how it could talk of saving the Japanese people sacrifice and suffering while opening hostilities. He sought clarification whether the declaration that a state of war would exist from the 9th meant that a state of peace would continue until then and that hostilities would begin the next day.[s] Molotov confirmed this and in response to a query from Satō said that he could send the text of the declaration and the content of their conversation to his government and that he could use code in doing so.[t]

---

[s] In asking this question Satō had in mind that there were another six or seven hours left in the day. He did not consider in the excitement of the moment that the hostilities would take place in the Far East, where only minutes separated the 8th from the 9th when he left Molotov.

[t] According to Toland, who interviewed Satō twice after the war, Satō did not bother with code in drafting the urgent cable. [56]

As Satō took his leave with a handshake, he said that
he was sincerely sorry over the outbreak of war between their countries. "Although I truly do not know
whether or not it would have been possible to continue the Neutrality Pact," he remarked in his memoirs,
"I wish to God it would have been possible to tide over
the period during which notification of cancellation
had to be given."[57]

Satō thanked the Soviet government for the hospitality
it had shown him during his three years in Moscow. Molotov replied with equal courtesy that he appreciated
Satō's words and reiterated that peace was now in
sight. Molotov assured Satō, who was fated to remain
in the U.S.S.R. for the duration of the conflict, that he
would not be slighted and that the Soviet Union would
abide by international law in the opening of hostilities.[58]

The telegram in which Satō reported the Soviet dec-
laration of war, though accepted by the Central Telegraph
Office in Moscow, never reached Japan. By the time that
Malik called at the Foreign Office on the morning of
August 9 to ask for an appointment with Tōgō, the Red
Army had invaded Manchuria. Tōgō, who had been
awakened in the early hours of the morning when a
TASS dispatch announcing Soviet entry into the war
had been picked up by a radio monitor of the Dōmei
News Agency, did not have time to see him that day.
Thus it was not until August 10 that Malik was able to
read the declaration of war to the foreign minister.[59]

All the frustration that had pent up in Tōgō during
his endless attempts to enlist Soviet mediation welled
up as he recapitulated to Malik his fruitless efforts and
rebuked the ambassador and his government. Question-
ing the source of information for the contention that
Japan had rejected the three power joint declaration,
he stated that it had been very careless of the Soviet

government to believe in the rejection without checking with Japan. It was not only incomprehensible, he said, that the Soviet Union should have suddenly severed diplomatic relations and opened hostilities without replying to the Japanese proposal for mediation, but it was very regrettable from the point of view of the future situation in East Asia.

Malik retorted that the Soviet declaration included a reply to everything that Tōgō had stated and that there was nothing to add. When Tōgō declared that since world history would soon prove Soviet action to have been incomprehensible and deplorable, there was no need to discuss it now, Malik shot back that history was an impartial judge and historical necessity inevitable.

After repeating that the Japanese government's request for Soviet assistance in ending the war had gone unheeded, Tōgō communicated its decision to surrender in view of the Emperor's desire for the establishment of general peace and a prompt end to the suffering from war. Tōgō's statement was not unqualified, however, and showed continued reliance on the Soviet Union for advice, if not assistance.

> Because it is its understanding that in the conditions stated in the joint declaration regarding Japan, made by the leaders of the three powers, the United States, England and China, on the 26th of last month and later joined by the Soviet Union, there is no demand for a change in the sovereignty of the Emperor as a ruler, the Imperial Government accepts the above declaration [for the unconditional surrender of its armed forces].
>
> The Imperial Government asks the Soviet Government to inform it as soon as possible whether its interpretation is correct.

Tōgō expressed the thought that Malik fully understood the position of the imperial family in Japan—that the Emperor could not be separated from the Japanese nation. He hoped that the Soviet government would understand this too and agree to it. Although the Japanese government had already taken steps to communicate its declaration to the Soviet government through Sweden, Tōgō requested Malik to send a telegram to Moscow.

Malik replied that although he was not empowered to accept the Japanese proposal, he would communicate it to his government. Stung by Tōgō's accusation that the Soviet Union had been misinformed in her belief that Japan had rejected the three power declaration—a criticism that was a reflection on his role as ambassador of keeping Moscow correctly informed of Japanese policy—Malik stated that such an assertion was contained not only in the declaration of the Soviet government but also in President Harry S Truman's declaration concerning the use of the atomic bombs. Tōgō replied that in view of the friendly relations that existed between Japan and the Soviet Union, their uninterrupted exchange of ambassadors, and the continued negotiations concerning the ending of the war, the U.S.S.R. should have discussed the matter with Japan before coming to such an important decision with other powers. Had the Soviet Union responded to the Japanese proposal and acted as peace maker in ending the great war, what a delightful and advantageous position she could have gained in world history and the present international political situation! Malik retorted that history would prove how much the Soviet Union had contributed to the strengthening of peace.[60]

9

Soviet Entry into the Pacific War

The United States and Great Britain had solicited Soviet entry into the Pacific War to tie down the Kwantung Army, whose return home from the mainland would have made the contemplated invasion of Japan more costly.[a] Soviet planning and preparations for the campaign were elaborate and the offensive against the Japanese forces in Manchukuo, northern Korea, South Sakhalin and the Kuril Islands was mounted on a large scale, with over 1½ million men, 5½ thousand tanks and self-propelled guns, 26,000 pieces of artillery and 3,800 warplanes being brought into play. The Russians put some of their most experienced generals in charge of the operations, with Marshal Aleksandr Vasilevskii, former chief of the General Staff, heading a special High Command of the Soviet Forces in the Far East.[1,b]

The main Soviet objective was to encircle the

[a] For an account of American requests for Soviet participation in the Pacific War, see Appendix E.

[b] For an account of Soviet plans and preparations, see Appendix F.

Kwantung Army in central and southern Manchuria in a surprise attack and, if it did not surrender, to destroy it. In his instructions to the General Staff, Stalin had insisted that the campaign must be concluded as soon as possible. Aside from the political advantages that would accrue from a maximum advance prior to the termination of hostilities, there were strategic arguments for a *Blitzkrieg*: to prevent the Japanese from falling back to the Great Khingan mountain range, a formidable natural line of defense, to thwart the reinforcement of the Japanese forces in Manchukuo by troop groupings in Korea and China proper, and to prevent the organized withdrawal of the Japanese forces to the Korean peninsula, where they might be able to make a more effective stand, or into the depth of China, where they would be more difficult to corner.[2] Furthermore, the Russians calculated that the Japanese had become accustomed to the relatively slow, methodical American assaults, which were preceded by prolonged artillery barrages and air bombardment, and would not be prepared psychologically for a swift, silent penetration.[3] So careful were the Soviets to preserve the element of surprise that all battle plans were kept in the personal safes of the commanders of the fronts and the commanders of the armies, and the marshals who were transferred from Europe to the Far East to lead the Soviet forces proceeded to their posts under assumed names and ranks.[4]

It was impossible, of course, for the Red Army to attain complete strategic surprise because the Japanese had long feared Soviet entry into the war, but it could and did achieve tactical surprise by transporting supplies over the Trans-Siberian railway faster than the Japanese thought possible, by striking during the rainy season, by attacking at night and with little or no artillery preparation, and by launching a massive tank attack through supposedly inaccessible terrain.[5,c]

The strategic plan of the Soviet High Command, which had been worked out by the General Staff in conjunction with the front commanders by June 27, entailed a simultaneous assault on central Manchuria from three directions and was expected to last between six and eight weeks. The First Far Eastern Front, under the command of Marshal Kirill Meretskov, was to move westward from the Maritime region toward Kirin and Harbin; the Second Far Eastern Front, under General Maksim Purkaev, was to advance southward from the region southwest of Khabarovsk toward Harbin; the Transbaikal Front, under Marshal Rodion Malinovskii, in a joint offensive with Mongolian forces, was to push eastward and southward from the Tamtsak salient on the border of the Mongolian People's Republic toward Changchun, Mukden, Hailar and Tsitsihar.

The plan of operations for the Transbaikal Front, the main front, was particularly bold. Designed to hit the enemy in the rear, since his major fortifications faced the Maritime region, it entailed the employment of a tank army as the first echelon of the main striking force and execution of the 500 mile drive through desert and mountain terrain in one swoop, without pause.[6] The very task of assembling a large striking force in Outer Mongolia[d] seemed forbidding, since the facilities

[c] The Japanese had calculated that the U.S.S.R. would enter the war in mid-September and, indeed, the Soviet General Staff had originally thought in terms of a September offensive.

[d] The Mongolian People's Republic, like the U.S.S.R., had signed a neutrality pact with Japan in 1941, but considered it voided by Japan's support of Germany, which had attacked the Soviet Union, and by her war against the United States and Great Britain, Russia's allies. At

of the Trans-Siberian railway could not be diverted to this purpose. Not only did all motorized units have to drive hundreds of miles to the assembly area, but the infantry had to cover hundreds of miles on foot, mostly in early morning and evening marches, as the temperature in the daytime was too high (up to 112°F) and the visibility at night too low because of heavy dust. There were few water wells—in some areas none at all—and the Soviets had to drill over 600 new wells and build water stations to supply their armies during assembly and to provision them for the offensive.[8]

At 00:10 Khabarovsk time, on August 9, the reconnaissance and advance units of the Transbaikal Front slipped silently into enemy territory. At 01:00 the advance units of the First Far Eastern Front crossed the frontier. A fifteen minute artillery barrage signalled the opening of hostilities on the right flank, but the main line of advance and the left flank moved under the cover of darkness and of a raging thunderstorm without preliminary artillery or air bombardment.[e] Advance units of the Second Far Eastern Front also went into action at 01:00, the main forces several hours later. The main forces on the Transbaikal Front moved out a dawn, at 04:30; the main forces on the First Far Eastern Front at 08:30. The Amur River flotilla attacked Japanese fortifications on the Sungari River and the 12th Air Army bombed major railway

---

Yalta the United States and Great Britain had gone along with the Soviet demand that the status quo of the Mongolian People's Republic be preserved afer the Second World War and thus, from the Soviet point of view, "had in fact recognized the independence of the MPR."[7]

[e] This had been a last-minute decision. The Russians had planned to soften up the ferro-concrete fortifications in this region by heavy artillery fire and air bombardment and blind the enemy with powerful searchlights, as they had done successfully in their attack on Berlin, but the unexpected thunderstorm, with its sheets of rain, had forced a change in tactics.[9]

stations, communication centers and military targets in the major cities of Manchuria.[10]

The situation map of the Transbaikal Front looked like a fan of arrows, radiating from the eastern projection of the Mongolian People's Republic into Manchuria and Inner Mongolia. The fan was pointed toward the Great Khingan range, toward which the main thrust was directed; the top edge of the fan touched Hailar and the bottom edge Kalgan, the objectives of secondary drives. As expected, the Japanese had not anticipated an offensive in this region and had withdrawn their main forces to the interior of Manchuria, to the area of Changchun and Mukden (Shenyang), so that the Russians encountered little resistance as they fanned out.

The 6th Guards Tank Army, which formed the mainspring of the Soviet offensive with its 1,000 odd tanks and self-propelled guns, raced toward Changchun in two columns, 40 to 50 miles apart, and, meeting practically no opposition, covered over 90 miles in one day; its advance units reached the approaches to the Great Khingan range. The 39th Army, to its left, which had tanks, self-propelled guns and motorized infantry and thus also was highly mobile, bypassed the Halun-Arshan fortified area from the south and, overcoming some resistance, advanced 37 miles into Manchukuo. The 17th Army, to the right of the Tank Army, headed toward Ch'ihfeng (Wulanhata). It penetrated some 30 miles, its advance units reaching Lake Tabun Nor, about 45 miles from the border that day. To the right of the 17th Army, and thus forming the right flank of the Transbaikal Front, a combined Soviet-Mongolian Mechanized Cavalry Group moved through the Gobi desert in the direction of Dolon Nor (Tolun) and Kalgan; it had several engagements en route and covered about 35 miles. To the left of the 39th Army and thus on the left flank of the Transbaikal Front, the 36th Army forged across the Argun River after engineers had constructed several bridges across the rainswollen river and proceeded toward Hailar, its reconnaissance units getting as far as the Moer Gol river by nightfall. The 53rd Army constituted the second echelon or reserve of the Transbaikal Front, and was to follow in the tracks of the Tank Army the next day.[11]

So bewildering was the surprise attack that the Japanese General Staff could not ascertain until noon what had happened.[12,f] Thinking in terms of border incidents, the Kwantung Army had believed that the Japanese forces, based in such fortified areas as Halun-Arshan, would be able to cope with Soviet inroads. But, as noted, the Soviets simply went around the fortified areas initially and with their mighty host ground isolated units into the dust. An attempt by the commander of the Japanese Third Front to withdraw the divisions caught west of the Changchun-Mukden line to the interior of Manchuria and make a stand in the Manchurian plain was thwarted by the swiftness of the Soviet advance.[14]

On August 10 the Japanese government announced its willingness to accept the Potsdam Proclamation "on the understanding that the Allied proclamation would not comprise any demand which would prejudice the prerogatives of His Majesty as a Sovereign Ruler."[15]

---

[f] Even when the Japanese learned that Soviet forces had penetrated through the desert in Inner Mongolia and across the Great Khingan range, they did not comprehend the magnitude of the offensive. As late as August 15-16 Japanese intelligence estimated that they faced only 4 tank brigades and 1 cavalry division in this region, whereas in fact six field armies had been thrown against them.[18]

The Soviets did not find the condition in compliance with the demand for unconditional surrender, and pushed on.[16,g]

On August 10 the combined Soviet-Mongolian Mechanized Cavalry Group advanced a dozen miles north of Bogdosume and the following day, on August 11, reached the southwestern spurs of the Great Khingan mountain range. By August 13 Dolon Nor was in the hands of one of its columns, on August 20 Ch'engte (Jehol). Changpeh fell to the other column on August 16 and Kalgan after two days of fighting on August 19.[19,h]

The 17th Army negotiated the desert without significant resistance, but the struggle against the elements was brutal, the footsoldiers covering over 25 miles, tortured by the burning sun and the choking dust; by the evening of the 11th they too had reached the foothills of the Great Khingan. The Japanese made a stand at Tapanshang and Ch'ifeng, but the former was captured on August 15, the latter surrendered on August 17, isolated units continuing their futile resistance.

The 6th Guards Tank Army had advanced quicker, of course. Beginning the ascent of the Great Khingan

---

[g] Foreign Minister Tōgō had given Ambassador Malik a copy of the declaration. As soon as Foreign Commissar Molotov had heard from Malik, he had called the British and American ambassadors to his office and had asked for their governments' attitudes, telling them that he felt that the Japanese reservation did not satisfy the Allied demand. "The American reply, to which Soviet adherence was requested, informed the Japanese that the surrender would be unconditional."[17] On August 12 a broadcast from Tokyo announced that the Japanese army and navy were taking the offensive in defense of their country.[18]

[h] The Soviet-Mongolian Mechanized Cavalry had continued farther, toward Peking, when recalled by Marshal Malinovskii on August 20 in line with Stalin's agreement to refrain from such an operation. Meanwhile the Chinese Communist 8th Route Army had mounted a new offensive in North China and crossing into Manchuria had made contact with the Soviet-Mongolian force at Kalgan and Jehol on August 18.[20]

mountain slopes on the afternoon of the 10th, the front brigade of the 5th Guards Tank Corps reached the divide by 23:00. Again nature proved a more formidable opponent than the remnants of the Kwantung Army, as the sappers had to widen roads, fill in sharp drops, and otherwise make possible the passage of the steel monsters over the rocks at night. As the tanks started down, heavy rains washed out the roads; the greater effort consequently required by the tanks increased fuel consumption at the same time that automobile transport was cut off, and the tanks had to be supplied by air.[21] By the evening of August 11 the advance unit of the 5th Guards Tank Corps took the city of Lupeh; the next day the 7th Mechanized Corps occupied T'uch'üan (Lich'üan). In spite of the difficult terrain, the 6th Guards Tank Army thus had covered about 280 miles in three days. Advance detachments of the 6th Guards Tank Army captured the cities of T'ungliao and K'ailu on August 16, the main forces following two days later, delayed by the fuel shortage. On August 20 units of the 6th Guards Tank Army entered Mukden, on the 21st Changchun. Two tank brigades were loaded on flatcars and sent to Dairen and Port Arthur, which had been secured by airborne troops.[22]

While the 6th Guards Tank Army was forcing its way over the mountain range, the 39th Army, to its left, with some of its units bypassed and blocked the Halun-Arshan fortified area, crossed the Great Khingan mountains, and advanced toward Solun. (The 94th Rifle Corps, which had been proceeding northward, toward Hailar, was ordered to sweep back and attack Halun-Arshan from the rear.) As the 39th Army moved past the fortified area, the Japanese 107th

Infantry Division tried to slow its advance and, as it approached Solun, sacrificed two regiments in a futile banzai charge. The city fell after a fierce fight on August 13, the Red Army displaying its share of heroism—a Russian soldier who had spent his last grenade blocked the muzzle of a Japanese machine gun with his chest to permit his comrades to pass by safely.[23,1]

The 36th Army, on the left flank, reached the outskirts of Hailar on August 10. While the Japanese 119th Division, which had tried to slow down its advance on Hailar, withdrew before the assault on the 11th in order to man another line of defense at Wunoerh and Bukhedu (P'ok'ot'u) on the way to Tsitsihar, the 80th Composite Brigade remained in its dugouts and withstood fierce ground and air attacks for a whole week—till after the capitulation of Japan, of which it had not learned in its isolation. But the main forces of the 36th Army had not stopped to take Hailar. They had hastened after the 119th Division and on August 13th engaged it at Wunoerh. Again the Japanese put up a valiant fight, surrendering on the 18th, only after having been ordered to do so by the Kwantung Army headquarters. On August 19 the 36th Army entered Tsitsihar without opposition.[24]

While the Transbaikal Front in the first days of the campaign, between August 9 and 14, had smashed the northwestern border defenses and hurled itself toward Changchun and Mukden and the Soviet Mongolian Mechanized cavalry had seized the lines of communication between Manchukuo and North China, cutting

---

[1] The same act of heroism was performed by Soviet soldiers elsewhere. They were following the much heralded example set by Aleksandr Matrosov in 1943 on the Kalinin front, where he had blocked the gunport of a German bunker with his chest.

the Kwantung Army off from strategic reserves in North China,[25] the First Far Eastern Front was advancing from the opposite direction. Its mission was as follows: the 1st Red Banner Army and the 5th Army and the 10th Mechanized Corps were to launch an assault from the Grodekovo-Voroshilov region toward Mutanchiang, then after reaching the Poli-Mutanchiang-Wangch'ing railway line, advance toward Changchun and Mukden. Auxiliary strikes were to be carried out by the 35th Army from Lesozavodsk to Mishan and by the 25th Army from an area southwest of Vladivostok to Ant'u.[26]

The southeastern border of Manchukuo had been fortified in the 1930's and 1940's, yet by stealing across the border in complete silence under the cover of darkness and in a raging thunderstorm, the Russians succeeded in catching a number of garrisons asleep in the barracks and overwhelmed them before they could rush to their stations. Due to the element of surprise the Russians managed also to slip past many Japanese fortifications and strongpoints and take them from the rear. By the time Japanese units which had escaped entrapment by virtue of the same darkness or which had been alerted by the outbreak of fighting elsewhere rallied in fierce resistance, they were faced by vastly superior Soviet forces.[27]

As noted, the first Russian units had crossed from the Maritime region into southeastern Manchuria at 01:00. The main assault of the 1st Red Banner Army and the 5th, 25th and 35th Armies came at 08:30. The 35th Army negotiated the Ussuri River and the Sungach, one of its tributaries, and making its way through swampland to a region about 9 miles southwest of Hut'ou, cut the highway and railway running parallel with the front.[28] Hut'ou itself was stubbornly defended, however, and though the city and wharf were taken on August 10, the Japanese remained entrenched in various strongpoints in the Hut'ou defense zone. But the main forces of the 15th Army pushed on and on August 12 took Hulin and Mishan.[29] By the evening of the 13th the city of Tungan was in their hands, four days later P'oli.[30]

The 1st Red Banner Army, to the left of the 35th Army, encountered little resistance as it attacked on a wide front on August 9. Its advance was slowed down by the lack of roads and by the terrain—mountainous taiga and wooded swamps—as well as by heavy rain, so that it penetrated an average of only 4 miles into enemy territory the first day, the main force reaching the right bank of the Tashiht'ou River.[31] On August 10 the 1st Red Banner Army rapidly pushed toward Muleng and Mutanchiang, taking advantage of the large distances between the centers of resistance and strong points of the enemy. At 21:00 on August 11 the important railway and highway junction of Muleng was taken by a simultaneous attack from the north, east and south.[32,j] On August 13 the 1st Red Banner Army captured the large highway junction of the city of Link'ou, and the forward units of the 26th Rifle Corps penetrated the northeastern edge of the city of Mutanchiang, where intense street fighting broke out.[34] By the evening of the 14th, units of the Soviet 5th Army broke into the city from the east, and engaged in house-to-house combat.[35]

A city of about 200,000 and an important administrative center, Mutanchiang was also the key defense

---

[j] On August 12 it cooperated with the 35th Army in taking Mishan and the surrounding fortified area.[33]

point of the Japanese First Area Army, manned by the Japanese 5th Army. The Japanese made every effort to hold Mutanchiang and block the way to Harbin. Japanese soldiers strapped grenades to their bodies and threw themselves under Soviet tanks. In spite of repeated air strikes on the city by the 9th Air Army, Japanese resistance continued and Marshal Meretskov had the 25th Army bypass Mutanchiang on the south and head directly for Kirin (Chilin) to link with the Transbaikal forces coming from the west.[36]

The Soviet 5th Army, which together with the 1st Red Banner Army to its north formed the center of the First Far Eastern Front, drove toward the Volynskii junction, the left flank of the Pogranichnenskii fortified region. Heavy fighting ensued, particularly over the tunnels between the border and Pogranichnaia Station. Leaving part of its forces behind to annihilate the Japanese pockets of resistance over a period of three days, the 5th Army advanced between 10 and 14 miles over a 22 mile wide front on August 9. Its right flank reached the eastern spurs of the T'aip'inglin mountain ridge that day; its left flank occupied the large road junction which constituted the center of the fortified area of the city of Pogranichnaia by the morning of the 10th.[37] On August 11 the 5th Army took the city of Muleng and crossed the Muleng River; on the 13th it joined in the attack on Mutanchiang and, as mentioned, penetrated the eastern rim of the city by the following night.[38]

The 10th Mechanized Corps, which had been held in reserve, assembled in the region of Tungnin on August 12 and the following day began to advance toward Kirin.[39]

Meanwhile, on August 9, the 25th Army, on the left

flank of the First Far Eastern Front, had bypassed and blocked the key points of the Tungnin and Tung-chingch'en fortified areas and had cut the Tungnin-T'umen railway line, which ran about 7½ miles from the border, in a number of places. Some of its units, supported by the guns of the Pacific fleet, had forced the Hunch'un and Tumen rivers and stormed the Japanese fortifications of the border of Korea.[40]

One column of the 25th Army continued westward, toward Wangch'ing and Kirin. Eager to link up with the Transbaikal forces as soon as possible, it bypassed heavily defended Mutanchiang on the south.[41] On August 12 forward units of the 10th Mechanized Corps joined with the 25th Army in its westward thrust, while another column of the 25th Army, moving southward, along the Pacific Coast, occupied the North Korean ports and cities of Yuki (Unggi) and Rashin (Najin), which had been secured by naval landing parties.[42] On August 18 the 25th Army advanced from Wangch'ing and Hunch'un into northern Korea. Soviet landing parties arrived by sea at the port of Odetsin (Etetin) the same day and at Genzan (Wonsan) on August 21; airborne troops secured Heijo (Pyongyang) and Kanko (Hamhung) on August 24.[43]

The surprise attack, which had literally caught the Japanese asleep, had deprived them not only of their border defenses but, as all their lines of communication were cut promptly, of the means and the time to organize a stand at the Muleng or Mutanchiang rivers. Individual Japanese units had fought back doggedly, but the struggle had been uneven and the Soviet advance had taken on the appearance of a pursuit until the First Far Eastern Front had come to Mutanchiang. As related, a major battle had developed over Mutanchiang between units of the 1st Red Banner Army and the Soviet 5th Army on one hand and the Japanese Fifth Army on the other hand. After two days of fighting, the 26th Rifle Corps of the 1st Red Banner Army entered the city, but was driven out and thrown back some six miles by a Japanese counterattack. Only on August 16, a day after the official capitulation of Japan, did the Soviets capture Mutanchiang in the last major battle in southeastern Manchuria.[44]

The Second Far Eastern Front, in the northeast, also opened hostilities at 01:00 on August 9. Its objective was to cross the Amur River and following its tributary, the Sungari, attack Chiamussu and then continue toward Harbin.[45] With the collaboration of the Amur flotilla, its 15th Army forced the Amur River to the north of the city of T'ungchiang (Lahasusu) on the night of August 9–10 and the following day captured the heart of the city of Fuchin. Heavy fighting, often in the form of hand-to-hand combat, continued over the well fortified military strongpoint of the Japanese 134th Infantry Division in the southern part of the city, however, and the Russians did not subdue it until the evening of the 13th.[46] Another column, the 5th Independent Rifle Corps, crossed the Ussuri River with the aid of the 3rd Brigade of the Amur flotilla and attacked the Jaoho fortified area; then it headed for Paoch'ing, which it captured on the evening of the 14th. The 10th Air Army gave air support to the operations of the 2nd Far Eastern Front.[47]

With the operations on the three fronts proceeding ahead of schedule,[k] the Soviet command decided to widen the offensive line of the Second Far Eastern Front from Bikin to Blagoveshchensk and to capture South Sakhalin and the Kuril Archipelago. On August 11 the 2nd Red Banner Army, which had been ferried across the Amur River by the Amur flotilla, seized the Manchurian cities of Sakhalian and Aigun. On August 14 it destroyed most of the Japanese positions in the Sunwu fortified area, then set out for Tsitsihar.[49]

The 16th Army, meanwhile, invaded South Sakhalin, whose defenders had first learned of Soviet entry into the Pacific War from an American newscast.[1] On the morning of August 11 units of the 56th Infantry Corps launched an offensive against Koton, northern railhead and axis of the Japanese line of defense. Stubborn resistance induced the Russians to skirt Koton—the 179th Regiment slushed through the Poronai swamps to the east of Koton, while the 165th Regiment moved through the tall grasses and dense mist around the western flank—and attack it simultaneously from the front and rear.[52] To cut off the Japanese defenders from reinforcements, naval landing forces and infantry were put ashore at Toro

---

[k] The Soviet advance on the Transbaikal front had been facilitated by the decision of General Ushiroku Jun, who commanded the Japanese Third Area Army, not to waste his troops in delaying maneuvers, but to withdraw the entire 44th Army to the Dairen-Mukden-Changchun railway line and make a stand there in the expectation that Russian lines would be overextended and Russian troops exhausted by that time. Ushiroku did not conceive, of course, that Japan would surrender before then.[48]

[1] The American broadcast had been heard on August 9 at 5 a.m.[50] Official notification of divisional headquarters at Toyohara came two hours later.[51]

(Shakhtersk), on the west coast of the island, on the 16th.[53]

At Koton and the nearby Horomi Pass, at Esu-toru, an important rail center, and at other points on Sakhalin, to which the conflict spread, the Japanese offered bitter opposition, and although some of their forces surrendered on August 19, others continued fighting until the 24th, some units holding out until the end of the month. As company and field grade officers laid down their lives in banzai charges, senior officers sought to restrain them. "Dying is a simple matter which can be done at any time," a regimental commander told a major who wanted to mount a sui-cide attack; "extract as much damage as possible from the enemy by fighting stubbornly instead."[54] Never-theless, when resistance proved futile, many civilians as well as soldiers committed suicide rather than sur-render to the Soviets.[55]

Those who surrendered, on the other hand, did so with exemplary discipline. Forces of the 125th In-fantry Regiment in the vicinity of Nairo, for example, meticulously brought their tables of strength up to date, serviced their weapons, then lined up in forma-tion at the side of the road on which the Russians were advancing, reverently bowed in the direction of the Imperial Palace, and stoically welcomed their cap-tors.[56]

On the night of August 17–18 the Northern Pa-cific Fleet of the U.S.S.R. launched its conquest of the Kurils with an assault on Shumshu, the Northern-most island of the archipelago.[57] Although fighting on Shumshu was heavy and its defenders did not sur-render until receipt of the cease-fire order from the Fifth Area Army, once Shumshu had fallen, the garrisons on the other islands did not resist and laid down their arms as landing forces of the Northern Pacific Fleet arrived between August 22 and September 1, when Kunashiri, the southernmost Kuril island, was occupied.[58]

As related, fighting had not ceased with the capitulation of the Japanese government. On one hand, the Soviet Union had brushed aside the imperial rescript of August 14, announcing Japan's decision to surrender, as merely a general declaration in regard to unconditional surrender; on the other hand, the Kwantung Army had not specifically ordered its forces until August 17 to cease hostilities by the afternoon of the 18th and even then had done so with the qualification that "self-defense actions" would be permissible under "unavoidable circumstances."[59] Various units had continued to fight, because in the breakdown of communications the surrender orders had never reached them; others had struggled on because they had not believed the orders or had chosen to ignore them.[60,m] Thus Soviet operations in Manchuria had continued until August 18, in some areas until the 30th.[62]

On August 18 Major General G. A. Shelakhov, deputy chief of staff of the First Far Eastern Front, had landed at Harbin airport with a group of airborne troops and had ordered General Hata Hikosaburō, chief of staff of the Kwantung Army who had hastened to the airport, to issue the necessary instructions for surrender. Japanese generals and officers had been allowed, "pending special instructions from the

---

[m] The idea of surrender was the more difficult to accept because the soldiers had been kept uninformed about Japan's losses. "Only yesterday the radio had told them of great victories."[61]

Soviet command," to retain their swords and stay in their quarters, if they surrendered "voluntarily."[63] Hata, Miyakawa, and other generals then had been taken to Meretskov's command post, where Vasilevskii, who had also proceeded there, had personally dictated the method of formal surrender, which was executed on August 20.[64] Soviet forces, meanwhile, had continued their penetration of Manchuria, the Liaotung Peninsula with Port Arthur being occupied on the 25th.[65]

The capitulation of Japan as a whole took place on September 2 in Tokyo Bay, aboard the American battleship *Missouri*. Soviet officers participated in the ceremonies, Lieutenant General K. N. Derevianko signing the instrument of surrender on behalf of the U.S.S.R. Two days later General Yamada Otozō, commander-in-chief of the Kwantung Army, and most general officers who had served in Manchukuo were flown to the U.S.S.R. to be tried as war criminals.[66] Soon afterwards the bulk of the Kwantung Army—some half a million men—were shipped to the Soviet Union for two or more years of forced labor to help rebuild the Soviet economy, devastated by Japan's Axis partner.[n]

[n] Professor Edward Norbeck, who interviewed some of the prisoners of war several years after their release, learned that aside from their detainment, which had been an obvious hardship, they had been well treated by the Russians. "In contrast with conditions in the Japanese army, the prisoners found life comfortable."[67] Upon repatriation they realized that they had suffered less than their families in war-ravaged Japan and were reluctant to talk of the good treatment they had received.[68]

10

Recriminations at the War Crimes Trial

Among the prisoners taken to the Soviet Union was Aisin-Gioro ("Henry") Pu Yi, the pathetic puppet-emperor of Manchukuo, who had been sitting at the Mukden airport waiting for a plane to whisk him to Japan, when Soviet airborne troops had seized the airport on August 19 and had chanced upon him.[1] Though Pu Yi begged his captors not to turn him over to the Japanese[2]—his hair stood on end when he thought that the latter might kill him to keep him quiet[3]—he feared the Russians too, for the Japanese had told him that he would be the first to be murdered by the Soviet troops. But most of all he dreaded being turned over to the Chinese, at whose expense he had presided over Manchukuo, and was terrified when upon landing at Chita and being taken from the airport, his car stopped suddenly and a Soviet officer, whom he could not recognize in the dark, shouted in Chinese: "Get out if you want a pee!"[4]

Pu Yi was well treated by the Russians, whom he supplied enthusiastically with information to be used against the Japanese, and made three written applications to become a permanent resident of the U.S.S.R.[5] But after the Chinese People's Republic came into being, Pu Yi and other Manchukuoan officials were extradited to China to be tried as war criminals.[6] Yet Pu Yi fared better than he had expected. He was neither shot nor imprisoned for life. After serving ten years, during which he was remolded ideologically and taught a useful trade, he received a special pardon.[7]

The Japanese officers who had been put on trial in the Soviet Union received stiffer sentences. In December 1949 General Yamada, Lieutenant General Kajitsuka Ryūji, head of the Medical Corps, and ten subordinates were convicted of planning and waging bacteriological warfare and were condemned to up to twenty-five years of corrective labor.[8,a]

The most severe sentences were meted out by the International Military Tribunal in Tokyo, which convicted 28 "major war criminals" of planning to secure Japan's domination over Asia by aggressive warfare. Seven were condemned to death, sixteen to life imprisonment. Hirota, who had vainly sought to negotiate a Soviet-Japanese rapprochement, was among those hanged.[9] Tōgō, who also had tried to reverse the course of Soviet-Japanese relations, was sentenced to twenty years of incarceration, but fell ill and died in a United States Army Hospital while serving his term.[10]

In trying the leaders of Japan for planning and waging aggressive war,[b] the international tribunal left

[a] The sentences varied; one was for only two years. It is possible furthermore that some or all of the prisoners were released before serving the full terms.
[b] The question whether the war crimes trials were—or by their nature could have been—just, is beyond the scope of this study. So is the ques-

the presentation of the case of alleged Japanese aggression against the U.S.S.R. to the Soviet prosecution. Stalin had recalled the Japanese surprise attack on Tsarist Russia, when informing the Soviet public of Japan's capitulation.[11] Like him the Soviet prosecutors evoked a long history of Japanese aggression against Russia and charged that the creation of Manchukuo had been an anti-Soviet act—the establishment of a base of operations against the U.S.S.R.[12] The Soviet prosecution alleged that Japan had concluded the Neutrality Pact under false pretenses, that Matsuoka had been well aware of German preparations for an attack against the Soviet Union when he had signed the Neutrality Pact and that "Matsuoka hoped he would be able to deceive the Soviet Government and reckoned that as soon as the war with Germany broke out, the Soviet Union, relying on the Pact, would transfer all her forces from the Far East to the Western front and then the whole of Eastern Siberia together with the Maritime Province would easily fall into the hands of Japan."[13] It accused Japan of having violated the Neutrality Pact, once it had been concluded, by furnishing Germany with information about the U.S.S.R., collected by Japanese diplomatic representatives stationed in the latter, and by sinking Soviet ships and hampering Soviet navigation.[14]

Evidence was introduced at the trial that the imperial conference of July 2, 1941, had decided not to intervene in the German-Soviet war "for a while," but make secret preparations for possible entry at a later time. The Japanese had agreed to continue the diplo-

tion whether the hands of all the judges were clean. For a discussion of these matters, see Lord Maurice Hankey, *Politics, Trials and Errors*, 139–42.

matic negotiations, but "take up arms to solve the Northern Problem" if German victories created conditions favorable for a Japanese attack.[15]

There was testimony that General Araki Sadao, one of the apostles of Japan's mission in Asia, had told the secretary general of the Imperial Rule Assistance Association in August 1941 that it was regrettable that at the time of the Siberian Intervention Japan had lacked the courage and the determination "to strive for the calculated ends" by making "the expected last stroke," but that "history repeats itself" and that the seeds of the Siberian Intervention had grown into "Japan's present ambition to dominate the continent."[16]

The Soviets adduced proof that the military had not been the only ones with contingency plans for an invasion of the Soviet Union, nor the only ones to contemplate the annexation of the Russian Far East. They documented that the Committee for Administrative Measures of the National Policy Investigation Society (the Kokusaku Kenkyūkai), an influential, semi-official organization with financial backing from the zaibatsu,[17] had made various proposals to the Japanese government and the military in the fall of 1941 concerning the administration of the Maritime region and had recommended the settlement of armed Japanese colonists in Siberia and the exclusion from the same area of Slavs whom the Germans might not wish to keep in "their" part of Russia.[18] The Soviets produced a secret "Plan for the Establishment of a Greater East Asia Coprosperity Sphere," issued in January 1942 by the Research Institute of Total War, which had been established by an imperial edict and had been directly under the prime minister, in which the Maritime Province had been included in the "East Asia Union" that

Japan was to head. They showed that the Research Institute had envisaged the annexation of the territory east of Lake Baikal, with the extension of "self-government of the lowest degree," once the region had been purged of "red influence."[19]

The Soviets contended at the War Crimes Trial that the Japanese had violated the state borders of the U.S.S.R. 49 times in 1940, 136 times in 1941, 229 times in 1942, and 414 times in 1943.[20] Eighteen Japanese ships had been detained by the Russians in 1940 for violation of Soviet territorial waters, twice that number in 1942. Japanese planes were alleged to have violated Soviet air space 56 times in 1940, 61 times in 1941, 82 times in 1942 and 119 times in 1943.[21]

The Japanese defense retorted that on the basis of data compiled by the Bureau of European and Asiatic Affairs of the Foreign Office, "unlawful acts" committed by the Soviet Union along the frontiers between the U.S.S.R. and Manchukuo and between Mongolia and Manchukuo had totalled 166 in 1938, 195 in 1939, 151 in 1940, and 98 in 1941. While regarding the decline in total number of incidents as "a phenomenon worthy of notice," the Foreign Office had warned at the time that it had been paralleled by "the rapid increase of such intentional acts as the violation of the territorial air and the plotted transgression of the border."[22]

The prosecution challenged the Japanese documents on the ground that they were "merely a compilation by a bureau, presumably of the Foreign Ministry, from unknown sources" and constituted at most "merely evidence that that bureau received such reports from somewhere, but no evidence of the truth of the reports." The defense countered that the tabulation of alleged Japanese frontier violations presented by the prosecution had been compiled by an official of the People's Commissariat for Home Affairs of the U.S.S.R. after the war for use at the trial and constituted "another of the self-serving declarations put into evidence by the Soviet prosecution." The Japanese document, on the other hand, had been prepared contemporaneously and confidentially by the Japanese government for its own use and was superior, the defense argued, "in probative value."[23]

While seeking to shift the responsibility for military preparations and war plans on Soviet shoulders, the defense sought to absolve the Japanese from hostile intentions against the U.S.S.R. Pointing to the improvement in Soviet-Japanese relations in the period after the Nomonhan Incident, it asserted that General Umezu had been named commander-in-chief of the Kwantung Army and concurrently ambassador to Manchukuo because he was known to favor peaceful relations with the U.S.S.R. and could be expected to forestall rather than initiate frontier incidents,[24] and that the chief of staff and the vice-chief of staff had been picked similarly for their determination to avoid trouble with the Soviet Union.[25]

The defense related that on February 1, 1940, Foreign Minister Arita had assured the Diet that "international feeling" between Japan and the Soviet Union had "taken a turn for the better," and that he had asserted, when informing it of the establishment of a commission to delimit the boundaries between Manchukuo and Mongolia and of negotiations for the formation of other commissions to demarcate the boundaries between Manchukuo and the U.S.S.R. and solve any contentions in the frontier districts, that "the Japanese Government have always desired to adjust relations with the U.S.S.R. and so contribute toward ensuring the peace of East Asia as a whole."[26]

To the question of the Soviet prosecutor whether the Kwantung Army special maneuvers were carried out in execution of the decision of the imperial conference of July 2, 1941, to make secret preparations for entry into the Russo-German war, Lieutenant General Tanaka Shinichi, who had been chief of operations of the General Staff Office at the time, responded that their purpose had been purely defensive.[27] The defense noted that the imperial conference of September 6, 1941, had resolved that Japan would not initiate military action against the U.S.S.R. "as long as the Soviet Union will respect the Russo-Japanese Neutrality Pact and will not threaten both Japan and Manchukuo."[28] The fact that Japan had not attacked the Soviet Union, in spite of repeated German urgings and protests to do so, was adduced as proof that she had never intended to do so.[29]

While the Soviet prosecution contended that the intensification of a military build-up in Manchukuo and the German invasion of the U.S.S.R. were not coincidental,[30] General Tanaka and other Japanese witnesses insisted that their plans for the occupation of the Maritime Province had been merely operational and "passive offensive." Asked whether they did not know that Japan planned to include the Soviet Far East in the Greater East Asia sphere, they retorted that this was a political question with which the general staff had no connection.[31]

The defense related that in November 1941 Army Chief of Staff General Sugiyama, who had been responsible for national defense and tactics, had told the vice-chief of staff, who had been in charge of coordinating policy and operations, and the chief of the First Department, who had been in charge of matters relating to operations, that in view of Japan's national policy of "adjustment" of relations with the Soviet Union, the basic strategy in drawing up plans of operations against the U.S.S.R. was to reserve part of the army to guard against possible Soviet attack and to maintain peace in the North.[32]

General Tanabe Moritake, who had become vice-chief of the army general staff in November 1941, asserted in an affidavit, introduced at the War Crimes Trial, that in 1941 Japanese military efforts vis-à-vis the Soviet Union had been defensive and that the Supreme Command had made it its principle "never to enter into a state of war against the U.S.S.R."[33] Plans of operations against the Soviet Union had been drawn up nevertheless, the Japanese contended, because the military planners, in spite of the conclusion of the Neutrality Pact, had envisaged from the very beginning of the Pacific War that the Soviet Union might eventually take an active part against Japan.[34]

General Kasahara Yukio, chief of staff of the Kwantung Army from 1942 to 1945, argued that a Japanese attack on the Maritime Province would have been "an offensive unavoidable for self-defense" in the event of hostilities with the Soviet Union, lest Japan proper and her vital sea communications be bombed from air bases in the Maritime Province.[35,e] Kasahara asserted that the strength of the Kwantung Army had never matched that of the Far Eastern Red Army, even after the trans-

[e] In discussing the 1935 Otsu plan of operations against the Soviet Union, General Ushiroku stated that "its operational aim was to occupy the Maritime Province and to eliminate air raids upon Japan by the air forces of the Soviet Army."[36]

fer of some Soviet forces to the European front,[d] and that in view of her other commitments, Japan had lacked the economic resources to expand military power sufficiently to cope with the U.S.S.R.

Interrogated about plans of aggression that Japan might have had against the territory of the U.S.S.R., Kasahara replied:

> I can testify only concerning operational plans, not war plans. The Army staffs drew up the plans of operations, but the war plans were under the jurisdiction of the cabinet and not matters for military staffs. In the plans of operations the only subject was the manner of operation in the event of an outbreak of war, and the object of war or the starting of war, etc.—matters connected with war plans—were never touched upon. I should think this is true in every country. I distinctly knew that the Army had no plan of war at all, and I had never heard that the Cabinet had any. But as for me, I thought there was no hope of victory in a war against the U.S.S.R., since I knew that our power was inferior to theirs. I believed that an aggressive plan against Soviet territory would be thoroughly impossible in view of our inferior armed strength.[38]

Under the circumstances, the actual strength of the Kwantung Army became an issue at the trial. According to American intelligence estimates, produced by the defense, the strength of the Kwantung Army had risen from 500,000 men in May 1943 to a peak of 785,000 in April 1944, had declined to 610,000 men in April 1945, then gone up to 660,000 in August 1945.

[d] The imperial army was ever conscious of the military superiority of the Far Eastern Red Army. According to Japanese intelligence estimates the Soviets sought to maintain three times the strength of the Kwantung Army and by the winter of 1940-41 had actually attained an even greater ratio of fighting power.[37]

The number of planes in Manchuria and Korea combined had fluctuated from 405 in May 1943, down to 150 in December 1943, up to 353 in April 1944, down to 139 in October of that year, and up again to 205 by April 1945.[39]

The Soviet prosecution rejected the figures, arguing that they excluded 1941–42, when the U.S.S.R. was most threatened by a Japanese attack and that Moscow's estimate that over 1 million troops or about one third of the entire Japanese Army were massed in Manchuria in 1942[40] was more relevant, because "the Soviet Union, being a neighboring country to Manchuria, knew better about the armed forces in that country." The defense retorted that the Russian figures had been prepared by a deputy chief of the Soviet general staff especially for the trial, while the American estimates had been made during the war as a basis for military planning and thus were of greater "probative value."[41,e]

The defense denied that the establishment of sea defense areas was an anti-Soviet measure; it contended that Soviet vessels were stopped and searched to forestall their confusion with hostile craft. The restriction of Soviet shipping to two water lanes was justified by the Japanese as a necessary measure for preventing the passage of United States submarines and thus indirectly as a safeguard for Japanese shipping.[43]

e The Japanese general staff had been aware that substantial Soviet forces were being moved from Europe to the Russian Far East from February 1945. Following the abrogation of the Neutrality Pact by the Soviet Union in April, it had expected the Soviet Union to enter the Pacific War by winter. With the issuance of the Potsdam Proclamation in July, it had moved up its estimate of the attack to autumn and had hastened to reinforce the Kwantung Army, ordering the total mobilization of able-bodied men in Manchuria and Korea. Though mobilization had not been completed when the Soviet Union entered the war, the Kwantung Army had been boosted to about 780,000 men.[42]

The defense produced evidence that when Ambassador Satō, in a conversation with Deputy Foreign Commissar Lozovskii concerning Japanese-German and Anglo-American-Soviet relations on July 19, 1944, had stated that the Japanese government, which had remained faithful to the Neutrality Pact, expected the U.S.S.R. to do the same, Lozovskii had retorted that the Soviet government always acted in accordance with the Neutrality Pact.[44] Satō himself testified that Molotov had assured him on April 5, 1945, after reading the denunciation of the Neutrality Pact, that it would remain in force for another year and that the attitude of the Soviet government would be determined by this condition.[45]

Asserting that Japan had given the Soviet Union no cause for attack, Satō declared:

> Prior to the Soviet declaration of war on Japan there had been in March 1944 a settlement of the Fisheries Convention question by extension of the convention for five years, and simultaneously a settlement of the troublesome Northern Sakhalin petroleum concessions question by Japan's relinquishment of its concession there. No protest was ever made during my tenure as Ambassador against the maintenance of Japanese forces in Manchukuo and Korea or along the Soviet border; and although border incidents were numerous during that time, they were very minor, involving only a few soldiers at a time, and no serious disputes ever developed from them. With removal of the long-standing sources of friction mentioned above, relations between the two countries during my tenure were good and bordering on the cordial, and no question was pending in August 1945 to suggest the possibility of an outbreak of war.[46]

The attempt of the defense to turn the tables on the prosecution and charge the Soviet Union with the violation of the Neutrality Pact and thus with aggression stung the Russians. They reiterated that Japan had repeatedly violated the Neutrality Pact and that her attack on the United States of America and Great Britain—the allies of the U.S.S.R.—had robbed it of meaning and had forced the Soviet government to denounce it as soon as the time for such denunciation had come under the terms of the pact.[47]

Reflections

The Neutrality Pact between the U.S.S.R. and Japan had been concluded under strange circumstances. It had been negotiated in the wake of the German-Soviet nonaggression pact and the deterioration of Japanese relations with the United States and Great Britain, the U.S.S.R. seeking to secure her rear in the event of another switch in German policy, Japan her rear in case of hostilities with the United States. The Neutrality Pact had remained in effect for most of its term in spite of the fact that the Soviet Union and Japan had been fighting desperately against each other's allies. "If Soviet-American relations during the war were called 'the Strange Alliance,' Soviet-Japanese relations during the war should be termed 'the Strange Neutrality,'" a Japanese diplomat wrote years later.[1]

The Neutrality Pact had been a blessing in disguise for the United States. Hitler had felt in the summer of 1940 that the Soviet Union and the United States were England's only hope for survival. "If hope in Russia is eliminated, America too is eliminated, because elimination of Russia means a tremendous increase of Japan's power in East Asia. Russia is England's and America's sword against Japan in East Asia."[2] The English journalist Alexander Werth, after weighing the positive and negative results of Soviet-American wartime collaboration, declared, all things considered, "Thank God for the Strange Alliance!" If one ponders that the Japanese invasion of the U.S.S.R. might have led to the collapse of Soviet resistance and to the fall of England and that the United States would have been left to face alone a victorious German-Japanese combination, drawing on the economic resources of Europe and Asia, Americans can only add, all things considered, "Thank God for the Strange Neutrality!"

At the same time, it can be argued that the United States contributed indirectly to Japan's observation of the Neutrality Pact. The Japanese government had contemplated breaking it at an opportune moment and the temptation to attack the Soviet Union, which was in a death-grapple with Germany, might have become irresistable, had the American economic embargo not forced the Japanese to devote their full strength to the conflict with the United States and Great Britain. "It may not be too much of an exaggeration to conclude from the situation in the summer of 1941," a German historian remarks, "that the United States, in drawing upon herself by her sanctions the fears, anger and aggression of the Japanese, unwittingly saved the Soviet Union from a perhaps catastrophic two-front war."[4]

The eventual denunciation of the Neutrality Pact by the U.S.S.R. and Soviet entry into the Pacific War before its legal expiration came at the urging of the United States and Great Britain. In view of the subsequent spread of Communism in Asia and the break-up of the Strange Alliance, Americans have come to blame themselves and their government for contributing to the expansion of Russian influence by facilitating the Soviet invasion of Manchuria and by rewarding the U.S.S.R. with Japanese and Chinese territory.

At the heart of the issue, from the American point

of view, are two questions: (1) Was Russian participation necessary to defeat Japan? (2) Was the price reasonable?

If one answers the first question on the basis of what was learned from Japanese sources *after* the war and confines it to the time of the Soviet Union's actual entry, the answer is, "No." Japan had been on the verge of surrender by the summer of 1945 and would have capitulated prior to the dropping of the atomic bombs and prior to the Soviet attack *if* the Allies had not insisted on unconditional surrender.

The concept of unconditional surrender was President Roosevelt's brainchild, delivered at Casablanca on January 23, 1943, during a luncheon with Prime Minister Churchill. Stalin, who was not informed of the principle before its promulgation, did not favor it when he first learned of it, for he realized that it would strengthen the enemy's will to resist. But he espoused it as Germany became weaker and the prolongation of the war in Europe and in Asia gave the Soviet Union time and opportunity to spread her influence.[a]

Ironically Roosevelt's insistence on "unconditional surrender"—a "fatuous fight for a phrase" and "one of the greatest errors of the war"—was an attempt not to repeat the mistakes of the past, but to profit from the lessons of history. One of the lessons of history, learned from the First World War, had been that the nebulous way in which it had ended, with minor figures affixing their names to the armistice

[a] Dr. Leonid Kutakov, a Soviet historian and diplomat, to whom I showed this chapter, questioned that the Soviet government would have wanted to prolong the war. The country had suffered so much, he contended, that Moscow needed peace.

agreement, had made it possible for Germans to claim later that their army had not been defeated, but sold out by the politicians, and whip up support for a return engagement. It had been the desire to demonstrate to the aggressors that they had been beaten beyond a shadow of a doubt that had given birth to the demand for unconditional surrender. Ironically too, after prolonging the war by their insistence on unconditional surrender, the Americans eventually accepted a surrender that was not really unconditional, for they assured the Japanese that they would not be stripped either of the emperor system or their independence. Moreover, whatever arguments of a political sellout may have been taken from the mouths of future militarists by the so-called unconditional surrender, the dropping of the atomic bombs provided them with another, namely that the defeat of Japan had been due to the technological (rather than military) superiority of the United States.

The question of the need of Russian participation in the Pacific War takes on a different light, if examined on the basis of military estimates of the time. Even General MacArthur, though he later criticized the call for Soviet help, had himself favored it. It is true that toward the end of the war Soviet participation was no longer regarded as *necessary,* but it continued to be viewed as *desirable* to save American lives, for until the last moment a bloody invasion of Japan was contemplated.

As to the price tag of the Yalta Agreement, it had seemed reasonable at the time; there had been little haggling over the Russian demands. South Sakhalin and the Northern Kuril Islands had once belonged to Russia, and Port Arthur and Dairen had been Russian leaseholds. To the Soviets, whose navigation had been restricted by the Japanese during the period of neutrality, possession of the entire archipelago was vital as an assurance of free access to the Pacific Ocean; they had sought to obtain it through negotiations with Japan even before the Pacific War. It has since been argued that the United States and Great Britain had no right to promise to the Soviet Union territory of an ally without prior consultation with the latter and that the Southern Kuril Islands had never been Russian.[b] To the former one can respond that more or less the same had been done at Portsmouth, N.H., when Japan had obtained these leases from Russia without prior Chinese approval. Less can be said in justification of the transfer of the Southern Kuril Islands to the Soviet Union, if one thinks in terms of Wilsonian principles.[c] If, on the other hand, one considers how much territory the Soviet Union would have lost to Japan, had Matsuoka's advice been followed and Japanese victory achieved, the Soviet booty appears modest in comparison.

Whether Roosevelt and Churchill were morally right or wrong in giving Stalin what he wanted is purely academic at any rate. The question is whether they were in a position to deny him what he wanted, and the answer is, no. There was nothing to prevent

[b] Papers by Professor George H. Blakeslee and Professor Hugh Borton recommending international trusteeship for the northern and central Kuril Islands and South Sakhalin respectively had been prepared for the presidential briefing book, but inexplicably had been left out.[6]

[c] Soviet historians do not distinguish between the Northern and Southern Kuril Islands, but claim that the entire archipelago was first discovered by the Russians, Japanese not being allowed to go abroad during the Seclusion Period, which lasted from the mid-17th century to the mid-19th century. However, Japanese did visit the Southern Kuril Islands secretly, and the Russo-Japanese Treaty of 1855 specified that Etorofu and the islands to the south belonged to Japan.[7]

the Soviets from entering the Pacific War anyway and taking even more territory; in fact, as had been seen, they could have obtained practically the same concessions directly from the Japanese by staying out of the war.

In entering the Pacific War the U.S.S.R. contended that Japan's attack on her allies had robbed the Neutrality Pact of meaning. While this was true to some extent, the Soviet government had made no rebuttal when Tōgō had asserted the opposite in 1942: that Japan's war with the United States and Great Britain had no bearing on Japanese-Soviet relations and that, indeed, it was with the outbreak of the war that the Neutrality Pact really took effect. Likewise, the Soviet Union had argued that the Neutrality Pact was not affected by her war with Germany or her aid to China, insisting that it did not govern relations with third powers.

That the Soviet Union violated the Neutrality Pact by attacking Japan before its legal expiration is obvious, as is the fact that the Allies share responsibility in urging her to do so. It is equally plain, however, that Japan had considered doing the same and that her change of plans had not been impelled by moral scruples. Privately neither Japanese nor Russian statesmen had regarded the pact as unbreakable—indeed, both sides had violated it repeatedly. Both powers were content to observe it formally as long as they needed protection from a two-front war.[d]

Technically the Soviets presented Japan with a declaration of war before opening hostilities. Since it is

---

[d] In reading these lines, Dr. Kutakov objected to my speaking of Japanese and Soviet violations in one breath, but, as we have seen, both sides were culpable to some degree in violating the Neutrality Pact.

inconceivable, however, that Ambassador Satō's telegram with the declaration of war was simply lost, it must be concluded that the U.S.S.R. in effect struck first and gave notice later. The success of the Soviet attack was greatly enhanced by the element of surprise, and though some Japanese statesmen professed outrage, others realized that Japan had acted in the same manner toward Russia and the United States. "It was true that a powerful section of our Army harbored hostile intentions against the northern neighbor," Kase wrote. "It must be recalled that when the Soviet Union was in peril Japan's attitude was none too reassuring for her. When Japan was in danger, therefore, it was natural that the Soviet Union should return the compliment in kind."[8]

The nature of the Russian contribution to the defeat of Japan, once the Soviet Union entered the war, has been the subject of much controversy. It is popularly believed in the United States that Russian operations, coming as they did five days before the decision of the Japanese government to surrender, were not a major military effort. One American writer has likened the Soviet attack, "while Japan's cities were going up in flames or evaporating in mushroom clouds," to that of "a thief at a fire."[9] It is implied that the U.S.S.R. did not join the struggle earlier because she had been biding her time to ride to victory on the coattails of Uncle Sam, that she had entered the war upon learning of the atomic bombing of Hiroshima, because by then it was all over except for the grabbing of territory.

Marshal Meretskov in his memoirs, on the other hand, insists that the dropping of the atomic bombs had almost no effect on Soviet plans. "Firstly," he writes, "the tragic events at Hiroshima and Nagasaki had no relationship whatsoever to our plans of smashing the Kwantung Army. Secondly, the actual results of the explosions were not exactly known at that time to the Americans themselves, and the Japanese naturally did not inform us."[10]

The date of the Soviet entry into the Pacific War had been dictated by the time required by the Russians for the transfer to their distant frontiers of the large forces, which they really thought they needed to defeat the Kwantung Army, and had been fixed long prior to the dropping of the atomic bombs. As Churchill told the House of Commons on August 16, 1945:

> It would in my opinion be a mistake to suggest that the Russian declaration of war upon Japan was hastened by the use of the atomic bomb. My understanding with Marshal Stalin in the talks which I had with him had been, for a considerable time past, that Russia would declare war upon Japan within three months of the surrender of the German armies. The reason for the delay of three months was, of course, the need to move over the Trans-Siberian Railway the large reinforcements necessary to convert the Russian-Manchurian army from a defensive to an offensive strength. Three months was the time mentioned, and the fact that the German armies surrendered on May 8, and the Russians declared war on Japan on August 8, is no mere coincidence, but another example of the fidelity and punctuality with which Marshal Stalin and his valiant armies always keep their military engagements.[11]

The French journalist Robert Guillain, who had been overtaken by the Pacific War in Japan and had remained there throughout the conflict, addressed himself to the same subject in his recollections of war-time Japan. Admitting that Soviet participation had lasted only a week, he questioned whether that was what the U.S.S.R. had wanted: "Can the Russian intervention be considered, as one does, a blow 'Italian-style,' analogous to Mussolini's entry into the war in 1940, when the [German] Reich had already beaten France? I do not believe so. . . . Far from wanting to intervene when all was over, Russia had believed she could take a large part in the end of the war; but the United States prevented her from doing so."[12] Noting that at Yalta, where Stalin had agreed to enter the war three months after the defeat of Germany, American planners had told the Soviets that the war with Japan would last until the spring of 1946, Guillain reasoned that the Soviets had expected to fight with the Japanese for some six to eight months and had thought that they would have ample time to "carve" for themselves a large part of the Japanese empire, and that the Americans had dropped the atomic bombs "as if . . . to forestall and avoid precisely having to share their victory."

> All plans are upset [Guillain surmised]. Events are quite different from those calculated by Russia. The war has but six days to go; in less than a month the United States, though acting nominally for all the Allies, will be installed in Japan, and alone, while Russia will have to content herself with peripheral positions on the circumference of the Japanese bastion. And all this will happen as if she had paid and paid very high for the excessive complaisance manifested toward Japan by her policy of neutrality.[13]

While Americans, conscious of their long and bloody struggle with Japan, tend to dismiss the Russian contribution to the termination of the Pacific War,[e] Soviet writers have gone to the opposite extreme, minimizing the American war effort. Professor David Gol'dberg, a distinguished scholar, takes issue with the view that the Pacific War was won primarily by the naval and air forces of the United States and labels the contention that the United States played a decisive role in the defeat of Japan as a bourgeois falsification of history. Relating the war in the Pacific directly to the war in Europe, he sees the turning point of the Second World War in the Soviet victories over the Germans, notably at Stalingrad. He denies that the employment of the atomic bombs affected the Japanese military potential, since neither Hiroshima nor Nagasaki were industrial centers, and asserts that the atomic bombs were dropped on the eve and on the day of the Soviet entry into the Pacific War to give the *illusion* that the United States had knocked out Japan.[15] While stressing that the dropping of the atomic bombs was at once "senseless" and "an unprecedented act of barbarism,"[f] Soviet historians contend that it was the crushing of the Kwantung Army in Manchuria by the Red Army that induced the Japanese to surrender.[17]

[e] Joseph Lawrence Marx does not so much as mention Soviet entry into the Pacific War in his discussion of whether or not the employment of the atomic bombs was necessary to hasten the end of the war.[14]

[f] Needless to say, while the Soviets sought to make political capital out of American use of the atomic bomb, they were not the only ones to condemn its employment. The noted English jurist Lord Maurice Hankey has pointed out that the use of the atomic bomb had been contrary to the Washington Treaty of February 6, 1922. Since the treaty had never been ratified, the United States had been legally within her rights to use it, but, in the opinion of Hankey, "if the Allied leaders had fallen into the hands of the enemy and had been tried as War Criminals the authors of the Charter would have made it their business to see that the use of the atomic bomb was declared to be a crime against international law."[16]

The truth lies somewhere between the equally chauvinistic American and Soviet views. As mentioned earlier, the Japanese might have laid down arms by the summer of 1945 if the unconditional surrender formula had not stiffened their resistance. Even unconditional surrender was brought close, however, when the dropping of the atomic bombs confronted Japan not merely with the possibility of the destruction of her polity but with national extinction. Yet the nature of the Hiroshima tragedy was not immediately comprehended in Tokyo and the Soviet entry into the war did hasten its termination. In the words of Lieutenant General Kawabe Torashiro, vice-chief of the Japanese Army General Staff at the time, "Russian entry was a great shock when it actually came, whereas the atom bomb impact was not so readily apparent.[18,g]

In his memoirs Foreign Minister Tōgō recalled that as soon as he had been informed of the Soviet attack by the radio room of the Foreign Office, he had called on Premier Suzuki to repeat that the war must be stopped at once. When he had expressed the same opinion at the Supreme Council meeting at 11 a.m., "now, after the employment of the atomic bomb and the Russian entry into the war" everyone agreed in principle.[20] Kase corroborates: "It is certain that we would have surrendered in due time without the terrific chastisement of the [atomic] bomb or the terrible shock of the Russian attack. However, it cannot also

---

[g] Since the radiation aftereffects were not foreseen at the time, the damage to Hiroshima appeared less extensive than that caused by the B-29 raids. The atomic explosion, furthermore, had done little damage below ground and the commander-in-chief of the Second General Army and his chief of staff reported, when they flew to Tokyo the following day, that although their headquarters had not been far from where the bomb had been dropped, they had not been hurt and only a few soldiers had died.[19]

be denied that both the bombs and the Russians facilitated our surrender. Without them the Army might have tried to prolong resistance."[21]

Major General S. Woodburn Kirby in the official British study of *The War Against Japan* goes so far as to state that "the Russian declaration of war was the decisive factor in bringing Japan to accept the Potsdam Declaration, for it brought home to all members of the Supreme Council the realization that the last hope of a negotiated peace had gone and that there was no alternative but to accept the Allied terms sooner or later."[22]

It is extremely difficult to give an objective assessment of so recent a period of history in which so many of us were personally involved.[h] The matter is complicated by the distortions and recriminations that have crept into standard histories in the wake of the Cold War and that have been supplemented rather than supplanted by the more recent distortions and recriminations of some revisionist historians of the right and of the left.

That false impressions can be given even when there is agreement on facts and neither side strays from the truth is well illustrated by a Soviet anecdote. President Eisenhower and Premier Khrushchev, the story goes, had a foot race and Eisenhower won. Though the two were the only contestants, the American

---

[h] I myself served as a United States Army Officer in India and China during the Pacific War and in Japan during the first year of the Occupation. On the other hand, I returned to Japan several times as a professor and became sufficiently fond of her people and life-style to consider seriously settling there. I hope that my sensitivity to other points of view has been enhanced by the fact that I was stateless for the first twenty years of my life and received my primary and secondary education in four different countries and that my first wife was from mainland China, my second wife is from the Soviet Union.

press wrote: "Eisenhower came in first, Khrushchev came in last." Soviet newspapers, on the other hand, declared: "Khrushchev came in second, Eisenhower next to last."

Nor need distortion be deliberate. It is natural that a history of the Pacific War written for American readers should contain a photograph showing General MacArthur seated aboard the *Missouri,* affixing his signature to the Japanese instrument of surrender, while a corresponding history written for Soviet readers should show the same scene, but with Lieutenant General Derevianko in a seated position, signing the document, with MacArthur and all the other officers standing in the background. Both pictures are true and their use fair, yet they leave different images in the minds of the American and Russian public of their countries' respective roles in the Japanese surrender.

The differences of opinion concerning the history of Soviet-Japanese-American relations in the years before, during and after the Second World War are less over facts than over motivations. Since motivations tend to be elusive and the attribution of subsequent events to prior intentions unreliable, writers fall back on their own perceptions of the nature of the Soviet, Japanese and American political systems in analyzing the course of events. Thus at the heart of one's evaluation of the Soviet entry into the Pacific War is one's view of the nature of the U.S.S.R.

The question is not whether one likes or dislikes Communism, but whether the Soviet Union by 1945 had become a nation state or continued to be an international, revolutionary power. Everyone agrees that during the war Stalin, Georgian though he was, extolled Russia's national interests. The dispute arises over whether he believed what he said or hoodwinked the Allies into giving him concessions—whether the Soviet Union after the war sought to Communize the world (and had planned to do so all along) or merely took advantage of revolutionary situations to advance her national interests.

Professor F. C. Jones takes the former view. Noting that "during 1941–5, the soft-pedalling of Communist ideological theory, the stress on Russian nationalist themes in Moscow's war propaganda, and the apparent abolition of the Comintern, all combined to give the impression that the fanatical and proselytizing epoch of the Russian Communist movement was beginning to give way to a mellower era in which permanent co-existence of other ideologies and Powers might be accepted," he asserts: "The idea that the Soviet Union could be regarded as a national State, with limited territorial ambitions, of which the satisfaction would content her, proved to be a fundamental misconception. The U.S.S.R. was and had never ceased to be, the citadel of the Communist revolutionary movement, which was world-embracing in its aspirations, in contrast to the relatively limited objectives of the Axis Powers and of Japan."[23]

Professor Adam B. Ulam, on the other hand, explains Soviet postwar policy in nationalistic terms. "The end of World War II left Russia the only Great Power on the Continent. . . . Russia was now clearly one of the two super-powers. Consequent upon this fact was the determination of Russia's leaders to enjoy all the prerogatives of that position, quite apart from any ideological considerations."[24] Ulam sees the roots of Soviet expansion in the eighteenth century Russian maxim "That which stops growing begins to rot" and in the desire to put as much territory as possible between Russia and her potential enemies, partly to prevent war on Russian soil, partly to isolate the Russian people from subversive foreign ideas, a policy reminiscent of 16th and 17th century Muscovy. To be sure, Communism proved a useful vehicle for the expansion of Soviet influence, but Ulam insists that the success was not only temporary but self-defeating. "The spread of Communism to other countries was to erode its monolithic unity to the point where, even before Stalin's death, the interests of world Communism and those of the Soviet state could no longer be considered as identical."[25] Russian aspirations were limited by the gradual realization that the proliferation of Communist states had ceased to produce satellites or dependable allies, that in fact it produced dangerous rivals."[26] "Who can doubt," Ulam asks, "that a Communist America would be a greater threat to the Soviet Union than a capitalist one?"[27]

Jones and Ulam both are first-rate scholars. Jones is an East Asia man, however—his analysis of Japanese foreign policy is brilliant—Ulam is a Russia specialist, writing, furthermore, from a later perspective. My own impressions of Soviet thinking and motivation lean toward those of Ulam.

The nationalism revived by the Great Patriotic War, as the Second World War is known in the U.S.S.R., has persisted and grown with the increase of Soviet power and has overshadowed ideological considerations in foreign policy. The objectives of the Soviet regime in Asia (both the Far East and the Near and Middle East) and in Europe are not very different from those that would have been espoused by any other strong Russian government. And while the Soviets still welcome Communist revolutions, they have come to realize the fruitlessness of the forceful imposition of friendly regimes on neighboring countries.[1] The Communization of Asia was the fruit of war, not of Soviet diplomacy or subversion. The Soviet Union was quick to exploit the opportunities that it perceived after the war, but it had not created them. In 1945 Stalin was as unprepared for the events that were to happen in China as was Truman. The nation that most contributed to the victory of Communism in China and Southeast Asia was Japan, which had plowed the political, social and economic systems of the region into the ground. Her own defeat and demilitarization had removed the historical counterweight to Russian power in East Asia; a vacuum was created into which the Soviet Union was drawn. That Japan achieved the opposite of what she had planned was ironical, but not uncommon. Every great power tends to be her own worst enemy, her very success bearing the seeds of failure, for sooner or later she overreaches herself, alienating her allies and uniting her opponents.

The emergence of the Soviet Union and the United States as the contending champions of the world was less the result of planning by either of them than of the elimination of the previous champions in the general melee. The contention of some revisionist historians that the American government wanted war with Japan or that she strove for imperialistic control of the world is grotesque. So is the Soviet contention that the military efforts of the United States and Great Britain in World War II were "slow and without spirit" because "the ruling circles of these powers hoped to save their forces

[1] Soviet troops were sent into Hungary and Czechoslovakia to prevent their disaffection, but few Russians have any illusion that this action contributed to the loyalty of these states in the event of a world war.

for the final epoch of the war in order to impose their will on the weakened participants and to dictate peace terms which corresponded to their interests."

The subject of world domination had actually come up during the Yalta Conference. According to the Soviet minutes, the following exchange had taken place between Stalin and Churchill:

> [*Stalin* declared] Churchill expressed the apprehension that there might be an impression that the three Great Powers wanted to dominate the world. But who was contemplating such domination? Was it the United States? No, it was not thinking of that. (*The President laughed and made an eloquent gesture.*) Was it Britain? No, once again. (*Churchill laughed and made an eloquent gesture.*) Thus, two Great Powers were beyond suspicion. That left the third— the U.S.S.R. So it was the U.S.S.R. that was striving for world domination? (*General laughter.*) Or could it be China that was striving for world domination? (*General laughter.*) It was clear that the talk of striving for world domination was pointless. His friend Churchill could not name a single Power that wanted to dominate the world.
>
> *Churchill* interposed that he himself did not, of course, believe in the striving for world domination on the part of any of the three Allies. But the position of those Allies was so powerful that others might think so, unless the appropriate preventive measures were taken.[29]

Although Stalin dismissed the idea of an American or British quest for world domination, his suspicions of the intentions of his wartime allies vis-à-vis the Soviet Union were deep. Since the actions of a country are determined less on the basis of what the foreign policy of another country actually is than on the basis of what it is believed to be, Stalin's mistrust was significant, whether justified or not. It is easy to brush aside Stalin's fears as part of his general mistrust of everybody, his own comrades and generals included. But his mistrust of the Western powers was shared by other Soviet statesmen and was not merely the product of Marxist thinking or an invention of Cold War scholarship.

Firstly there was the memory of the Allied Intervention at the time of the Russian civil war. Then there was the matter of the long-delayed American recognition of the Soviet regime and the refusal of the Western powers to join with the U.S.S.R. in blocking Hitler's seizure of Czechoslovakia. The surmise that the Western powers welcomed Germany's *"Drang nach Osten"* was not without foundation, though the eastward drive may have been desired not so much out of hostility toward the Soviet Union as out of the wish to turn German expansion away from themselves.[j] The Allied landing in Africa toward the end of 1942 had not satisfied the Russians; the "second front" in Europe, which they had demanded with increasing bitterness, had not been realized until the summer of 1944! Dictated though the slowness of the Allies in relieving German pressure on the U.S.S.R. by the opening of the second front had been by America's military unpreparedness, it appeared as intentional to the Soviets—to let Hitler bleed their country white.

There was disagreement among Communists about the form which the struggle between Communism and Capitalism must take—whether a military confrontation was inevitable or whether the battle could be won on economic lines—but none of them questioned the Marxist

[j] In the same way, the Soviet Union, while not encouraging Japanese expansion, preferred to see it directed against China or the United States rather than against herself.

premise that such a conflict underlay the course of history. As a result the Soviets did not accept various American proposals at face value, but read hostile motives into them. When the Allies sought closer contacts with the Soviet Union in their common struggle against the Axis powers, the Soviets suspected that they meant to collect intelligence to be later used against them.[30] When the United States sought to bomb Japan from bases in the Soviet Far East, the Russians feared that the Americans wanted to trigger a Japanese attack on their country to bring them into the Pacific War.[31]

Truman's failure to tell Stalin forthrightly of the atomic bomb was bound to increase Stalin's misgivings when it was dropped, as was the rejection of the Soviet requests that the Red Army be allowed to accept the surrender of Japanese forces on Hokkaido[32] and that a Soviet Supreme Commander for the Occupation be appointed alongside with General MacArthur.[33]

To the Americans the Soviet demands seemed preposterous.[k] The Americans felt that they had earned pre-eminence in Japan by virtue of having borne the major burden of the Pacific War for four years. To the Soviets, on the other hand, the Pacific War was but one phase of the Second World War, and they believed that their contribution to victory in blood and suffering had exceeded that of the Americans.[35] Their virtual exclusion from the Occupation, though justified from the American

[k] When Stalin requested on August 16, 1945, that the Soviet Union be allowed to accept the surrender of Japanese forces in northern Hokkaido, arguing that since the Japanese had occupied the entire Russian Far East in 1919–21, "Russian public opinion would be seriously offended if the Russian troops would not have an occupation region in some part of the Japanese territory," Truman refused, convinced that "Stalin was trying to bring to Japan the same kind of divided rule which the circumstances and necessities of the military situation had forced upon us in Germany."[34]

point of view, made them genuinely fearful of American intentions and contributed to the spread and intensity of the Cold War, for the presence of American bases in Japan, however "defensive" in American eyes, constituted a threat to the national security of the U.S.S.R. and gave an enormous advantage to the United States in the century-old contest between the two powers for economic and political cooperation with Japan. In the words of a "dissenting" American historian: "Just as the United States found it difficult to accept the explanation that the Soviet Union was acting in accordance with basic security concerns in expanding its frontiers of influence, particularly in Eastern Europe, so the Communists (including the Chinese as well as the Russians) became more and more unable to believe that American-controlled 'democratization' of Japan was not primarily remilitarization and capitalist exploitation in new guise, or that American 'defense posts' in the Pacific were not in fact advanced bases for the launching of an American attack against the Asian continent."[36]

Revisionist historians have challenged the wartime image of "naked Japanese aggression." In their attempt to arrive at an understanding of Japanese policy, some of them lean over backwards when they show that the Pacific War was not solely of Japan's making. The resulting depiction of Japan as no more responsible for the outbreak of the Pacific War than the United States or the Soviet Union is as much of a caricature as the traditional picture of Japan as a buck-toothed villain bent on world conquest. Justifying Japanese aggression as "the inevitable result of the West's efforts to eliminate Japan as an economic rival after World War I, the Great Depression, her population explosion, and the necessity to find new resources and markets to continue as a first-rate power," John Toland adds as a source of conflict "the threat of Communism from both Russia and Mao Tse-tung which had developed into paranoiac fear."[37] Criticizing the United States for insisting on the liberation of China, "an issue not vital to her interests," and for driving Japan into a corner, giving her "no option to capitulation but war," Toland gives equal blame for the coming of the war to "the rise of two great revolutionary ideologies—Communism and Fascism—working sometimes in tandem and sometimes at odds."[38]

Granted that the torrent of moralistic and legalistic American protests—a policy of walking loudly and carrying a little stick—and the attempt to halt the Japanese war machine by withholding fuel proved counterproductive, the image of Japanese policy as but a reaction to American and Soviet pressure is false. Japan was not being cornered by the U.S.S.R. when Matsuoka, whose signature on the Neutrality Pact was barely dry, proposed that Japan attack her. It is true that the military did not go along with the foreign minister's recommendation, but not because they were more pacific; merely because they were not ready to do so.

Whether or not the United States, whose trade with China dates back to the American Revolution, should ever have become involved in Asia is a matter of opinion. One might argue, I suppose, that if Commodore Matthew Calbraith Perry had not opened Japan, Japan could not have attacked Pearl Harbor less than a century later. But had the Americans not opened Japan, the Russians would have, or indeed the Japanese themselves. The fact that Japan was opened at gun point did impress on the Japanese the importance of military power, as did the Tripartite Intervention of 1895, when Russia, Germany and France deprived Japan of some of her spoils of victory in the Sino-Japanese War. But anyone familiar with the history of Japan knows that the country had been dominated by the warrior class since the 12th century and that Japanese militarism was not American or Russian made or inspired. This is not to suggest, of course, that all Japanese favored war, merely that to place the major or even equal blame for the Pacific War on the United States or the Soviet Union is absurd.

Japanese ultranationalists—military and civilian—had pulled Japan into conflict after conflict and the government had not dug in its heels to resist, partly because it was powerless and did not want to lose whatever prestige it had left, partly because it disagreed over tactics more than principle. As Sir George Sansom, who had lived in Japan since 1904 and knew the country and many of her leaders intimately, wrote in 1932:

> The political doctrines now current in Japan cannot be simply ascribed to the triumph of militarists over civilians. To suppose that a military clique has ruthlessly overruled a substantial civilian opposition to its domestic and foreign policies is to misunderstand the political development of Japan. In all government departments (and particularly in the Ministries of the Interior and Education) there was, for some years before the Manchurian affair of 1931 and increasingly thereafter, an influential body of officials, especially in the middle and junior ranks, who were thoroughly imbued with totalitarian thought. Behind them was a numerous class of salaried workers and small property owners from whom they largely sprang; and to many of these a belligerent national-socialist regime seemed to offer prospects of place or profit.[39]

Soviet fear that Japan, given the opportunity, would seek to neutralize, if not seize, the Maritime region and North Sakhalin was rooted in historical fact. During the Siberian Intervention in the wake of the October Revolution, Japan had tried to seize control of the Siberian railways and integrate the economy of the Russian Far East with that of Japan;[40] she also had sought to set up a puppet state under someone like Ataman Grigorii Semenov.[41] In 1921 she had presented to the Far Eastern Republic, which governed the Russian Far East less independently from Moscow than Tokyo realized, a list of demands, including the demands that the Far Eastern Republic "take down and if necessary blow up all forts and fortifications along the whole Pacific coast," "admit the official residence and travel of special Japanese military missions and of individual Japanese military officers throughout its whole territory," and "never maintain a naval fleet in the Pacific and . . . destroy the existing fleet." Secret articles, attached to the so-called Seventeen Demands, bound the Far Eastern Republic to observe strict neutrality in case of armed conflict between Japan and a third power (even Russia), while it allowed for Japan's withdrawal of her troops from the Maritime Province "at the time which in its own judgment will be convenient, when this shall be necessary." North Sakhalin was to be given to Japan as a lease for eighty years and troops not withdrawn until such lease had actually been received.[42] Japan's inability to attain her demands was no reflection on her aspirations and though she withdrew from the Maritime Province in 1922, largely because the cost of the occupation had become prohibitive, she did not pull out of North Sakhalin until 1925 and then only in return for economic concessions.[43]

When Japan had invaded Manchuria only six years later, in 1931, the United States and Great Britain, in spite of their nonrecognition policy, had actually acquiesced to her domination of the region.[44] The Soviet Union, on the other hand, while recognizing Manchukuo *de facto* when she sold the Chinese Eastern Railway to her in 1935, had not reconciled herself to the new situation, for it constituted a direct threat to her national security. Not only did Manchukuo border on the U.S.S.R., but it jutted into Russian territory in such a way that the vital Maritime province became exposed to possible Japanese attack from three sides—Manchukuo, Korea and the Pacific Ocean. But the Soviet Union like the Western powers was not in a position to court war with Japan and Soviet-Japanese relations remained relatively good until 1937, when the Japanese invasion of China signalled further Japanese expansion on the continent. Even thereafter, the border conflicts of the late 1930's did not lead to war, and the attitudes of Moscow and Tokyo toward each other alternated between hardness and softness, depending on their respective strength or weakness in the rapidly changing world situation.

Japanese expectation of Soviet assistance in 1945 has been a puzzlement to many writers; it has been ridiculed by Soviet, Japanese and American authors, wearing the golden spectacles of hindsight. In the context of the time, the Japanese hopes, though desperate, were not beyond the realm of possibility.

Firstly the history of Russo-Japanese rivalry was matched by a history of Russo-Japanese agreements, whereby the two countries adjusted their differences and joined in defense of their common interests in East Asia. Secondly, in spite of their noisy anti-Communism, the radical rightists of Japan were attracted by many aspects of the Soviet social and economic system. While George Bernard Shaw had been needling

General Araki when he had told him to his face that
he was the same type of man as Stalin and that the
Japanese Army was an example of pure communism,[45]
some of the military, impressed by the strength shown
by the Red Army against the Kwantung forces and
against the Germans, were oriented toward the Soviet
Union. One need not accept the grouping of Japanese
and Russians as fellow-Asiatics, advanced by Stalin,
Matsuoka and Kido as a common bond, to recognize
that the Japanese shared with the Soviets a group-
centeredness and collective bent alien to Western individualism.[1] There is evidence, furthermore, that anti-
Communism was in part but a vehicle for national
mobilization and possible foreign support. As Tani
Masayuki, then director of the Asia Bureau of the Japanese Foreign Office, had stated in the 1930's: "It
seems advantageous for Japan, from the standpoint of
foreign policy, to leave Russia as Red Russia. If it
changes to White Russia, the sympathies of the European powers would all be transferred to Russia. It is
advisable, in view of Japan's position, for Russia to be
hated to a certain degree."[46]

So striking was the paradoxical attraction of radical
rightists to Communism that Prince Konoe regarded
them as "simply Communists clothed in national essence, secretly intending to bring about a Communist
revolution."[47] Japanese Communists as well as the Soviet master spy, Dr. Richard Sorge, who prided himself on his understanding of the Japanese national char-

---

[1] Two examples come to mind. A class of Japanese school girls went
on a bus tour in the mountains. Asked by a correspondent if she was
not afraid that the vehicle might go off the narrow road and she might
be killed, one of the girls replied, "No, for then we would all die together." The Russian compulsion to act in step with the group is illustrated by the popular saying *"Za kampaniiu i evrei povesilsia"* (To keep
company even the Jew hanged himself).

acter, in turn conceived of the possibility of a Communist Japan with an emperor, at least as a figurehead.[48]

A third reason why Soviet assistance had seemed possible to the Japanese was that they (and not only they) regarded the alliance between the Soviet Union and the capitalist countries as unnatural and temporary. Anticipating a struggle for power between the United States and the U.S.S.R., they thought that the U.S.S.R., to whom they had returned the Sakhalin concessions and with whom they had maintained normal diplomatic relations, might welcome the offer. Finally, American and English insistence on an unconditional surrender discouraged peace feelers to the United States and Great Britain directly, while Sweden and Switzerland were not regarded as influential enough to sway the Allies to modify their demand.

The Japanese overtures to the Soviet Union were destined to fail because the Allies had met the Soviet price for entry into the Pacific War. There is no way of telling, however, what their reception would have been had the United States and Great Britain turned down the Soviet demands—not an impossibility, considering public reaction upon their disclosure. It is not inconceivable that the Soviets, who believed their claims to be justified, might have made an agreement with the Japanese to secure the same territory, if not more.[49] It would have cost them nothing; in fact, it would have saved them money and lives. All they would have had to do was to do nothing!

Patriotic pronouncements by Stalin and *Izvestiia* notwithstanding,[50] the Russians entered the Pacific conflict with little grudge or hostility against the Japanese. The Soviet declaration of war aroused no enthusiasm in the U.S.S.R. News of the dropping of the atomic bomb had come as a great shock to the Russian people who regarded the new weapon as a threat to their security. Not knowing of the Yalta Agreement, the Russian public felt that the war on Japan had been precipitated, if not forced on Russia, by the atomic bomb. "The feeling of resentment against those who had dropped the atom bomb was so acute," wrote Alexander Werth, who was in Moscow at the time, "that any feeling of animosity against Japan was conspicuously absent."[51] Meetings were organized at which factory workers denounced the Japanese imperialists, but, as Werth noted, "in reality, the Russians who felt passionately about Germany, had no feelings about Japan at all, and the new war against Japan was distinctly unpopular, except possibly among Russians in the Far East."[52]

In spite of recurring attempts on the part of the Soviet government to mobilize public opinion against Japan, there was no hatred of the Japanese among the Russian masses when the break occurred. Recalling how the Japanese diplomats were moved from the Hotel Metropole to the Japanese Embassy on August 8, Werth wrote: "Shortly before midnight, as they were piling their last trunks on lorries, something of a crowd gathered around, but no hostility was shown and many people even lent a hand with the trunks. It was like a subtle little demonstration of sympathy."[53,m]

[m] The Japanese diplomats and newspapermen were moved to the embassy building and the personal residence of the ambassador. Although they were forbidden to use radios and the delivery of newspapers to them was stopped, they were allowed to go out and could read the newspapers that were posted everywhere and later could buy copies at kiosks. They had permission to go to the theater and to the movies, but refrained from doing so as a matter of self-discipline until sometime after the war. They were not able to leave Moscow until April 25, 1946, and returned

The assertion of Soviet historians and some American revisionists of the left that American "imperialists" had hostile intentions toward the U.S.S.R. during the Second World War is as distorted as the view that world revolution was uppermost in Soviet thinking at the time. To be sure, the American decision to provide lend-lease aid to the Soviet Union was not motivated by a penchant for Communism, but by military necessity. The survival of England and the West depended on Russian resistance to Germany so long as the American public was unwilling to become directly involved in the European conflict.[55] Yet the heroic defense of their fatherland by the Russian people pulled at the heartstrings of the United States and it was not merely self-interest that prompted Roosevelt on July 4, 1941, after American interception of a Japanese Foreign Office statement summarizing the decisions of the imperial conference of July 2, to take the unprecedented step of sending a personal message directly to Premier Konoe expressing the "earnest hope" of the United States government that reports of Japanese plans to attack the Soviet Union were not based on fact.[56]

The idea that Soviet interests in East Asia must be respected antedated the emergence of the U.S.S.R. as a superpower. Replying to a questionnaire by the American Foundation in New York City in 1933, such American scholars as H. N. MacNair, J. Leighton Stuart, Dexter Perkins, and Amry Vandenbosch linked United States recognition of the U.S.S.R. with the

to Japan together with consular officials who had been interned elsewhere on May 30 of that year.[54] The relatively good treatment of Japanese prisoners of war by the Russians has already been mentioned. See Professor Norbeck's fascinating article for a description of the daily life and political activities of the Japanese in Russian captivity.

Far Eastern Situation. Perkins declared: "It is important to present a united front against Japan and useless to deal with the Oriental situation except on a basis of cooperation with Russia." Vandenbosch agreed: "To neglect consultation with Russia, whose interests in Manchuria are far more vital than our own, is to play with fire."[57] In a letter to the State Department that year an American citizen, born in Riga, argued that the United States should recognize the U.S.S.R. because she constituted "the breastwork against the Yellow Peril."[58]

American views changed as People's Republics were left in the wake of the Soviet Army and the Communization of China assumed in American eyes the character of the Yellow Peril and the Red Peril, all wrapped in one. Justified as the removal of Manchurian factories by the Russians may have been from the Soviet point of view—be it as reparations from Japan or as traditional war booty—it was regarded as despoliation by the Americans, who were helping to rebuild the economies of the defeated countries.

Although the contest over Japan, that developed at the end of the Pacific War, was depicted by both sides in ideological terms,[59] it actually hearkened back to the mid-nineteenth century, when Commodore Matthew C. Perry and Vice Admiral Evfimii Putiatin had competed in the opening of the country. While Perry had envisioned a "fierce and final encounter" between "the Saxon and the Cossack," on which "the freedom or the slavery of the world" would depend,[60] the Japanese had taken advantage of the rivalry between the two powers to play them against each other, eliciting from Perry and Putiatin pledges of protection. Thus the Japanese attempts during the Second World War to divide the

United States and the Soviet Union also had deep historical roots. In fact, the history of Japanese relations with Russia and the United States may be likened unto a triangle, whose sides remain in continuous relationship to each other.

In 1904 Japan had fought against Russia with American financial support; the war had ended through the mediation of President Theodore Roosevelt, who was to receive the Nobel Peace Prize for his efforts. Two years later Japan had turned toward Russia and in the decade from 1907 through 1916 had made common cause with the latter against American encroachment in Manchuria. The Communist Revolution of 1917 had brought Japanese armies back to the Russian Far East side by side with United States troops, but her attempt to sever part of the Russian empire had been frustrated partly by American opposition. In 1925 the Japanese pendulum had swung toward Russia again as Japan had recognized the Soviet government eight years before the United States was to do so. When Washington had interfered in the Soviet-Chinese conflict of 1929 in Manchuria, Tokyo had sympathized with Moscow. When the Kwantung Army had conquered Manchuria, Russo-Japanese relations had deteriorated again, yet the strength and determination which the U.S.S.R. had displayed in the defense of her borders had prompted another switch in Japanese policy, and thought had been given to an alliance with the Soviet Union as well as with Germany and Italy against the United States. Following the German invasion of the Soviet Union, Japan had wavered for some time between attacking the U.S.S.R. and attacking the U.S.A. As she had bombed Pearl Harbor, she had tried to remain on good terms with the Soviet Union; as the tide of battle had turned against her, she had revived the idea of an alliance with the Soviet Union against the United States, and when the proposal had borne no fruit had appealed to Moscow to mediate an end to the war with the United States.

While the Soviet Union had rejected Japanese requests for aid or mediation and had attacked Japan in accordance with her agreement with the United States and Great Britain, her entry into the Pacific War had also constituted a move against the United States to the extent that the latter might have blocked Russian aspirations. As Harriman had told Navy Secretary Forrestal, the Soviets feared a separate peace treaty between the United States and Japan even more than the Americans a Soviet-Japanese deal.[61] With the Strange Alliance giving way to the old rivalry between the United States and Russia, both powers had been determined to administer the "decisive" blow to Japan. To the extent that the decision to drop the atomic bomb may have been influenced by the desire to impress the Soviet Union with American power,[62] Japan had fallen victim to a conflagration of rivalry whose embers she had fanned.[n]

[n] The chaos and hunger which had engulfed Europe after the war had already given rise to fear in Washington that much of Europe would go Communist and the Soviet Union had been viewed increasingly as a rival and a potential enemy rather than an ally. Soviet desire to share in the occupation of Japan, to end the monarchy, and to keep Japan economically and politically weak gave impetus to the revival of the traditional American policy, advocated by Secretary of State James F. Byrnes, Assistant Secretary of State Joseph C. Grew, Secretary of War Henry L. Stimson, and Secretary of the Navy James V. Forrestal, of using Japan as a counterweight to the U.S.S.R. It is, however, an exaggeration to assert, as P. M. S. Blacket does, that the dropping of the atomic bomb was not the final military operation of the Second World War but the first diplomatic move in the Cold War and that, as Gar Alperovitz argues, " a combat demonstration [of the devastating power of the atomic bomb] was needed to convince the Russians to accept the American plan for a stable peace."[63] The *primary* motivation for dropping the atomic bomb was to end the war quickly to save American lives. But the desire to terminate

With Japan's defeat, the clock of history seemed to have been turned back to the middle of the nineteenth century, when the Japanese pendulum had begun swinging back and forth between the United States and Russia, for stripped of her conquests and armies, Japan once again had to assure her safety by diplomatic means. In playing the United States and the Soviet Union against each other, Japan was not governed by likes or dislikes or by ideological considerations. Her independence lay in the balance of power between the two giants and she sided occasionally with one in order to improve her relations with the other. One is reminded of the advice Colonel Hashimoto Kingorō, president of the Greater Japan Young Men's Association and a member of the Japanese Army General Staff until the abortive military Putsch of 1936, had uttered on the eve of the Pacific War: "Japan will be lacking sense if she consciously refrains from shaking hands with Soviet Russia, who is now seeking good political and economic friendship with Japan, only for the reason that it will hurt the feelings of the U.S.A. Is it not wise at this time to adopt a policy that will compel the U.S.A., whether she likes it or not, to seek our friendship by our shaking hands with Soviet Russia and touching the sore spot of the U.S.A.?"[66]

Interrogated by his Soviet captors after the war, General Matsumura Tomokatsu asserted that Japan had never had any aggressive designs on Russia, that she had acted in the Russo-Japanese War and the Siberian Intervention under English and American influence, rather than out of her own conviction. "As for relations be-

---

the conflict before the Soviet army overran East Asia was one of the *additional* reasons. The wish to end the war before mounting English and American differences on the meaning of "unconditional surrender" had to be worked out[64] and the bureaucratic compulsion to use the atomic bomb to justify the two billion dollars expended in its development were other reasons.[65]

tween Japan and Russia," Matsumura declared, "they have been unstable in the past—at times good, at times bad—although Japan and the U.S.S.R. had no aggressive intentions against each other. In the future, relations with Japan will depend only on the U.S.S.R. Japan would like to have friendship with the Soviet Union, as it is easier for Russia and Japan to have friendly relations than it is for Japan on one hand and England and America on the other hand."[67]

Within a generation mounting Soviet-Japanese economic collaboration in the Russian Far East had led to a steady improvement in relations between the two countries, notwithstanding Japanese demands for the return of at least some of the islands acquired by the Russians during the Pacific War.° The Soviet-Japanese rapprochement was accompanied by a deterioration in Japanese-American relations, which had traversed the gamut from hostility to friendship, because of American attempts to transfer part of the burden of the "containment" of Communism in East Asia onto Japanese shoulders, American failure to consult with the Japanese government in the formulation of a new policy toward the Chinese People's Republic, and heavy-

° In clamoring for the return of Etorofu and Kunashiri, the Japanese Foreign Office contends that these islands were never part of the Kuril archipelago, that article II of the treaty of 1875, whereby Russia ceded her rights to the Northern Kuril Islands in exchange for Japanese rights to South Sakhalin, "defined the 18 islands from Shimushu down to Uruppu as the Kuriles, that is, the islands south of Uruppu were excluded."[68] This does not correspond with my reading of the treaty. The islands south of Uruppu were excluded, because the treaty listed merely "the group of the Kuril Islands" which Russia possessed and was ceding, i.e. the Northern Kuril Islands. Such impartial reference works as the *Columbia Lippincott Gazeteer of the World* identify Kunashiri as the southernmost Kuril Island. Whatever chance Japan may have to recover Etorofu and Kunashiri will be for value received—conceivably for major contributions in the economic development of the Russian Far East, as I suggested in Tokyo in 1968—and not because of "historical" arguments of this sort.

handed American efforts to curtail Japanese economic competition.

While a historian may be amused by the irony that the United States (like the Soviet Union) has fallen victim to her success, that the opposition of young Japanese to full rearmament is the result of lessons masterfully taught during the occupation and that the same industrial power of Japan which is souring Japanese-American relations at the same time as it is sweetening Japanese-Soviet relations was built with American aid, he cannot but take alarm at Japanese equation of the situation in the 1970's with that on the eve of the Pacific War.ᴾ It may be well to recall the warning of the *Japan Weekly Chronicle* in 1934, when the clouds of war were beginning to gather all over the world:

> Too easily do we take it for granted that people do not want war. Those who cultivate patriotism rage when a few young men at a university pass a resolution against serving "king and country," but those who approve the sentiment probably exaggerate the importance of such demonstrations even more than those who disapprove. When the next war comes, those

ᴾ "Intellectually I know that another war between Japan and the United States is unthinkable, but emotionally I sense a kind of pre-Pearl Harbor atmosphere in the relations between our countries," a Japanese official declared at the beginning of August, 1971.⁶⁹ Within a fortnight Japanese-American relations deteriorated further as President Richard M. Nixon suddenly announced drastic measures to curtail foreign imports into the United States. News analyst Eric Severeid likened the surprise offensive, directed primarily against Japan, to a "Pearl Harbor" inflicted on the latter. Although he voiced the fear that the United States was driving Japan into the hands of the Chinese People's Republic, the Soviet Union, in my opinion, is more likely to become the beneficiary of the "Nixon Shocks." However much the Japanese may wish to trade with China, Chinese hatred of the Japanese remains strong; the Russians, on the other hand, are eager to deal with the Japanese and have a stable economy which can provide a safer and richer market for Japanese businessmen than China.

of fighting age will fight just as they have always done, and those who dodge the fighting will make money just as they have always done. . . . The majority of people in the world do not like the idea of war, but they are not very actively against it, and are not in positions of such influence, as the men who regard it with benevolence if not with active desire. . . .

If the men of peace would save the world from a bigger and better war, they will have to throw themselves into the struggle quickly and earnestly.[70]

Appendix

A

Border Problems

Border disputes have been a perennial problem in Russo-Japanese relations. The Kuril Islands, which were divided between the two powers in 1855, became entirely Japanese in 1875, entirely Russian in 1945. Sakhalin, which had remained in joint possession in 1855, was declared to be entirely Russian in 1875; the southern half of the island was taken by the Japanese in 1905, retaken by the Russians in 1945. With Japanese expansion to the Asian continent, the points of physical contact and, therefore, of friction multiplied. In the late 1930's, as mentioned already, large-scale fighting occurred along the Manchukuo-Soviet and Manchukuo-Mongolian frontier.

The high cost of the Nomonhan incident put Soviet-Japanese relations back on the diplomatic track. A commission was formed to study the boundary problem, and a series of conferences was begun in December 1939. On June 9, 1940, Foreign Commissar Molotov and Ambassador Tōgō initialled an agreement delineating the disputed portion of the frontier, but when it came to marking the border on the terrain itself, the Mongolian and Manchurian representatives advocated conflicting procedures.[1]

223

The major problem was to locate the exact spots where the borderlines broke. The suggestion of the Mongolian delegates that the highest point in a disputed area be used for demarcation was rejected by the Manchurians for military reasons, lest the Mongols entrenched themselves in the strategic heights. The Mongols then proposed in the case of one disputed place that the breaking point in the borderline be determined on the basis of the map, its location calculated in terms of longitude and latitude, and then found and marked in nature. The Manchukuoan side was willing to go along with this method, if it were applied to all boundary breaking points.[2]

The conclusion of the Neutrality Pact generated a spirit of cooperation and on April 15, 1941, Molotov agreed with Tatekawa, who had replaced Tōgō as ambassador, to complete demarcation of the border by the end of the year.[3] On May 4 Tatekawa communicated to Deputy Foreign Minister Lozovskii that Manchukuo requested a meeting of plenipotentiaries at Manchuli or Chita. Lozovskii's immediate reaction was that he did not object in principle to such a meeting of plenipotentiaries, but that it must take place after preliminary technical agreements had been reached in Moscow; yet several days later, on May 9, he informed the Japanese ambassador that the Mongolian plenipotentiaries had agreed to enter into negotiations at Chita, with a final agreement to be concluded at Harbin or Manchuli.

On May 28 the representatives of Manchukuo, Shimomura Shintei and Poyan Mantu, duly met with their Mongolian counterparts, Doloi Patou and Dmitrii Smirnov. During the negotiations that continued in Chita until June 10, the Mongolian side, which had been relatively inflexible prior to the conclusion of the Neutrality Pact, made considerable concessions, and a friendly atmosphere of mutual compromise prevailed.[a]

_____

[a] While the Neutrality Pact marked a turning point in the boundary

Field work had been extremely difficult because the Soviet map attached to the preliminary agreement initialled by Molotov and Tōgō on June 9, 1940, had been on a scale of 1:200,000 and many important places had been marked only by vague lines. Now a topographical map of the border area between Manchukuo and the Mongolian People's Republic, prepared by the Japanese Kwantung Army on a scale of 1:100,000, was used, and each break in the line could be clearly indicated.

The line from Lake Buir Nor to the Arshun river, Muhar Oboo and Bofaobō, bending southward at the Halha river, was fixed mainly on the basis of actual topographical considerations, as the Manchurian side had demanded. Manchukuo also received an island in the eastern part of the Halha river and a modification of the border in its favor in the vicinity of the Numergin river. The Mongolian People's Republic won out in the Shiliin Bogdo region and was given an island in the western part of the Halha river, half of its maximum claims in the Nomonhan region, and compensations equivalent to its concessions.[4]

On June 14 the representatives of Manchukuo and Mongolia signed a preliminary agreement, including provision for further on-the-spot study and filming of the border regions; a final agreement was to be concluded at Harbin. The field study was duly conducted by the plenipotentiaries of both sides at Shiliin Bogdo from June 27 to August 17. The outbreak of war between Germany and the U.S.S.R. on June 22 did not hinder the work; on the contrary, it expedited it, Mongolia leaning backwards to reach a settlement. Upon completion of the local investigation, the plenipotentiaries began their third round of meetings at Harbin on September 23. On October 15—almost two years after the termination of the Nomonhan incident and over a year

negotiations, Tokyo attributed Soviet willingness to arrive at a settlement not so much to the pact *per se* as to the changes in the world situation, notably the growing menace of Germany.

after the Molotov-Tōgō decision to demarcate the frontier—
they signed a general agreement and attached documents,
on which the border had been mapped out in detail.[5]

The exchange of ratifications of the agreement was scheduled to take place at Harbin on December 5, but on October 31 Manchukuo notified the Soviet consul general at
Harbin that it preferred to exchange ratifications at Ulan
Bator on December 4. When the consul general, complying
with the request, transmitted one copy of the Soviet letter
of ratification on December 3, the Manchukuoan side
would not approve it on the grounds that two copies were
required and that it contained unauthorized modifications.[6]
Mutual ratification was not to be completed until May
1942.[7]

The Manchukuo-Mongolian frontier was only one area
of dispute. The Soviet Union and Japan realized that other
boundaries must be clarified too and had been studying
draft agreements for the establishing of commissions for
general border demarcation and for the settlement of border disputes, when the eruption of the Nomonhan incident
had prompted Moscow to withhold approval for the formation of such commissions.

In a conversation with Tōgō on January 1, 1940, Molotov linked the solution of the frontier question with the
establishment of a maritime incidents commission. Afraid
that such a commission might rule against the escorting
of Japanese fishery fleets by naval vessels in disputed waters, the Japanese in turn linked it with a halt in Soviet
interference with the exploitation of Japanese oil and coal
concessions in North Sakhalin and the conclusion of a
fishery agreement.[8]

A memorandum submitted by Japan on January 31,
modifying her earlier draft proposal, had remained unan-
swered. Requests made by Tōgō to Molotov on August 5
and to Lozovskii on August 28 of that year for a Russian
reply were to no avail.[9]

On May 16 Foreign Minister Matsuoka took advantage of the decrease in tension following the signing of the Neutrality Pact to ask Ambassador Smetanin for an answer to the Japanese memorandum; he proposed that the editing of the draft agreement be begun in Tokyo between the director of the Bureau of European and Asian Affairs of the Foreign Office, Sakamoto Tamao, Counselor Zhukov of the Soviet embassy, and the counselor of the Manchukuoan embassy. When another month passed without an answer, Sakamoto made use of the conclusion of Soviet-Japanese trade talks (June 11) to query Zhukov about the matter.

Zhukov replied on June 16 that the Soviet government agreed to the resumption of negotiations concerning the establishment of commissions for border demarcation and for the settlement of disputes on the basis of the Japanese draft proposals, but would prefer to do so in Moscow. It would shortly transmit to the Japanese embassy there a reply to the Japanese memorandum of January 31, 1940; it would also submit soon a proposal of its own for the formation of a commission to settle maritime disputes; negotiations concerning this could be conducted in Tokyo.

The Japanese government decided to agree to the conduct of negotiations in Moscow if the promised Soviet reply did not differ markedly from the Japanese memorandum and there was likelihood of a quick agreement; in such a case the Japanese ambassador would represent both his country and Manchukuo. On the other hand, if the Soviet reply was such that lengthy negotiations would be required, Japan would insist on Tokyo, which the U.S.S.R. had accepted as a meeting place at one time toward the end of the preceding year. With the German attack on the Soviet Union, Moscow made no further proposals, however, and the matter remained in abeyance.[10]

The struggle with Germany alone was desperate, and the U.S.S.R. made every effort to avoid a simultaneous con-

flict with Japan. Soviet agitation against Japan and Manchukuo declined, and the number of incidents where Soviet
guards fired across the frontier or arrested people along
the border decreased sharply. According to Japanese statistics there had been 133 such incidents in 1938, 148 in
1939, 94 in 1940 and only 44 in 1941. Yet fear that
Japan would join her German ally and open a second front
haunted the Russians and they placed their Far Eastern
regions on a semiwar footing. Soviet reconnaissance planes
flew over Japanese territory and Soviet mines appeared in
the Japan Sea. (While alleged Soviet border crossings,
shooting incidents and arrests of Japanese and Manchurians decreased sharply in 1941, reconnaissance flights increased from a reported 27 in 1938, 42 in 1939, and 17
in 1940, to 47 in 1941). When Japan launched the Pacific
War in December 1941, the U.S.S.R. made preparations to
ward off an expected Japanese attack. Once again the frontier between Manchukuo and the Mongolian People's
Republic grew tense.

Japanese Foreign Office documents detail dozens of border incidents in which individual guards or small units of
Soviet, Japanese and Manchukuoan soldiers exchanged fire
and a number of persons were killed. Protests and counter-
protests were traded by Japanese and Soviet officials, each
side accusing the other of being responsible. The Soviet
Union and Japan similarly produced evidence to show repeated violation of their air space by planes of the other
side. The Japanese tabulated almost 100 incidents for which
the Soviet Union was allegedly responsible in 1941.[11] Soviet sources list 28 violations of the border of the U.S.S.R.
by Japanese planes from July to October 1941 and 19 major violations of the Mongolian frontier by Japanese forces
from August to November of the same year.[12,b]

[b] The question of the reliability of such statistics was brought up by
the defense at the War Crimes Trial in Tokyo, when the Russian prosecutor charged the Japanese military with a total of 1,850 violations of
the Soviet frontier between 1932 and 1945. "Who is the arbiter in this
situation where there are supposedly violators of what and by whom?"[13]

The arresting of Japanese, Manchukuoan and Soviet soldiers who crossed the frontier on purpose or by accident led, of course, to demands for their release, and much time and energy was expended over the years in this connection. Planes of either side would make emergency landings, their crews would be detained, the equipment impounded, and investigations begun. Anyone familiar with Japanese and Soviet bureaucratic procedure, can visualize how document after document piled up, duly stamped and signed, with the appropriate seals attached.

Two examples, taken at random, will serve to illustrate the sort of problems that formed a minor but constant factor in Soviet-Japanese relations. In November 1940 a Japanese noncommissioned officer and three of his men set out in a snow storm to repair some telephone lines. When they failed to return, Counselor Miyakawa in Moscow requested Soviet assistance, expressing the apprehension that they had strayed into the Mongolian People's Republic. Six months later, in May 1941, Semen Tsarapkin of the Far Eastern section of the Foreign Commissariat informed Miyakawa that the frozen body of a Japanese soldier had been found in the Mongolian People's Republic, some three miles from the border, and that the Soviet Union was willing to return it. But this proved to be the beginning rather than the end of the matter, as negotiators argued for almost a month about the place and date of transfer while the corpse decomposed.

The second example concerned a Manchukuoan plane, chartered by the Kwantung Army. When it failed to return from a mission in June 1941, the Japanese suspected that it might have lost its way and made an emergency landing in the U.S.S.R. In response to a Japanese request for assistance, the Soviet Union replied that the plane had indeed crossed the border and that Soviet fighter planes had signaled it to land and, when it had refused to do so, had opened fire and forced it down. In the crash landing the pilot had been killed and the two passengers, a lieutenant colonel and a sergeant major, seriously wounded. The Russians agreed to the prompt surrender of the plane, but counseled against the immediate return of the gravely injured men. Meanwhile the German-Soviet war broke out and Japan deemed it advisable to have them moved anyway, as was done successfully.

To repeat, the number of incidents represented a decline over previous years and showed restraint on both sides. None of the incidents were serious or were allowed to become serious, and 1941 ended quietly as far as Soviet-Japanese relations were concerned.[14]

B

Commerce and the Transit of Goods

The conclusion of a treaty of commerce with the Soviet Union had long been an elusive objective of Japanese foreign policy. By April 1940 the general form and period of a treaty of commerce had been worked out,[a] but several major issues had remained unresolved. The Japanese had rejected the Russian request for the establishment in Japan of a Soviet trade mission with diplomatic status. They had rebuffed also Moscow's demand for free transit trade with other states via Japan in exchange for the free transit of German and Japanese goods via the U.S.S.R. The Soviets in turn had refused to accept the substitution of a clause stipulating merely the duty-free transit of goods in lieu of the specific provision for transshipment.

During the fishery negotiations in January 1941, Tatekawa and Molotov discussed the desirability of resuming trade talks. The Russians appeared more eager for a commercial agreement than they had in 1940. Tatekawa stated that the Japanese government was prepared to make a new proposal, if the U.S.S.R. consented to the resump-

[a] For the English text of the draft treaty of commerce, presented by the Japanese on January 10, 1940, and of the Soviet draft treaty, submitted in reply three days later, see Hubertus Lupke, *Japans Ruszlandpolitik von 1939 bis 1941*, pp. 151–56.

231

tion of negotiations. It was ready to accept most of the demands made by the Soviets in 1940, if the Soviet side on its part would go along with most of the Japanese points. Molotov expressed approval, and it was agreed to hold a second round of trade talks.[1]

In mid-February[b] 1941 Tatekawa submitted the Japanese proposals—the draft of a commercial treaty, a protocol concerning a Soviet trade mission in Japan, and a protocol concerning the transit of goods. The Soviet government deemed the Japanese draft unsatisfactory, because it did not provide for most-favored-nation treatment in regard to import duties and other commercial matters and because it made no allowance for an increase in trade.[2]

On February 27,[c] Tatekawa gave to Commissar of Foreign Trade Anastas Mikoian a copy of the new Japanese proposal and pointed out that Japan had agreed almost completely with the Russian demands for absolute freedom of transshipment of goods in transit and the establishment of a Soviet trade mission in Tokyo with diplomatic immunity for the trade representative and his two deputies. Regarding the first question Japan proposed unconditional and duty-free transit of goods through either country, regardless of their origin or destination; freedom of unloading and transshipment to be guaranteed, as was to be most-favored-nation treatment of the cargo in general. Japan also desired an exchange of documents, which would give governmental validation to the Soviet-Japanese agreements of June 29 and July 7, 1931, concerning the sending of parcels and cargo from Japan and European countries through Siberia, agreements that had been signed merely by the local railway authorities.

Mikoian replied that the free transit of goods through Siberia would be of sole benefit to Japan and that the

[b] On February 17 according to Japanese sources, on February 18 according to Soviet reckoning.

[c] On March 27 according to Soviet sources.

U.S.S.R. would consent to it only if Japan, in compensation, would agree in principle to the transportation by Japanese vessels of the same amount of Soviet cargo to the South Pacific and to North and South America as carried by the Siberian railway. The Soviet Union demanded, furthermore, that the difference in freight charges be paid by Japan not in American dollars but in goods needed by the U.S.S.R., notably rubber, copper, tungsten and tin. She would not give governmental status to the parcel and cargo agreement of 1931, stating that they were and should remain properly agreements between local railway authorities.

In late March the U.S.S.R. proposed free transit through Japanese territories of Soviet products bound eastward to the Indian Ocean, the Pacific Ocean and various American countries and free transit through the Soviet Union of Japanese products bound westward to Germany, Rumania, Switzerland and Sweden; special approval was to be required each time for products of other countries. The U.S.S.R. repeated the demand that Japanese vessels carry Soviet cargo up to the amount of Japanese cargo transported through the Soviet Union and demanded specifically that the Ministry of Communication make available to the U.S.S.R. 1,000 kilotons of shipping for the first month following the conclusion of the agreement, and in subsequent months sufficient shipping to carry the same amount of cargo as transported from Japan and Manchukuo via Soviet territory the preceding month. The Soviet Union reiterated also that Japan meet the difference in freight charges with rubber, tin, tungsten, and copper and rubber products, that unloading and transshipment of cargo be guaranteed and no duties be imposed and that most-favored-nation treatment be extended to transit cargo.

Japan objected to Soviet limitation of Japanese transit cargo to four countries and regarded the equation of land and sea transportation as unreasonable; as for the products from Southeast Asia that the U.S.S.R. wanted in payment for the difference in freight cost, Japan had difficulty in obtaining them herself. She replied, therefore, that she insisted on the right to ship goods via the Soviet Union to any European country; she agreed in principle to the shipping by Japanese vessels of the same amount of Soviet cargo as of Japanese cargo transported the preceding month by the Siberian railway but narrowed the range from the Indian Ocean, the Pacific Ocean and its seas and various American countries, proposed by the Soviet Union, to transportation between China, the South Seas, the Pacific Coast of North America and Vladivostok. Japan consented to provide 10,000 kilotons of shipping the first month, and requested mutual assurance of the transportation of a minimum of 3,000 kilotons a month. She said she was unable to pay for the freight charges with the Southern products demanded by the Soviet Union.

Negotiations dragged on until summer, with the Soviet Union yielding little even after the conclusion of the Neutrality Pact. But trade with Europe, especially with Germany, was important to Japan and use of the Siberian railway vital, the more so because of increasing British pressure on Japanese shipping and the need for a safe supply line in the event Japan entered the Second World War. Thus Japan made additional concessions, and the following compromise was reached: Freedom of transit through Japanese territories was guaranteed for products from any country with which Japan had a transit agreement to the Soviet Union regardless of place of origin and for Soviet products only from the U.S.S.R. to any of the above countries; freedom of transit through Soviet territories was authorized similarly for any cargo from Germany, Rumania, Switzerland and Sweden to Japan and for Japanese products to these four countries. Japanese vessels would transport to the Soviet Union from the Indian Ocean, the Pacific Ocean and neighboring countries and various American states to Vladivostok the same amount of cargo as shipped by the Siberian railway to Manchukuo and Japan, calculation to be made by three-month periods; Japan consented to provide 10,000 kilotons of shipping the first month, the U.S.S.R. guaranteeing the transportation of at least 3,000 kilotons of eastbound cargo a month thereafter. It was agreed that Japan pay for the difference in freight in commodities to which she could consent.

The question of the legal status of the Soviet trade mission and its property entailed no less discussion. Japan expressed willingness to recognize its two representatives as part of the Soviet embassy, with corresponding privileges and diplomatic immunity. Japan refused to extend this immunity to local branches of the trade mission; nor was such immunity to be invoked in regard to transactions of the trade mission. Furthermore, Japan insisted that all Soviet property in Japan, other than the property of the embassy and of consulates, be subject to Japanese legal jurisdiction. But the Soviets countered that trade mission property which was required for the performance of official duties must be exempt from Japanese jurisdiction. This Japan would not accept. A compromise was reached whereby the two sides agreed to work out appropriate measures. Much as she tried, Japan could not persuade the Soviet Union to grant similar privileges and rights to representatives of a Japanese trade mission in Moscow, even though she argued that she had no intention of establishing such a trade mission and merely desired the provision as a token of reciprocity.

Negotiations concerning the transit of goods and the establishment of a trade mission were concluded on June 9 after about a dozen small committee meetings, eight conferences between Tatekawa and Mikoian and one between Tatekawa and Molotov. On June 11[d] an agreement was initialled.[3]

[d] On June 12 according to Soviet reckoning.

Japan and the U.S.S.R. were interested, of course, not only in the transit of goods through their territories but in direct commerce with each other—the *raison d'être* for the trade mission; and the dispute about the commodities that the Soviet Union wanted from Japan in payment for the difference in freight charges was merely a reflection of the running controversy over trade items in general. Firstly there was a question about the amount of trade. By 1940 Soviet imports from Japan had fallen to a total of about 3½ million rubles, Soviet exports to Japan to less than 1 million rubles. In 1939 Japan had proposed that the level of trade be raised to 100 million yen of exports and imports respectively;[6] in 1940 she had lowered her sights to 70 million yen, but the amount was whittled down further by the Soviet Union to 30 million yen.

The trade was to be carried out on a barter basis. On February 23, 1941, Japan proposed to export raw silk thread, cocoons, rayon, tea, electric heaters, transformers, rubber tires, fruit, canned pineapple, and hemp and wire rope. She stated that she was unable to supply immediately the South Asian products that the Soviet Union desired, but that she would be willing to deliver rubber, tin, copper and aluminum. For her part, she wished to import crude oil, manganese, pig iron, asbestos, ammonium sulphate, potassium, and platinum. The Soviet Union agreed to take Japanese electrical appliances; she did not want raw silk thread, cocoons and tea, and desired only one quarter of the amount of fruit proposed by Japan; on the other hand, she needed larger quantities of hemp and wire rope and desired soy bean oil. She tied the export of crude oil and manganese to the import not only of the proposed rubber tires but of rubber, tin, cooper, aluminum and tungsten and related products. The U.S.S.R. could provide Japan with the items that Japan desired, even if in somewhat different amounts, except for pig iron, which she declined to supply, at least in 1941.

Japan revised her proposal and after considerable discussion agreement seemed to have been reached on March 25. A Soviet request for further modification, made on April 5, caused new delay, a compromise plan not being accepted until June 3.

As indicated, the exchange of vital raw materials was stipulated so that the Soviet Union would barter, for example, crude oil for rubber rather than bananas. For this purpose the various items of trade were classified into two categories. Crude oil, manganese, rubber, tin, tungsten and the like were in category A; potassium, asbestos, platinum, electric appliances, fruit and the like were in category B. During negotiations concerning trade payments—a matter quite separate from the question of the items to be exchanged—conducted in March and April, the Soviet Union was extremely sensitive about the maintenance of a balance of trade. She insisted that the necessary adjustments be made every three months in groups A and B respectively and that if one side did not supply certain merchandise, the other could halt the delivery of corresponding items.[7]

With the intensification of the war in Western Europe, the Soviet Union, which maintained a position of neutrality vis-à-vis Great Britain, brought up the subject of the shipment of war supplies through her territory. Referring back to the Customs Rate Law of 1929, which prohibited the import of weapons and ammunition and medical supplies for military purposes, and an order of the Soviet Commissariat of Foreign Trade, dated March 18, 1941, which forbade the import of weapons, ammunition and military supplies, airplane parts, machine tools and machinery used in the manufacture of the above, as well as of explosives and deadly poisons, the Soviet Union prohibited in April 1941 also the transit of such items. By this action the U.S.S.R. made a gesture of her neutrality at the same time that she strengthened her bargaining position vis-à-vis Germany and Japan; she required transit licenses and license fees but did not in fact stop the transportation of all the above items.

Although the Soviet Union refused to make any changes in the text of the prohibitions, as requested by Ambassador Tatekawa during the trade talks in Moscow at the beginning of June, she was willing to interpret them liberally and to make unofficial exceptions. Thus Mikoian told Tatekawa that in view of the friendly relations between the U.S.S.R. and Japan he would as an exception allow the transit not only of machinery and machine tools but of certain kinds of arms and even of airplanes. Mikoian would not put this in writing—whether for fear of creating a precedent or of compromising Soviet neutrality—but he gave Tatekawa a "top secret" oral promise, with which the Japanese ambassador expressed himself satisfied.[8]

The German attack on the U.S.S.R. on June 22 nullified all the labors of the negotiators. The treaty of commerce, which had been initialled less than two weeks before, was never signed or put into effect.[9]

The sudden conflagration caught a large amount of Japanese and Manchukuoan cargo, en route to and from Germany, in Soviet territory. Exact figures were not at hand, but it was estimated that 11,000 tons of cargo sent westward via Vladivostok since May 1 and 90,000 tons dispatched via Manchuli since that date were still in the Soviet Union, as were over 1,500 tons of east-bound goods. An unknown quantity of freight shipped earlier was also believed to be in the U.S.S.R. Payment had not yet been received by Japanese exporters for many of the westbound goods and they were thus still Japanese property. The cargo headed east consisted mainly of machinery for which payment had been completed and which was of great importance for the expansion of Japanese industrial capacity. Japan requested, therefore, immediately after the outbreak of the German-Soviet war, that goods which were being sent westward be returned to the stations of origin, while freight intended for Japan and Manchukuo be shipped on, without delay.

Desirous to remain on good terms with Japan, as she reeled under the German onslaught, the U.S.S.R. ordered on June 30 that goods which were on route from Germany to Japan and Manchukuo should be forwarded to the addressees and that Germany-bound Japanese goods, which were still at Vladivostok and Otpor (in the vicinity of Manchuli) should be returned to the Japanese senders. West-bound goods which were already in transit through the Soviet Union could not be returned, however, the U.S.S.R. informed Japan.

Discussions ensued about the payments that had to be made to the Soviet Union for return transportation and about the confiscation by Soviet authorities of what they regarded as German property, including, for example, a shipment of rubber tires for the Ford plant in Cologne.[10,e]

---

[e] Negotiations were held simultaneously between Japan and Germany, Japanese goods bound for Germany and German machinery bound for Japan both having been shipped at German risk according to an agreement concluded in January 1941. Thus Germany was responsible, for example, for the cost of returning the German-bound Japanese goods from Vladivostok to Japan.

C

Miscellaneous Problems

Maritime Danger zones.

Two weeks after the German invasion of Russia, the Soviet government, in a note to the Japanese embassy in Moscow, dated July 7, 1941, proclaimed specified waters in the Far East to be maritime danger zones. The Japanese government protested in a strongly worded note handed by Vice Minister of Foreign Affairs Ōhashi Chūichi to Smetanin in Tokyo on July 18. It regarded the Soviet measure as a blow to Japanese national interests, because it would interfere with Japanese navigation to and from Vladivostok and with Japanese fishing in Korean waters and because if mines were laid in that area, some would no doubt drift away and endanger Japanese shipping in general. The note, therefore, not only demanded that the U.S.S.R. rescind the declaration, but warned that Japan reserved the right to take any action to preserve tranquility in the waters of the Far East.

The Soviet Union tried to overcome Japanese objections in a note delivered to the Japanese Ministry of Foreign Affairs on July 26. While defending the action as neces-

sary because of the repeated appearance of vessels, believed
to be German warships, in Far Eastern waters since the outbreak of war between the U.S.S.R. and Germany, the Soviet government promised not to impede Japanese navi-
gational contact with Vladivostok and denied that Japanese fishing would be affected adversely, since the danger
zone was confined to coastal waters. But Japan did not
assent. In a note handed by Amau, who had succeeded
Ōhashi as vice minister of foreign affairs, to Smetanin, she
asserted that there was no danger of an attack by German
warships on the Pacific coast of Russia; reiterating that
Soviet creation of a danger zone in the Far East might
damage Japanese navigation and fishing, she asked again
for the rescinding of the declaration and for the payment
of compensation for any losses suffered by the Soviet action.
Japan repeated the warning that she reserved the right to
take any action in this connection.

A fortnight later, on September 5, Amau protested to
Counselor Zhukov against the occurrence of the sort of
incident which Japan had anticipated. A Japanese fishing
boat had struck a drifting mine and sunk. Amau demanded
reparations and insisted again on abolition of the restricted
zones. When no Soviet answer was forthcoming, Amau
summoned Smetanin on September 18 and demanded a
prompt reply to the Japanese protest. Alleging that more
and more Soviet mines were floating into the open sea,
causing loss of lives, he reiterated the demand that the restricted zones be abolished.

Smetanin brought the reply of his government to Amau
on September 22. It was a rejection of the protest, brand-
ing Japanese demands for compensation as groundless. The
Soviet Union insisted that her Pacific coast was menaced
by German warships and that her action, as a belligerent,
in laying mines within her territorial waters was in accordance with international law and had been executed
properly. There was no proof, she added, that the accident

to which the Japanese referred had been caused by a Soviet mine.[1]

On the evening of November 5 another, more serious, incident occurred. The *Kibi Maru,* a steamer of the Japan Sea Steamship line, on her way from Chongchin to Tsuruga, hit a drifting mine at latitude 40°40′ N. and longitude 131° E. and went down with the loss of 156 lives. Vice Minister of Foreign Affairs Nishi summoned Smetanin and demanded that the Soviet Union pay reparations and abolish the restricted zones.

Smetanin rejected the contention that the *Kibi Maru* must have struck a Soviet mine—he said it was merely an assumption—and asserted that, as he had already explained to Amau, Soviet mines were so designed as to become harmless if accidentally torn from their mooring. The vessel, he claimed, could have been the victim of a boiler explosion or of a contact mine; in fact, he suggested, it might have been sunk intentionally by a third power in order to impair Soviet-Japanese relations. The Japanese side countered that there was no question that the disaster had been caused by a Soviet mine and that it expected a serious answer.

Additional information about the incident was furnished to Second Secretary Fedor Khalin of the Soviet embassy by Section Chief Narita on November 7 and five days later, on November 12, Sakamoto Tamao summoned Counselor Zhukov and pressed for a prompt reply to the Japanese demand for reparations. He gave to Zhukov a number of documents which charted the drifting of Soviet mines, listed accidents attributed to these mines, and detailed reparation demands for the *Kibi Maru* incident. Zhukov once again insisted that Soviet mines were automatically deactivated if set adrift and that the ship had probably been sunk by a German vessel, but promised to transmit any reply from his government as soon as received.

On November 13 Ambassador Smetanin personally presented the Soviet answer to Foreign Minister Tōgō. It rejected Soviet responsibility for the sinking of the *Kibi Maru,* asserting that the causes of the incident were obscure. The disaster had occurred 125 nautical miles from the danger zone proclaimed by the U.S.S.R., and Soviet mines could not have been there, and even if any should have drifted there by chance they would have been harmless by then the way they had been laid. The note reiterated the assertions made by Smetanin and Zhukov that the *Kibi Maru* may have been the victim of a boiler explosion or of a political plot by a third power. The Soviet government refused to abolish the danger zone, insisting that the threat of attack by German and Italian vessels was real.

Tōgō asked that the Soviet government reconsider the the matter. There was no doubt, he said, that the accident had been caused by a Soviet mine; it was nonsensical to suggest that it had been the result of a boiler explosion or an attack by a third power. He accused the Soviet government of insincerity in trying to shift the blame on somebody else's shoulders and at the same time appealed to its reputed humanitarianism, reminding it that many lives had been lost in the incident. But within a week, on November 19, Smetanin reported that the views of his government remained as set down in the note of November 13; it did propose, however, that a joint Soviet-Japanese investigation be made to check whether Soviet mines were indeed harmless if set adrift. When Tōgō replied that he would agree to such an investigation if the Soviet Union would accept responsibility for the *Kibi Maru* incident in the event that the investigation supported Japanese claims, Smetanin could not agree on his own authority and referred the matter back to Moscow.

No reply had been received nine days later, on November 2, when Tōgō checked with Smetanin. As another week passed without word, Tōgō on November 28 handed

to the Soviet ambassador a lengthy memorandum in which
the events of November 5 were reconstructed on the basis
of the testimony of the captain and other responsible survivors. Briefly, a sudden explosion at 10:14 p.m. had ripped
a gaping hole in the port bow of the *Kibi Maru,* close to
the bulkhead between cabins No. 1 and 2. Half of the 50
third class passengers who had lived in cabin No. 1 were
killed or critically wounded—some were torn to pieces—
and billows of onrushing water smashed the bulkhead and
forced the abandonment of the ship, which went down
at 11:25, bow first. Smashed window glass and other evidence
indicated that the blast had occurred at the water level rather
than under the surface and thus was caused by a floating
mine rather than a torpedo. Iron fragments found in the
bodies of the victims were believed to be of Soviet manufacture. The memorandum rejected the notion that there
might have been a boiler explosion. The boiler had been
in the hind section of the ship, not where the explosion
had occurred, and the first engineer had inspected the boiler
following the blast and had found it in normal condition.
Since all evidence pointed to the fact that the *Kibi Maru*
had been sunk by a drifting mine, Japan branded the allegation that the incident had been plotted by a third
power "a wickedly conjectured obvious absurdity."[2]

The memorandum countered the contention that the
ship had been too far away from the restricted area to hit a
Soviet mine by noting that three Soviet mines had been
recovered in that very area on November 6, 8 and 12 and
that one mine had been picked up in Korean waters, over
200 miles from the nearest Soviet maritime danger zone.
In the wake of storms along the Russian coast, since the
end of August, many mines had been torn loose and carried by the current toward North Korea; mines had been
found along the west coast of southern Sakhalin and even
in Tsugaru Strait. Two documents appended to the memorandum listed the number and location of Soviet mines

found adrift or washed ashore as of November 26. Significantly many of them had exploded automatically or upon contact. In addition to the *Kibi Maru,* a Korean sail boat and another Japanese ship had been sunk by mines and Koreans and Japanese had been killed or wounded in a number of explosions aboard ships or on land while trying to deactivate Soviet mines. Japanese investigation showed that the safety devices of Soviet mines were often missing or defective; at any rate, the fact that many explosions had actually occurred spoke for itself. The report added that not a single mine of another country had been located.

Although the Soviet government insists that the establishment of the Far Eastern maritime danger zones is a lawful measure of national defense to provide against surprise attacks by German and Italian [surface] ships and submarines [the memorandum concluded], there is no substance to the theory that German and Italian vessels might attack the Soviet Far East. We cannot overlook the fact that the national interests of our empire, a peaceful neighbor of the Soviet Union, are seriously threatened by such an unrealistic hypothesis. Nor can we see any reason why an innocent neutral state should have to suffer from a war, whatever rights the belligerent power might possess. So long as the Soviet government finds it technically impossible to lay perfect mines and our fishing and navigation are restricted, our empire is forced to demand the retraction of the restricted zones.[3]

On December 1 Smetanin reiterated the willingness of his government to participate in a joint investigation to verify whether or not floating Soviet mines were dangerous. The Soviet Union was prepared to share in compensation for material losses suffered in the *Kibi Maru* incident, if the investigation were conducted at Vladivostok and it were found that Soviet mines were dangerous when adrift and it were proven that the vessel had been sunk by one of these mines. Tōgō replied that the investigation must be

conducted also at Chongchin and that more than reparation for material loss was required, since there had been
also human casualties.

As the two sides argued over the type of investigation
that should be conducted, the degree of responsibility that
must be proven, and the extent of compensation that the
Soviet Union should pay, the solution of the maritime danger
zone question receded ever farther.[4]

The Exchange of Detained Crew Members.

In June 1941 the Soviet crab-packing ship *Snabzhenets
Vtoroi,* en route from Vladivostok to the west coast of
Kamchatka in a dense fog, ran aground on Nijo-iwa at the
southern tip of Sakhalin Island. On June 28 the Soviet
embassy requested Japanese assistance in rescuing the vessel. Upon notification from Tokyo, the local authorities in
South Sakhalin sent a steamer and two motorboats to the
aid of the stranded ship. The Japanese rescued the 21 crewmen of the *Snabzhenets Vtoroi,* transferring them to the
Bystryi, a small auxiliary vessel which had accompanied
her, but then arrested the crews of both ships, a total of
33 men, for having trespassed into waters closed to foreign
shipping without prior permission in violation of the Military Secrets Protection Law, and on July 2 brought them
before the public procurator of the Sakhalin district court
at Rutaka.

On July 16 the Soviet government proposed the exchange
of the *Snabzhenets Vtoroi* and *Bystryi* and their crews for
the *No. 3 Chokichi Maru* and *Eisho Maru,* two Japanese
fishing boats seized in April of 1941 with a total comple-
ment of 17 men. Japan agreed to an exchange, but demanded that the Soviet Union release all Japanese in her
hands—a total of 27 fishermen, including the crews of 10
fishing boats, some of whom had been imprisoned since
November of 1938—and pay for the cost of the rescue
operation. Moscow agreed. The 33 Soviet fishermen were

handed over at Taihaku, South Sakhalin, on July 25, and departed on the *Bystryi* for Vladivostok the same day. The Soviet embassy completed payment of the rescue bill on the 29th. That day the 17 crewmen of the *No. 3 Chokichi Maru* and the *Eisho Maru* were returned to the Japanese representative at Vladivostok. They departed on a Japanese liner the same day, the two fishing boats being taken in tow. The transfer of the remaining ten Japanese fishermen, some of whom had been sentenced to four years imprisonment, was to take place upon their arrival at Vladivostok from various prisons; it was effected between August 27 and October 4.[5]

Two days before his scheduled release, on August 25, one of the Japanese, Kosaka Tomezo, telephone operator of the *Myoko Maru,* had died of tuberculosis in the Vladivostok City Hospital. To the Japanese request for his ashes the Soviets replied that they were not familiar with the process of cremation; instead they delivered the embalmed body, which was then cremated by the Japanese, the ashes being carried back by the captain of the deceased.

Another Japanese, Captain Nakagawa of the *Hakuyo Maru,* had died in captivity prior to the exchange agreement. He had served his two year sentence (November 1938–November 1940), but had apparently not yet been released when death had overtaken him in Kazakhstan in January 1941. A request by the Japanese government to send a representative to investigate the circumstances on the spot and witness the cremation was turned down on the ground that the area was not open to foreigners; an alternate demand that the body be shipped to Moscow for cremation was also denied, since it had been buried for over half a year and its exhumation would be difficult. The Soviets did produce the deceased's belongings and a death certificate by the local authorities, attributing the captain's demise to nephritis, myocarditis, tuberculosis and dropsy of the entire body.[6]

Meanwhile, on July 21 in Moscow and again on August 6 in Tokyo, the Soviet government presented the Japanese side with a bill for damages inflicted on a Russian guard-boat by the *No. 3 Chokichi Maru* and for maintaining the crews of the *No. 3 Chokichi Maru* and the *Eisho Maru* and guarding the vessels. The Japanese replied that they were ready "to be practical" in considering the question, yet when the Soviet government renewed its request two or three times thereafter, they evaded payment by saying that the matter was still under investigation.[7]

On March 25, 1942, the Soviet freighter *Molotov*, en route from Petropavlovsk to Vladivostok, cast anchor two miles off the Hokkaido coast, within the Tsugaru fortified zone without prior permission in violation of the Military Secrets Protection Law. She did so allegedly to avoid a blizzard, but although the Japan Sea was stormy, the weather in the Tsugaru Strait was good enough that day for Japanese ferry boats to make their usual runs, and, at any rate, shelter could have been found in a nonrestricted zone. The Japanese, therefore, ordered the ship to proceed to Hakodate, where her skipper, Captain Kozlov, was fined 1,000 yen by the Hokodate District Court. For the record Captain Kozlov appealed the verdict and the Soviet consul protested against the detention of the ship, but since it was obvious that the Japanese would not reverse their decision (any more than the Soviets would have in a similar situation) the fine was paid on April 8, and the *Molotov* was promptly released.[8]

The Treatment of Diplomatic and Consular Personnel.

The treatment of diplomatic and consular personnel varied with the state of Soviet-Japanese relations in general. Following the signature of the Neutrality Pact in April 1941 Soviet shadowing of Japanese diplomats had eased, customs inspections had become less rigorous, and the purchase of supplies and medical treatment had been facilitated. The German invasion of Russia made Soviet officials apprehensive about Japanese intentions but at the same time eager not to antagonize Japan. Thus until the spring of 1942—until several months after the attack on Pearl Harbor—Soviet treatment of Japanese diplomatic and consular personnel remained relatively good, though not as good as of Allied personnel.

The Japanese embassy, which was in Kuibyshev at this time, was guarded around-the-clock by three to four militiamen and officials of the security police (the People's Commissariat of Internal Affairs or NKVD); four security agents were assigned to the ambassador and two to the military attaché. Japanese couriers received every assistance from railway officials and local authorities in charge of hotel accommodations. Telegraph communication with Tokyo was improved—telegrams took from 4 to 15 hours— and no restrictions were placed on the acquisition of newspapers and magazines. On the other hand, the Japanese embassy was not allowed to send officials to Moscow to fetch an embassy car, nor were Japanese reporters permitted to proceed to the Soviet capital like British and American newspapermen.

The Japanese consulate general in Vladivostok was guarded by one or more militiamen around the clock. Visitors were closely checked before being allowed in, though the whole procedure was less severe than before the signature of the Neutrality Pact, when the back gate had to be used for entering and leaving the consulate general. NKVD agents, stationed in the building vis-à-vis the consulate general, trailed the deputy consul general and his staff whenever they went out. As in the case of the embassy, telegrams were duly delivered, though some delay was noted following the outbreak of the Pacific War. Mail service, on the other hand, was unreliable and whenever they could, the Japanese forwarded letters and messages by other means. Letters from Japan to Vladivostok took over a month and a half; they were delayed in Vladivostok up to a week while being read by censors, and sometimes, the Japanese suspected, were not delivered at all. National newspapers, published in Moscow, could readily be obtained, but local newspapers had to be purchased at newsstands in the morning after waiting in line. A subscription to the Khabarovsk paper *Tikhookeanskaia Zvezda* was not accepted on the pretext that the circulation was too small.[a] Officials in Vladivostok also experienced difficulty traveling. In one instance Intourist, through which foreigners had to make travel arrangements, refused to sell a ticket to a consular employee to proceed to his new post in Kuibyshev on the pretext that the train was not running, when in fact it was operating. In January 1942 food rationing was enforced and the acquisition of beef, fish, soap and cigarettes became difficult.

The consulate general in Aleksandrovsk also experienced difficulties with food rationing, subscription to local newspapers and mail service, but less so than the consulate general in Vladivostok. In response to a protest to the Soviet diplomatic mission in 1941 against the unsealing of personal letters and censorship in general the practice seemed to have been discontinued, at least in Aleksandrovsk. There was a police box in front of the consulate general and the building and the official Japanese residence were well illuminated from the outside, but the Japanese were not shadowed as they went about town. Local officials were friendly and accommodating and no customs duties were levied unless articles were imported in large quantity. As elsewhere, medical treatment was readily available and often free of charge.

The consulate in Okha, like the consulate general in

---

[a] The Soviet Union still restricts the circulation of local newspapers. Though I was free to buy Khabarovsk newspapers at a stand when I was in the city in April 1969, they were confiscated at Nakhodka as I embarked for Japan.

Aleksandrovsk, had no occasion to test the attitude of local officials about travel permission, but Japanese vessels were allowed to visit Okha quite freely. As a result the Japanese there could obtain from home whatever food they required without regard to Soviet rationing. Mail for the Okha consulate did not seem subject to censorship. The Japanese officials experienced no particular discomfort or inconvenience from the presence of a Soviet militiaman at the entrance gate and, as far as they knew, were not followed when they left the building. The Japanese felt that the attitude of the Soviet diplomatic mission was "extremely good and sincere" and that the customs office too treated them well after its old director was replaced in the summer of 1941. In general they lived comfortably in Okha, unaffected either by the German invasion of Russia or the outbreak of the Pacific War.[9] With the liquidation of the Japanese oil and coal concessions on North Sakhalin in 1944, the Japanese consulates at Okha and Aleksandrovsk lost their raison d'être and were closed at Soviet insistence.[10]

The closing of the two Japanese consulates was precipitated by the recall of Soviet consular officials from Tsuruga after seven years of fruitless dickering over the location of the Soviet consular building, the local authorities at the bidding of the army having tried to remove it from its scenic position, overlooking the harbor, to a less sensitive spot.[11] As the Japanese consulates at Okha and Aleksandrovsk were shut down, the U.S.S.R. had to close a second Soviet consulate on the basis of reciprocity and discontinued her representation at Hakodate.[12]

The life of Soviet officials in Japan was as restricted as that of Japanese diplomats in the U.S.S.R. In July 1941 Third Secretary Mikhail Privalov was arrested for allegedly purchasing military information through the owner of a nightclub in Yokohama and detained overnight at a police station. He was released the following day into the custody of Second Secretary Victor Zaitsev. When Counselor

Zhukov filed a protest with Sakamoto, the director of the Bureau of European and Asian Affairs, concerning the arrest and treatment of Privalov, he was told that the latter was suspected of having violated the Military Secrets Protection Law, a serious crime, and that the delay in his release had been his own fault—he had been unwilling to show his identification card. Later Sakamoto informed Zhukov that the Japanese involved was still being investigated and that action might yet be brought against Privalov, but as the matter dragged on, the Soviet government transferred Privalov, and the case was dropped.[13]

In June 1941 Ambassador Smetanin fell ill. When local physicians could not determine the cause of his high fever, the Soviet government requested permission to send a plane with three Russian specialists to Tokyo. The Japanese government allowed the visit of the doctors, but sent a plane of the Manchukuo Airline to fetch them.[14]

Diplomatic and consular officials liked to see motion pictures produced in their own countries. In August 1940 it was agreed that films intended exclusively for showing to embassy personnel would be cleared reciprocally free of duty and censorship. A subsequent proposal by the Soviet embassy that the agreement be extended to consular use was turned down by the Foreign Office. When the Soviet consulate in Dairen showed such embassy films—and showed them not only to consular personnel but to outsiders—the Japanese government insisted that the practice be stopped. The Foreign Office also demanded in the spring of 1941 that the Soviet embassy desist from showing Russian movies to Japanese guests. When the Soviet embassy requested tacit approval for the performance for which invitations had already been mailed, the Foreign Office consented after being told the outline of the plot. The question of the showing of movies in embassies and consulates may appear trivial, but it deserves mention as being symptomatic of Japanese fear of Communist subversion.

Travel between Japan and the Soviet Union was complicated by the fact that visas were issued on a reciprocal basis—for the same number of visitors from each country. As a result, with the exception of diplomatic couriers, visas were issued generally to groups rather than individuals. No numerical balancing was required in the case of transit visas, but the procedure was extremely slow, as permission had to be obtained from Moscow. A considerable number of Japanese passed through Siberia—over a thousand from the outbreak of war in Europe to the German invasion of the U.S.S.R.—because it was the only land route between Europe and Asia, and the time-consuming and costly process of obtaining the necessary papers proved burdensome for both sides. As a result agreement was reached that transit visas without right to stopover could be issued directly by the Soviet consulates general in Tokyo and Berlin and the Japanese consulates general in Moscow and New York. But the new procedure, which went into effect on June 1, 1941, was shortlived. The outbreak of war between Germany and the U.S.S.R. on June 22, halted Japanese transit through the Soviet Union and the agreement was abrogated by Japan on August 6.[15]

D

Soviet Treatment of American Fliers

Unwilling as the Soviets were to endanger their relations with Japan by permitting American operations from the Russian Far East, they did extend a friendly hand to United States fliers downed in the U.S.S.R. That some of the Americans who had not been warned by their superiors that the Russians were obligated by international law to intern them resented their detention and found living conditions in wartime rural Russia, Central Asia and the Soviet Far East severe did not alter the fact that the Soviets did more to assist the Americans than international law required, in fact more than international law allowed.

The number of American fliers who landed in the Soviet Union after raids on Japanese territory was greater than the Japanese realized. At least 335 airmen were involved over a period of three years.[1]

First to land, in mid-April 1942, was a B-25 of the 17th Bombardment Group of the United States Eighth Air Force. One of sixteen medium bombers which had taken off from the aircraft carrier *Hornet* 800 miles east of Japan in the

254

celebrated Doolittle raid on Tokyo, Yokohama, Kobe and Nagoya, it was supposed to have proceeded to Free China, which was in Nationalist hands. Because of inclement weather and miscalculation of fuel consumption, none of the planes reached their final destination, however. Most of them crash-landed in Occupied China, where some of the airmen were captured and executed by the Japanese. Only the one B-25 reached safety by landing at a Soviet airfield near Vladivostok.[2]

After interrogation by the commanding general of the Far Eastern Red Army, the five uninjured crewmen were interned at Khabarovsk.[3] Stalin sought assurances from the American ambassador that the plane had come to the Soviet Union unintentionally, and Molotov reiterated when the desired assurance was received from Washington that the United States must take steps to prevent similar incidents.[4] But faced with capture and possible execution by the Japanese if they landed in Occupied China and with death by exposure if they ditched their planes in the icy waters of the North Pacific, other crews chose refuge in the Soviet Union. Crippled or lost in stormy weather after attacking the heavily defended Japanese military installations on Paramushiru Island from far-off Adak, most of them landed at an airfield near Petropavlovsk on the Kamchatka Peninsula.[5]

In August 1943 one of nine B-24's which had raided Paramushiru crash-landed on a lake in Kamchatka. The ten survivors were interned in a small town near Tashkent.[6] In September the number of American fliers interned at what now became a special detention center southwest of Tashkent greatly increased as seven of nineteen bombers which had attacked the Kuril Islands landed on Soviet soil.

In July and early August 1944 another 34 American airmen reached Kamchatka. Stung by Japanese protests, the Soviet government had demanded the preceding year that the United States order her pilots not to fly to Soviet territory. Now the Soviet Union protested again, this time not only against the landing of planes but against other incidents resulting from expanded American air activity over the Kurils—the violation of Soviet airspace (105 times in the first eight months of 1944), the dumping of unexploded incendiary cases and high explosives on the Kamchatka peninsula (presumably before landing) and air attacks on Soviet vessels (mistaken for Japanese). Yet Americans continued to seek refuge in the U.S.S.R., United States navy planes making forced landings at Petropavlovsk in the latter part of 1944.[7]

American B-29's in distress over Manchuria or Japan proper landed at Uglovaia airfield, just north of Vladivostok, probably the airfield where one of the Doolittle raiders had made the first landing. In July 1944 a B-29 which had taken part in the first raid on Anshan, Manchuria, from Ch'engtu, in southern China, developed a runaway propeller and in conformity with emergency briefing instructions headed for Soviet territory, destroying the Norden bombsight, the radio equipment, and documents about communication and aircraft maintenance and operations.[8,a] In mid-August a B-29 crew which had raided the iron works at Yawata, Japan, bailed out near Vladivostok; two more B-29 crews set foot on Soviet soil that year, one voluntarily, the other being forced down by Soviet fighter planes after violating Soviet airspace.[9]

Japanese accusations that the Soviet Union had conspired with the United States to provide landing fields for the American bombers were unjustified. The Soviet government sincerely protested against American endangerment of its peaceful relations with Japan and actually forced down a number of the planes. Yet there was more

[a] The Russians and the Americans tried to learn and hide all they could from each other. The impounded B-29's were used by the leading Soviet aeronautical engineer Andrei Tupolev as a model for his TU-4. At the same time, American officials who debriefed the downed pilots queried them not only about the combat missions, but about what they had seen in the Soviet Far East.

comradeship among the allies than postwar literature reflects, and the Soviets, in response to American requests for the parole or return of the internees, staged a number of "escapes" to release the fliers without arousing Japanese wrath.

In the spring of 1943 the five Doolittle raiders, who had landed almost a year before, were moved to Ashkhabad and put to work rehabilitating civilian aircraft. An official from the Commissariat of Trade introduced them to an Iranian merchant who with the blessings of the Soviet security police "smuggled" them across the nearby Iranian frontier. Two other "escapes" were engineered in 1943 with the personal approval of Stalin, who demanded, however, that the airmen be transferred to the European theater of operations to fight against the Germans.[10] General John R. Deane was privy to the plot and an American military attaché played the role of contact man with the NKVD. As the aviators were put on a train for the Caucasus, a breakdown was faked near the Iranian frontier, and they were induced to "bribe" some truck drivers and Iranian border guards to whisk them to freedom.[11] The elaborate show was staged for the benefit of the aviators and of the Japanese, lest the Soviet Union stand in open violation of the Neutrality Pact.

A fourth "escape" in 1944, involving 110 American airmen, was postponed and almost cancelled when a report by the American news agency United Press on April 19, 1944, that one of the Doolittle raiders interned by the U.S.S.R. in 1942 had left for England and participated in air raids on Germany, aroused the anger of Stalin and Molotov. Used to a tightly controlled press, the Soviet leaders regarded the dispatch as intentionally provocative, designed to draw the Soviet Union into war with Japan.[b] Eventually Stalin relented and let the internees escape, as he did another large group in 1945.[13]

[b] The same month English newspapers wrote that Japan played blind when she saw ships steam from the United States to Vladivostok right through Tsugaru Strait, between Hokkaido and the main island.[42]

E

American Requests for Soviet Participation in the War

The entry of the Soviet Union into the Pacific War had not come as a surprise to the Allied powers. On the contrary, the United States and Great Britain had solicited Soviet participation since the very beginning of the Pacific War. On December 8, 1941, President Roosevelt and Secretary of State Hull had suggested to Ambassador Litvinov that the U.S.S.R. join the war effort against Japan, a proposal made to Moscow also by Chiang Kai-shek the same day.[1] But the Soviet government had chosen to remain neutral, informing Washington that it was "not then in a position" to cooperate, as it could not risk an attack by Japan while being deeply involved in war with Germany.[2]

Reeling under the Japanese onslaught, American strategists pressed for Soviet collaboration. On December 10 General MacArthur cabled Chief of Staff General George C. Marshall that he had definite information that Soviet entry into the Pacific War was Japan's "greatest fear." He advised that "most favorable opportunity now exists and immediate attack on Japan from north would not only inflict heavy punishment but would at once relieve pressure from objectives of Jap drive southward."[3]

The question of Soviet participation in the Pacific War was kept alive in 1942 partly because Japanese successes in the Pacific and Southeast Asia raised the possibility of an attack on the Maritime region so that the U.S.S.R. would be brought into the conflict against her will, partly by the desire of American planners to weaken the Japanese offensive by bombing Japan, something that could have been done at this time only from nearby bases in the Russian Far East.[4] An offer by the United States to commit three heavy bomber groups to Siberia was declined by Stalin.[5]

A restatement of Allied strategy by the Combined Chiefs of Staff of the United States and Great Britain at a conference in Washington in May 1943 confirmed the desirability of Soviet participation in the Pacific War following the defeat of the Axis powers in Europe.[6] In an estimate of the situation in August of the same year the American Joint Chiefs of Staff noted that "a basic conflict of interests" existed between Japan and the Soviet Union. On one hand, Japan could not have "complete strategic security" without control of the Maritime region; on the other hand, Soviet strategic security required the expulsion of Japan from the mainland and from South Sakhalin. The Joint Chiefs of Staff felt that neither Japan nor the Soviet Union wished to detract from their operations elsewhere by opening hostilities against each other at the time, but that the latter was "likely to intervene in the war against Japan at some stage, but not before the German threat to her has been removed."[7] In their instructions to Major General Deane, a member of the United States delegation to the Foreign Ministers' Conference in Moscow, the Joint Chiefs of Staff stressed "the great importance to the United States of Russia's full participation in the war against Japan after the defeat of Germany as essential to the prompt and crushing defeat of Japan at far less cost to the United States and Great Britain."[8]

During the Foreign Ministers' Conference in Moscow in October the Soviet leaders made known their intention to enter the Pacific War eventually. Stalin "astonished and delighted" Hull when he told him during a banquet "clearly and unequivocally" that the Soviet Union would join in defeating Japan after the Allies had brought Germany to her knees.[9] When Molotov told Anthony Eden and W. Averell Harriman that a Soviet film about the Japanese occupation of Siberia would be shown after dinner, the British foreign secretary expressed wonder whether this might not be an inappropriate film for a neutral country to show, but the American ambassador asserted that it was appropriate and offered a toast to the day when they would be "fighting together against the Japs." Although he had told the Soviet foreign commissar that he would understand it, if he did not wish to join in the toast, Molotov replied, "Why not—gladly—the time will come," and downed the drink.[10]

At the Cairo Conference a month later, Stalin hinted at Soviet entry into the Pacific War. As he congratulated Roosevelt on American successes in the Pacific, he remarked that Soviet forces in the Russian Far East would have to be tripled before they could launch an offensive against Japan and that this could be done only after the defeat of Germany. "Then by our common front we shall win," Stalin declared.[11,a]

At Teheran later in the month Stalin reiterated that the Soviet Union would make common cause against Japan after the defeat of Germany.[14] But while Stalin had made

---

[a] Like the Americans the Soviets by then overestimated Japanese strength. Just as the Americans had been led to believe by the valor with which the Japanese had been fighting that Japan would not surrender until her armies on the continent had been destroyed and Japan proper invaded, so the Soviets were convinced that the Japanese could invade the Maritime Province and devastate Russian territory unless struck in a lightning blow with overwhelming force. To assemble such overwhelming force prior to the defeat of Germany would have meant to divert troops from the main front and thus to prolong rather than to shorten the Second World War.[18]

no mention in Moscow the preceding month of a price for Soviet participation, he now told Roosevelt and Churchill that the Soviet Union desired South Sakhalin and all of the Kuril Islands. When he mentioned that the U.S.S.R. lacked an ice-free port in the Far East, Roosevelt proposed Soviet use of Dairen (Dalny) as a duty-free port under an international guaranty.[b] While Stalin agreed to enter the Pacific War eventually, he was not prepared to authorize joint planning or joint operations; nor was he willing to grant bases to the United States Army Air Corps, lest Japanese retaliation plunge the Soviet Union into the conflict prematurely.[c]

American military plans in July 1944 called for the invasion of Kyushu on October 1, 1945, and an assault on the Tokyo region at the end of December of that year. Although Soviet support was not required, United States strategists noted that a Russian drive into Manchuria "coincident with or prior to" the American invasion of Kyushu would tie down the Japanese forces on the mainland and facilitate the American invasions of Kyushu and Honshu.[17]

In September Stalin assured Harriman of continued Soviet willingness to enter the Pacific War and sought information about Allied plans. At the same time he implied that he was not overly eager to do so and left the impression that he would welcome a specific invitation by the Allies.[18]

During the Churchill-Stalin meetings in Moscow in October, at which Harriman and Deane represented the United States, the Allies exchanged information about their mili-

---

[b] General Shtemenko suggests another quid pro quo: Allied opening of the second front in Europe. "Our Western Allies were anxious to draw us into the war in the Far East as soon as possible, but only at the Teheran Conference, where a definite agreement was reached on the opening of the Second Front in Europe, did the Soviet delegation agree in principle that the U.S.S.R. would take armed action against imperialist Japan."[15]

[c] See Chapter Six for American attempts to obtain air bases in the Soviet Far East.

tary plans. In speaking about American operations in the Pacific, including the projected invasion of Japan, Deane declared that "the most important factor in the development of the overall strategic situation will be in the part which the Soviet Union is to play," and asserted that while various plans had been worked out for advancing on Japan from the east, south and west, "these plans can be most effectively selected and applied, if they are thoroughly concerted with plans to be developed for operations against Japan from the north."[19]

In response, General Aleksei Antonov, deputy chief of the Soviet general staff, revealed the magnitude of the campaign planned by the Soviet Union and detailed five possible operational routes. The Soviets (like the Americans) overestimated Japan's remaining strength and believed that the Japanese might rush reinforcements to Manchuria from China proper and Japan and that it would take the Soviets three months after the defeat of Germany to move sufficient forces to the east to double their current strength there and launch a massive offensive.[20,d]

Stalin thought of a Russian flanking movement against Peking, but agreed to confine operations in China to minor landings to seize air fields.[21] Stalin and Antonov repeated that the Soviet Union would be ready to enter the war against Japan about three months after the defeat of Germany. Although Stalin made it plain that this was contingent on the receipt of large quantities of American supplies and on clarification of the political aspects of Russian participation, suggested at Teheran, i.e. on Chinese recognition of Soviet use of the Manchurian railways and the internationalization of Dairen,[22] the American officials were not discouraged. Roosevelt and the Joint Chiefs of Staff were delighted with the large-scale Soviet contribu-

---

[d] The Soviets calculated that the Japanese might assemble between 720,000 and 900,000 men on the mainland; they themselves had only about 300,000 men in the Russian Far East at this point.[20]

tion, as it would make it unnecessary for the United States to employ substantial forces in that region.

In November 1944 American planners reiterated that Soviet entry into the Pacific War was not essential but desirable. They were confident that "Russia's interests in the Far East and in postwar world politics will undoubtedly force her entry into the war against Japan," but were concerned about the timing, which they regarded as all important. "While the maximum advantage to us results from Russian entry prior to our invasion of Japan, the reverse is true from the Russian viewpoint. The maximum military advantage for them will obtain if they attack after our initial lodgment has been affected and Japanese forces in Manchuria have begun to move to reinforce Japan."[23]

It was at the Yalta Conference in February 1945 that the Soviet entry into the Pacific War "in two or three months after Germany has surrendered and the war in Europe has terminated" was put in writing in a top secret agreement together with the Soviet conditions accepted by the United States and Great Britain. By the Yalta agreement the Soviet Union was to recoup her losses in the Russo-Japanese War of 1904–1905: she was to recover South Sakhalin and adjacent islands, regain the use of Dairen as a free port (though it was to be internationalized) and of Port Arthur as a naval base, and win back control of the administration of the South Manchurian Railway. She was to recover administrative control also of the Chinese Eastern Railway which had been constructed with Russian money and had been sold to Manchukuo in 1935 under Japanese pressure, if not duress.[24] She was to get back the northern Kuril islands, which she had ceded to Japan in exchange for South Sakhalin in 1875, plus the rest of the archipelago. The *status quo* in Outer Mongolia, where the Mongolian People's Republic had been established under Soviet auspices two decades before, was guaranteed.[25] As in the Treaty of Portsmouth, which had ended the Russo-Japanese War, it was stipulated that Chinese consent be attained for the provisions pertaining to Chinese territory and property.[26,e]

The war in Europe was still under way. Since the United States Joint Chiefs of Staff believed that it was not likely to end before July 1 and since they had estimated at Malta that it would take from four to six months to redeploy American troops from the European to the Pacific theater of operations, the American and British Combined Chiefs calculated that the war against Japan might last until the end of 1946 *with* Soviet involvement and, of course, longer without it.[29]

The American and Soviet military staffs coordinated their plans and timetables at Yalta. Soviet entry into the Pacific War, three months after the German surrender, would come, it was figured, just when the Americans would be getting ready for the first landing in Japan. As Herbert Feis has observed, "the Americans admired the Soviet program; the Russians had nothing but praise for the vast range of American enterprise."[30]

General MacArthur, with whom Washington planning officers conferred on February 25, 1945, did not know of the Yalta Agreement. He did believe that the Soviets wanted a warm water port and that it would be "impracticable" to deny it to them in view of their military power; at the same time he thought it was right, therefore, for them to participate in the defeat of Japan. "From the military standpoint we should make every effort to get Russia into the Japanese war before we go into Japan, otherwise we will take the impact of the Jap divisions and reap the losses, while the Russians in due time advance into an area free of major resistance."[31]

On May 12, 1945, Acting Secretary of State Joseph C.

---

[e] There was one interesting difference. While at Yalta the American president agreed to "take measures in order to obtain this concurrence on advice from Marshal Stalin,"[27] article VI of the Treaty of Portsmouth put the burden of obtaining Chinese consent equally on both parties.[28]

Grew, who had not been consulted about the Yalta agreement in spite of his lengthy service as ambassador to Japan, inquired of Secretary of War Henry L. Stimson and Secretary of the Navy James V. Forrestal whether Soviet entry into the Pacific War was so vital as to preclude any attempt to obtain prior Soviet agreement to certain desirable political objectives in the Far East. Stimson replied that there was no objection to seeking a political agreement with the U.S.S.R., but that it was considered by the War Department that the Russian decision to intervene would be made "on their own military and political basis with little regard to any political action taken by the United States" and that "while the U.S.S.R. will seek and will accept any political inducement proffered by the United States as a condition to her entry into the war against Japan, such political inducements will not in fact affect the Russian decision as to when, if ever, she will enter the war."[32],[t]

Harry Hopkins, who was sent to Moscow to make preparations for the Potsdam Conference, reported that Stalin had told him and Harriman on May 28, 1945, that "the Soviet Army will be properly deployed on the Manchurian positions by August 8th."[33] Stalin was "very anxious" to discuss problems concerning Japan at the forthcoming conference with President Truman, Hopkins reported. Noting that Japan was putting out peace feelers, Stalin wanted the Allies to consider their joint attitude and act in concert about the surrender of Japan. "He expressed the fear that they will try to split the Allies," Hopkins wrote.[34] While Stalin preferred to go through with "unconditional surrender," he was willing to accept a modified surrender and then impose the Allied will during the occupation. "Stalin expects that Russia will share in the actual occupation of Japan and wants an agreement with us and the British as to zones of occupation."[35]

[t] In view of the American experience with the Russians in the occupation of Germany, the War Department did add that an exclusively American occupation of Japan might be wise.

In June 1945 the Joint Chiefs of Staff still felt that "the impact of Russian entry on the already hopeless Japanese may well be the decisive action levering them into capitulation at that time or shortly thereafter if we land in Japan."[36] In July they had moved up the planning date for the end of "organized resistance" by Japan by only a month and a half, i.e. to November 15, 1946.[37] On July 28, two days after the leaders of the United States, Great Britain and China had joined in issuing the Potsdam Declaration, calling for the unconditional surrender of the armed forces of Japan, Stalin informed the tenth plenary session of the Potsdam Conference of the Japanese request to send a special envoy to Moscow to seek Soviet mediation in ending the war. He related that he had rejected the original proposal as too vague. Another message had just been received from the Japanese government, detailing the objectives of the mission, including an offer of collaboration with his country, but, he stated, he would turn it down too. "It was clearly evident," Fleet Admiral William D. Leahy, Truman's chief of staff, remarked, "that Stalin was at that time determined to enter the war against Japan, which plainly was to the advantage of Russia, now that Japan was certain to be defeated."[38]

Leahy's comment reflects a change of heart on the part of the American and English leaders, that had occurred during the Potsdam Conference, when word had been flashed on July 17 of the successful explosion of the first atom bomb in the New Mexican desert. "We should not need the Russians. The end of the Japanese war no longer depended on the pouring in of their armies," Churchill recalled thinking. He minuted to Eden: "It is quite clear that the United States do not at the present time desire Russian participation in the war against Japan."[39]

There was no way in which the United States and Great Britain could withdraw their invitation or block Soviet participation in the Pacific War short of a direct confrontation with the U.S.S.R. The Americans tried apparently to end the war before the Russians could enter it, for Chiang Kai-shek, whose approval of part of the Yalta agreement was a condition for Soviet participation, was advised by Washington on July 23 to prolong the negotiations with Moscow; Truman evaded telling Stalin as he had told Churchill that the United States had exploded a nuclear device—he spoke merely of an "entirely novel form of bomb"—and the United States showed haste in dropping the atomic bomb on Hiroshima on August 6, shortly prior to the expected Soviet entry, and a second one on Nagasaki only three days later without waiting to see what effect the first might have had on the will of the Japanese government to resist unconditional surrender.[40] But the Red Army, as originally planned, struck swiftly into Manchuria, and secured the Yalta concessions with Russian blood.

F

Preparations for War

Japanese Plans

Japan's decision to attack the United States and Great Britain had been a desperate gamble, with the odds agonizingly weighed. Navy Minister Shimada had cautioned that "the risks attendant upon the opening of hostilities" against the United States, Great Britain and the Netherlands would be "enormous" and had warned that unless the war could be terminated within two years, it would be difficult for Japan to have "any measure of confidence" in victory; the Joint Army-Navy Supreme Council had echoed that in a war against the United States and Great Britain, Japan had "no sure way of bringing the enemy to his knees."[4] Yet after comparing the risks involved in continuing the negotiations without likelihood of diplomatic success and thus postponing hostilities until a less opportune time with the hazards of an immediate conflict, in which the breath of the more powerful opponent would be temporarily knocked out by a surprise blow, Japan had chosen the latter course in the hope that the stunned giant would be willing to come to terms.

One factor in the decision had been the realization that

the addition of the Soviet Union to either side of the equation would alter the entire calculation. Arguing that Japan might not be in a position to fight at all if she did not fight at once, Army Chief of Staff Sugiyama had insisted that if Japan waited until the spring of 1942, operational action in the North Pacific and Siberia would be possible and Japan might be faced fatally with a two-front war.[2]

This does not mean that Japan, in November 1941, had expected a Soviet attack. On the contrary, in view of the conflict with Germany, the U.S.S.R. had moved large numbers of tanks, airplanes and men from the Russian Far East to Europe, and Sugiyama had believed that so long as the Kwantung Army maintained its strength, there was little likelihood that the Soviet Union would initiate hostilities against Japan. But he had feared that war between the Soviet Union and Japan might be precipitated by the United States—"there is the possibility that the United States might force the Soviet Union to allow the United States to build air and submarine bases in its Far Eastern territory as northern bases of attack against Japan, and the Soviet Union might not be in a position to reject the demand."[3]

There had been disagreement among the military leaders which way to strike. Thinking in terms of sea power, the Japanese navy had seen the United States as the primary menace to Japan's security. It had favored Japanese expansion in the South Pacific, whose resources (notably oil and rubber) would have made Japan self-sufficient and thus free of American economic pressure. The Japanese army, on the other hand, land-bound by its nature, had pictured the Soviet Union as the major obstacle to Japanese prosperity, which required, in its view, the acquisition of resources on the continent (notably iron and coal).[4]

Once Japan had decided to go to war with the United States and Great Britain, operations against the Soviet Union had assumed a lower priority. It had been determined that in the event of a Soviet attack during the initial phase of Japanese operations, the Japanese navy would play a defensive role until forces could be diverted from the south. Even if the Soviets struck later, Japanese efforts were to be limited essentially to gaining control of the sea and air and securing strategic points in the Russian Far East.[5]

All military staffs have (or should have) contingency plans for operations against potential enemies. Such plans are not of themselves proof of hostile intent, though they may reveal the extent of a power's ambitions. Operational planning in the context of a national defense policy, mapped out jointly by the chief of the army general staff and the chief of the navy general staff with the approval of the prime minister and the sanction of the Emperor, had been initiated in Japan in 1907. Although relations with Russia had been becoming increasingly good and were to culminate in an alliance during the First World War, planning had been directed at first primarily against Russia for fear that she might wish to regain territory and prestige lost in the Russo-Japanese War of 1904–1905.[6]

In the wake of the Russian Revolution and the Siberian Intervention, during which the Japanese army had made futile efforts to set up a Japanese-dominated White Russian buffer state in the Russian Far East, Japanese planners had concentrated on possible operations against the Soviet Union. Between 1923 and 1931 Japanese strategists had envisaged a collision with the Red Army in Manchuria; following the establishment of Manchukuo they had thought in terms of fighting on Russian soil, penetrating as far west as Lake Baikal. During 1937–1940 both sides had girded for war. As the Japanese invasion of neighboring China had forced the Soviets to shore up their defenses, the Russian build-up had appeared as a threat to the Japanese, and the Soviet Far Eastern Army and the Kwantung Army had raced to excel each other in military strength.[7]

The German invasion of the Soviet Union had been, of

course, a tempting opportunity for Japan to solve the Northern Question, but after coolly reexamining her national policy, Japan had decided on June 24, 1941, to give priority to the southward drive in order to "establish a foundation for self-sufficiency and self-defense."[8] Military preparations for war against the Soviet Union were to proceed in secret. "If the progress of the German-Soviet War becomes very favorable for Japan," the newly formulated "Outline of Japan's National Policy to Meet Changes in the International Situation" had declared, "she shall use armed force to solve the problem in the north, and secure stability on the northern front."[9] The Japanese military build-up in Manchuria, Hokkaido and Sakhalin had been carried out under the guise of special maneuvers of the Kwantung Army and had been accompanied by the expansion of railway and shipping facilities, including the double tracking of most of the Dairen-Harbin-Mutanchiang-Suifenho line, the Mukden-Antung line, the Seoul-Sinuiju line and the Seoul-Pusan line.[10]

Informing the Kwantung Army of Japan's decision to wage war against the United States, Great Britain and the Netherlands and of the plan of the Imperial General Headquarters "to occupy immediately the strategic areas in the South and at the same time to end the China Incident," the army had ordered on December 3, 1941, that "during the time the outbreak of war with Russia will be avoided as much as possible."[11]

As Japan failed to bring the United States to her knees, more and more troops had to be withdrawn from Manchukuo. By the summer of 1944 it was obvious to the imperial general headquarters that offensive operations against the Soviet Union were no longer possible. The choice had narrowed down to two defensive concepts—holding operations on all fronts and delaying operations on all fronts. On September 18, 1944, the Imperial General Headquarters decided on the former, partly because it felt a moral obligation to defend Manchukuo, partly because maximum use could be made of the strong border installations. Ordering the Japanese troops in the border zone, "to fight until annihilated," it conceived of a last stand in the mountain region of southeastern Manchuria and northern Korea. By the end of May 1945, however, the strength of the Kwantung Army had been depleted further while the Soviet Far Eastern Army had been reinforced greatly.[a] The Imperial General Headquarters thus switched to the delaying plan, rejected the previous year, and called for a gradual fall-back of the Japanese forces from the border to the mountain barrier astride the Korean-Manchukuoan frontier.

The Kwantung Army headquarters duly drafted a corresponding operational plan and ordered full mobilization. Yet the 24 divisions, which it mustered in execution of the plan in August 1945, had a limited combat effectiveness, as low as 15 per cent of normal in some divisions.[12]

Soviet Plans

The Soviet General Staff had kept a wary eye on the Kwantung Army throughout the European War. Its fear of a Japanese attack had been greatest at the time of the German invasion. In 1938 the Far Eastern Military District had been reorganized as a front and in 1941 the same was done with the Transbaikal Military District. In 1942 the post of deputy chief of the General Staff for the Far East was established. In June 1943 the deputy chief of the General Staff, Major General Nikolai Lomov, switched positions with Major General F. I. Shevchenko, the head of the special Far Eastern Sector of the Operations Department of the General Staff, so that there were in the General Staff and in the Far East officers personally familiar with the Far Eastern situations as well as with the views of General Headquarters and the demands of the General

[a] For tables showing changes in the strength of the Japanese and Soviet forces between 1941 and 1945, see U. S. Army, Far East Command, Military History Section, "Japanese Operational Planning Against the U.S.S.R.," 170–71.

Staff. High ranking officers without combat experience were sent to the German front and battle-tested veterans to the Far East, General Purkaev, former commander of the Kalinin front, being entrusted with the command of the Far Eastern front.[13]

Although Stalin had intimated to the Americans as early as October 1943 that the Soviet Union would enter the war against Japan following the defeat of Germany, he did not instruct the General Staff until September 1944 to draw up estimates for the concentration and logistical support of troops in the Far East. The estimates were used by Stalin in his meetings with Churchill the following month and formed the basis for the Soviet request for Allied fuel, food and means of transport to reduce the volume of deliveries that had to be made from central Russia and thus hasten Soviet entry into the Pacific War. Although Soviet participation was set for "two or three months" after the surrender of Germany, however, no particular strategic planning of operations in the Far East was initiated at this point, as the collapse of German resistance was not yet in sight.[14]

By the time of the Soviet denunciation of the Neutrality Pact on April 5, 1945, it was clear that victory in Europe was but thirty to forty days away, and Stalin ordered the reinforcement of the staffs and higher command posts of the Transbaikal and Far Eastern fronts and the Maritime Group as well as the transfer of troops and their headquarters to the east. The movement was begun that month and was accelerated following the German surrender.[b] In choosing the armies to be sent east, the general staff looked for combat experience under similar conditions. Thus the 39th and 5th Armies were transferred from Eastern Prussia and the 53rd Army, the 6th Guards Tank Army and a motorized cavalry group from Prague, because they were used to mountainous terrain and the penetration of fortified areas.[16]

[b] Some units set out for Siberia at the end of March. Marshal Meretskov dates his own involvement in the Far Eastern campaign as of March 28.[15]

The Red Army put some of its most experienced generals in charge of the operations against Japan, the commanders who were familiar with local conditions staying on as deputy commanders. Marshal Vasilevskii, who had been chief of the General Staff, became head of a special High Command of Soviet Forces in the Far East, with Colonel General S. P. Ivanov as his chief of staff. Marshal Rodion Malinovskii took command of the Transbaikal Front, the main front, based at Chita, with General of the Army Matvei Zakharov as his chief of staff; Marshall Meretskov was appointed head of the First Far Eastern Front (the Maritime Region group), based at Vladivostok; Purkaev remained in command of the Second Far Eastern Front, based at Khabarovsk.[17]

It is a matter of controversy to what extent the Soviet timetable for operations against Japan was affected by extraneous factors. On one hand it is asserted in the United States that the U.S.S.R. procrastinated in her entry into the war until a cheap victory could be obtained, on the other hand—in what is perhaps the other side of the same coin—that she rushed into the war earlier than planned when the atomic bomb was dropped. The magnitude and intensity of the Soviet preparations on the Transbaikal front dispose of the argument that the U.S.S.R. was playing a waiting game, that she struck later than possible. There is evidence also that as far back as May, Stalin had named August 8 as a target date for the completion of preparations for the campaign against Japan, but that the General Staff had been unsure of its ability to meet the deadline.[18] The General Staff eventually moved up its schedule of operations, but it is not clear whether this was done as the result of the atomic bomb (either the original testing or its employment against Hiroshima) or for other reasons; even Soviet generals disagree on the subject.

According to General Sergei M. Shtemenko, who had served as chief of the Operations Department and deputy chief of the General Staff, the plan of operations worked out by the General Staff in conjunction with the front commanders in June set the time for the beginning of hostilities between August 20 and 25.[19,c] Shtemenko asserts that Truman's allusion to the atom bomb had been so veiled as not to alert Stalin or Antonov, to whom Stalin had passed on the information, and that no additional instructions were given to the General Staff.[20] He traces a change in the target date for operations to a meeting between Marshal Vasilevskii and Stalin on August 3, upon the latter's return from Potsdam, and attributes the initiative to Vasilevskii. Shtemenko claims that in making his report about the state of preparations for the offensive "which were already nearing completion," Vasilevskii proposed that hostilities be begun not later than August 9 or 10, partly because weather conditions were relatively favorable and should not be missed, partly because the Japanese seemed to be strengthening their forces in Manchuria and Korea.[21] The General Staff agreed to the change in date as did Stalin, though his directive to begin hostilities in the early hours of August 9 was not signed until the afternoon of the 7th. Since this was a day after the dropping of the atomic bomb, Shtemenko makes a point of stating that "atomic bombardment did not . . . influence Japan's ability to continue fighting or our military plans."[22]

A different picture emerges from the memoirs of Vasilevskii. While Shtemenko contends that Stalin had been hoodwinked by Truman, an impression gained by Churchill and by Truman himself at the time, Vasilevskii recalls that Stalin had telephoned him from Potsdam on July 16 after his talk with Truman and had ordered him to start hostilities on August 1, but that upon being told that an offensive could not possibly be launched before the 9th, Stalin had reluctantly settled for that date.[23] Yet while it is possible, therefore, that word of an American super-bomb had contributed to the advance of the Soviet date, the dropping of

c The transfer of the last troop units was to be completed by August 5.

the atomic bomb on Hiroshima probably had no further
impact on Soviet plans.[d]

[d] Garthoff argues that Soviet preparations were not fully completed
by August 9, but it is unlikely that the General Staff would have ventured
to deviate from the set date and invite Stalin's wrath; all fronts had been
informed on August 7 that the offensive would begin on the 9th.[24] While
it is true, as Garthoff says, that the Soviet Union could not afford to be
left out of the Pacific War, whatever acceleration there had been in
Russian plans had occurred, it appears, before August 6. To this extent
Shtemenko and Meretskov are correct when they say that the atomic
bombing of Hiroshima did not affect Soviet plans.

G

Documents

The Neutrality Pact[1]

The Presidium of the Supreme Soviet of the U.S.S.R. and His Majesty the Emperor of Japan, guided by a desire to strengthen peaceful and friendly relations between the two countries, decided to conclude a pact on neutrality, for the purpose of which they appointed their representatives:

For the Presidium of the Supreme Soviet of the U.S.S.R., Viacheslav M. Molotov, Chairman of the Council of People's Commissars and People's Commissar for Foreign Affairs.

For His Majesty the Emperor of Japan, Yosuke Matsuoka, Minister of Foreign Affairs, Jusanmin, Cavalier of the Order of the Sacred Treasure, first class; and Yoshitsugu Tatekawa, Ambassador Extraordinary and Plenipotentiary in the U.S.S.R. Lieutenant General, Jusanmin, Cavalier of the Order of the Rising Sun, first class, and the Order of the Golden Kite, fourth class.

Who, after the exchange of their credentials, which were found in due and proper form, agreed on the following:

ARTICLE 1

Both contracting parties undertake to maintain peaceful and friendly relations between them and mutually respect the territorial integrity and inviolability of the other contracting party.

ARTICLE 2

Should one of the contracting parties become the object of hostilities on the part of one or several third powers, the other contracting party will observe neutrality throughout the duration of the conflict.

ARTICLE 3

The present pact comes into force from the day of its ratification by both contracting parties and remains valid for five years. In case neither of the contracting parties denounces the pact one year before expiration of the term, it will be considered automatically prolonged for the next five years.

ARTICLE 4

The present pact is subject to ratification as soon as possible. Instruments of ratification shall be exchanged in Tokyo also as soon as possible.

In confirmation whereof the above-named representatives signed the present pact in two copies, drawn up in the Russian and Japanese languages, and affixed thereto their seals.

Done in Moscow April 13, 1941, which corresponds to the 13th Day of the Fourth Month of the 16th Year of Showa.

Signed by:

MOLOTOFF,
YOSUKE MATSUOKA,
YOSHITSUGU TATEKAWA.

Frontier Declaration

In conformity with the spirit of the Neutrality Pact concluded April 13, 1941, between the U.S.S.R. and Japan, the Governments of the U.S.S.R. and Japan, in the interests of ensuring peaceful and friendly relations between the two countries, solemnly declare that the U.S.S.R. pledges to respect the territorial integrity and inviolability of Manchukuo, and Japan pledges to respect the territorial integrity and inviolability of the Mongolian People's Republic.

Moscow, April 13, 1941.
Signed on behalf of the Government of the U.S.S.R. by:

MOLOTOFF

On behalf of the Government of Japan by:

YOSUKE MATSUOKA,
YOSHITSUGU TATEKAWA.

* * *

Protocol on the Liquidation of the Japanese Oil and Coal Concessions in North Sakhalin[2]

The Government of the Union of Soviet Socialist Republics and the Imperial Government of Japan, as a result of negotiations which had been conducted with a view to the implementation of an understanding they had reached in connection with the Neutrality Pact of April 13, 1941, concerning the liquidation of Japanese oil and coal concessions in Northern Sakhalin, have agreed on the following:

ARTICLE I

The Government of Japan transfers to the Union of Soviet Socialist Republics all rights to the Japanese oil and coal concessions in Northern Sakhalin in accordance with the provisions of the present Protocol and the terms of application of the Protocol appended hereto.

The concession contracts concluded between the Government of the Union of Soviet Socialist Republics, on the one hand, and Japanese concessionaires, on the other hand, concluded on December 14, 1925, as well as the supplementary contracts and agreements concluded subsequently, are annulled by the present Protocol.

ARTICLE 2

All the property (structures, equipment, materials, spare parts, provisions, etc.) in the possession of the Japanese concessionaires in Northern Sakhalin is to be turned over to the Government of the Union of Soviet Socialist Republics in its present condition insofar as nothing different is provided for by the present Protocol and the terms of application of the Protocol appended hereto.

ARTICLE 3

In connection with the provisions of the two preceding articles the Government of the Union of Soviet Socialist Republics agrees to pay to the Government of Japan the sum of five million rubles in accordance with the provisions of the terms of application of the present Protocol appended hereto.

The Government of the Union of Soviet Socialist Republics also agrees to supply annually to the Government of Japan on the usual commercial terms 50,000 metric tons of oil extracted at the Okha oil fields in the course of five consecutive years from the time of the termination of the present war.

ARTICLE 4

The Government of the Union of Soviet Socialist Republics guarantees to the Government of Japan unobstructed and free of duty removal from the concession territories of oil and coal stocked in stores and belonging to Japanese concessionaires, in conformity with the provisions of the terms of application of the present Protocol appended hereto.

ARTICLE 5

The present Protocol comes into force on the day of its signing.

The present Protocol has been drawn up in the Russian and Japanese languages; both texts possess equal force.

In witness whereof the undersigned, duly authorized by their respective governments, have signed the present Protocol and affixed their seals to it.

Drawn up in two copies in the city of Moscow on March 30, 1944, which corresponds to the 30th day of the third month of the 19th year of Shōwa.

S. A. LOZOVSKII	NAOTAKE SATO
Delegate of the Union of Soviet Socialist Republics. Assistant People's Commissar of Foreign Affairs of the U.S.S.R.	Delegate of Japan, Ambassador Extraordinary and Plenipotentiary of Japan to the Union of Soviet Socialist Republics.

* * *

Protocol on the Extension of the Fisheries Convention[3]

The Government of the Union of Soviet Socialist Republics and the Imperial Government of Japan, as a result of negotiations they recently conducted on the subject of fisheries, have agreed on the following:

ARTICLE 1

The fisheries convention between the Union of Soviet Socialist Republics and Japan, as well as all documents appended thereto which were signed on January 23, 1928, and whose term of operation after the yearly prolongation beginning with 1936, expired on December 31, 1943, shall remain in force for five years as from January 1, 1944, on the terms laid down in the present Protocol.

ARTICLE 2

All matters relating to the fishing activities of fishery-owning organizations and citizens of the Union of Soviet Socialist Republics shall not be regulated by the provisions of the fisheries convention and the documents appended thereto as being exclusively within the competence of the Union of Soviet Socialist Republics.

In conformity with the provision of the preceding paragraph, all the provisions contained in the fisheries convention and in the documents appended thereto and relating to the fishing activities of fishery-owning organizations and citizens of the Union of Soviet Socialist Republics, lose their force and henceforward shall not be applied.

ARTICLE 3

The following modifications and additions are made in Article 1 of the Protocol (A), appended to the fisheries convention:

a) The provisions of the last paragraph of Article 1 of the Protocol (A) shall be modified and replaced by the following provisions:

"In addition fishing is to be forbidden to Japanese subjects as well as to other foreigners in the following bays:

1. Avachinskii Bay—the area within the boundary formed by a line from Cape Krutov to Bechevinskaia Bay (inclusive).

2. De-Kastri Bay within the boundary formed by a line drawn from Cape Iuzhnyi to Krestovaia Bay (inclusive).

3. Sovetskaia Gavan'—in the area within the boundary formed by a line drawn from the point at latitude 49°26′ North and longitude 140°27′ East to the point at latitude 48°40′ North and longitude 140°11′ East.

4. St. Olga Bay and Vladimir Bay—the area within the boundary formed by a line drawn from the mouth of Lafula River to Cape Nakhval'nyi.

5. The Bay of Peter the Great (including Pos'et Bay)— the area within the boundary formed by a line drawn from Opasnyi Island to the mouth of the Tiumen-Ula River."

The bays figuring in Article 1 of the Protocol (A) with numbers 16, 27, 30 and 32 henceforward will not be mentioned with these numbers as included respectively in the above five areas.

The precise boundaries of the above-mentioned five areas barred for fishing have been fixed in notes Number 2 appended to the present Protocol, which the delegates of the Union of Soviet Socialist Republics and Japan exchanged simultaneously with the signing of the present Protocol.

b) The list of bays which constitute the exception mentioned in Article 1 of the fisheries convention, contained in Article 1 of Protocol (A) shall be supplemented by the following two names:

1. Ossor Bay

2. The northwestern part of Taui Inlet.

ARTICLE 4

The lump sum of the taxes and duties provided for in notes Number 1 exchanged on January 23, 1928 and appended to the fisheries convention shall be raised and fixed at 30 per cent of the rent of the respective fishery lots.

ARTICLE 5

The rates of special payments (share payments for the work of canneries) fixed in Section Six of Paragraph (B) of Protocol (C) appended to the fisheries convention, shall be raised and established as follows:

1. For cartilaginous fish—25 kopeks per case;
2. For Siberian salmon, kizhuch and chavycha—20 kopeks per case;
3. For humpback salmon—12 kopeks per case;
4. For crabs—50 kopeks per case.

ARTICLE 6

The present Protocol comes into force on the day of its signing.

The present Protocol has been drawn up in the Russian and Japanese languages; both texts have equal force.

In witness whereof the undersigned, duly authorized by their respective governments, have signed the present Protocol and affixed their seals to it.

Drawn up in two copies on March 30, 1944, which corresponds to the 30th day of the third month of the 19th year of Showa.

S. A. LOZOVSKII.
Delegate of the Union of Soviet Socialist Republics, Assistant People's Commissar of Foreign Affairs of the U.S.S.R.

NAOTAKE SATO.
Delegate of Japan, Ambassador Extraordinary and Plenipotentiary of Japan to the Union of Soviet Socialist Republics.

Exchange of Notes Regarding the Fisheries

LOZOVSKII TO SATŌ

Moscow, March 30, 1944.

MR. DELEGATE,

In connection with the signing on this date of the Protocol leaving in force for a period of five years the fish-

eries convention between the Union of Soviet Socialist
Republics and Japan and the documents appended thereto
signed on January 23, 1928, I have the honor to inform
you of the following:

1. The Government of the Union of Soviet Socialist Republics agrees to renew on the former terms, unless the
Protocol and the documents appended thereto contain different provisions, for a period of five years as from January 1, 1944, the operation of special contracts for the
exploitation by Japanese subjects of the canneries and
fishery lots attached to them, signed on November 3, 1928,
together with the documents and the subsequent supplementary agreements relating to these contracts.

2. The 24 fishery lots listed below which were leased to
Japanese subjects but were not exploited by them for two
years in succession in 1939 and 1940, irrespective of the
date of expiration of the lease terms, are to be closed and
will not be put on auction in the future.

Numbers of the fishery lots:

41, 42, 269, 271, 273, 367, 497, 498, 543, 555, 556, 561,
638, 641, 1002, 1003, 1004, 1082, 1104, 1190, 1265,
1266, 1267, and 95 (crab fishing).

The lease contracts for the above listed lots, the terms
of operation of which have not yet expired, are to be
severed.

3. The fishery lots which by the end of 1943 were
rented by Japanese subjects, with the exception of the lots
listed in the preceding Articles 1 and 2, after the expiration of their lease terms will be leased by auction for the
corresponding periods provided by the first section of
Article 6 of Protocol (A) appended to the fisheries
convention.

It is specified in this connection that the number of
fishery lots which will be rented by fishing organizations
and citizens of the Union of Soviet Socialist Republics on
the auctions provided for in the preceding paragraphs,

which will take place every year in the course of five years beginning with 1944, will not exceed 10% of the total number of lots that will be placed on auction in the respective years, and that fishing organizations and citizens of the Union of Soviet Socialist Republics have no intention to rent on auction those fishery lots on which there exist canneries.

I avail myself of the opportunity to renew, Mr. Delegate, my assurances to you of my highest esteem.

> S. A. LOZOVSKII,
> Delegate of the Union of
> Soviet Socialist Republics,
> Assistant People's Commissar
> of Foreign Affairs of the
> USSR.

SATŌ TO LOZOVSKII

Moscow, March 30, 1944

MR. DELEGATE,

On behalf of my Government I have the honor to inform you of the following:

1. Complying with the wish of the Government of the Union of Soviet Socialist Republics, the Government of Japan agrees to guarantee that all fishery lots rented by Japanese subjects and situated on the eastern coast of Kamchatka and in the Olyutorsk district will not be exploited by leaseholders before the termination of the war in the Pacific.

2. It is understood in this connection that the fact of Japanese subjects refraining from exploitation of the above-mentioned fishery lots will not serve as a pretext for the severing of contracts for the exploitation of any fishery lots or canneries situated in the said areas.

I avail myself of the opportunity to renew, Mr. Delegate, my assurance to you of my highest esteem.

> NAOTAKE SATO,
> Delegate of Japan. Ambassador Extraordinary and Plenipotentiary of Japan to the U.S.S.R.

Source Notes

1. NEGOTIATION OF THE NEUTRALITY PACT.

1. Tanaka Bunichirō, *Nisso koshō-shi*, 517 ff.

2. Leonid Nikolaevich Kutakov, *Istoriia sovetsko-iaponskikh diplomaticheskikh otnoshenii*, 246.

3. Hubertus Lupke, *Japans Ruszlandpolitik von 1939 bis 1941*, 5–53; Kutakov, *Istoriia*, 164–245; Sandra Winterberger Thornton, "The Soviet Union and Japan, 1939–1941," 86–89.

4. Classified Japanese Foreign Office material, "Secret" but made available for this study, hereinafter cited as "Classified"; Tōgō Shigenori, *Jidai no ichimen*, 132–33; Dr. Paul Schmidt, *Statist auf diplomatischer Bühne 1923–45*, 515–26; Kutakov, *Istoriia*, 245–59.

5. Frank William Iklé, *German-Japanese Relations 1936–1940*, 171–91; Theo Sommer, *Deutschland und Japan zwischen den Müchten 1935–1940*, 426–49.

6. Kutakov, *Istoriia*, 263.

7. *Ibid.*, 275.

8. *Ibid.*, 262–63.

9. *Ibid.*, 263.

10. Morishima Gorō, *Kunō suru chū So taishikan*, 7-8.

11. *Ibid.*, 264–65.

12. *Ibid.*, 263.

13. Classified; Kutakov, *Istoriia*, 275.

14. Kutakov, *Istoriia*, 275.

15. Toshikazu Kase, *Journey to the Missouri*, edited by David Nelson Rowe, 156–57.

16. Sommer, 469

17. Classified; Kutakov, *Istoriia*, 276.

18. Classified; Sommer, 480.

19. Kutakov, *Istoriia*, 276.

20. Classified; Lupke, 93–95, 173–75; Robert J. C. Butow, *Tojo and the Coming of the War,* 205–207.

21. Lupke, 95–96; Kutakov, *Istoriia,* 283.

22. Kase, 158.

23. Classified; Kutakov, *Istoriia,* 286–87; Lupke, 98–99; Thornton, 177.

24. Classified; Lupke, 95–101; Kutakov, *Istoriia,* 281–89.

25. Kase, 158.

26. International Military Tribunal Far East (hereafter cited as "IMTFE"), mimeographed transcript of proceedings, Prosecution exhibit No. 45, "The Neutrality Pact Between the Union of Soviet Socialist Republics and Japan, April 13, 1941."

27. Japan, Ministry of Foreign Affairs Archives, hereafter cited as "Japanese Archives," Library of Congress microfilm series, S 2.1.0.0.–23, pp. 374–79.

28. Classified.

29. Schmidt, 537.

30. *Ibid.*

31. Michael Libal, *Japans Weg in den Krieg,* 112.

32. Thornton, 184.

33. Kutakov, *Istoriia,* 289.

34. Otto D. Tolischus, *Tokyo Record,* 99.

35. Kutakov, *Istoriia,* 288.

36. Tolischus, 106–107.

37. *Ibid.,* 106; Kase, 159.

38. Tolischus, 106–107.

2. THE NEUTRALITY PACT AND THE GERMAN-SOVIET WAR.

1. Kase, 161.

2. Robert E. Sherwood, *Roosevelt and Hopkins: An Intimate History,* 303–304.

3. Classified; Kutakov, *Istoriia,* 305.

4. Classified.

5. Kase, 48.

6. Classified; Nobutaka Ike (transl. and ed.), *Japan's Decision for War,* 64–67; U.S. Army, Far East Command, Military History Section, "Japanese Operational Planning Against the U.S.S.R.," hereafter cited as "Japanese Operational Planning," 145–46.

7. Tolischus, 142.

8. Ike, 86.

9. Classified; Ike, 77–90.

10. Ike, 112.
11. Libal, 107.
12. Kutakov, *Istoriia,* 306.
13. *Ibid.,* 307–308; Classified.
14. Kutakov, *Istoriia,* 307–308.
15. Kase, 43.
16. Ike, 115.
17. Classified.
18. Ike, 116–17.
19. Colonel Gordon K. Pickler, "United States Aid to the Chinese Nationalist Air Force, 1931–1949."
20. Iu. N. Oskolkov, "Aggressivnaia politika iaponskogo imperializma protiv SSSR v 1939–1941 gg," 425; Classified; Kutakov, *Istoriia,* 375.

3. THE NEUTRALITY PACT AND THE OUTBREAK OF THE PACIFIC WAR.

1. Classified.
2. *Ibid.*
3. *Ibid.*
4. *Ibid.*
5. *Ibid.*
6. Morishima, 7–27.
7. Satō Naotake, *Kaiko hachijū-nen,* 71–114, 176 ff.
8. Morishima, 2–30.
9. *Ibid.,* 28–30.
10. Classified.
11. *Ibid.*
12. Pickler, "Features of Soviet Wartime Relations in the Pacific: American Internees and Air Rights," 11.
13. Kutakov, *Istoriia,* 397.
14. Classified.
15. Pickler, "Features of Soviet Wartime Relations," 11; United States, Department of State, Foreign Relations of the United States, hereafter cited as "FRUS," 1943, III, 698; IMTFE, 23,581.
16. Kutakov, *Istoriia,* 396–97.
17. Classified.
18. *Ibid.*
19. FRUS, 1941, IV, 742–44.
20. Richard C. Lukas, *Eagles East. The Army Air Forces and the Soviet Union, 1941–1945,* 98–99.
21. *Ibid.,* 100.

22. United States, Department of Defense, "The Entry of the Soviet Union into the War Against Japan: Military Plans, 1941–1945," hereafter cited as "Entry of the Soviet Union," 7.

23. FRUS, 1942, III, 693–95.

24. *Ibid.*, 545–47 and 702–703.

25. Union of Soviet Socialist Republics, Ministry of Foreign Affairs, *Correspondence between the Chairman of the Council of Ministers of the U.S.S.R. and the Presidents of the U.S.A. and the Prime Ministers of Great Britain during the Great Patriotic War of 1941–1945*, hereinafter cited as "*Correspondence*," II, 26–27.

26. Lukas, 125–28.

27. *Ibid.*, 135–36.

28. *Correspondence*, II, 50; Kutakov, *Istoriia*, 399.

29. Lukas, 193 and 223.

30. John L. Snell (ed.), *The Meaning of Yalta*, 150.

31. Lukas, 225–26.

32. Pickler, "Soviet Aid to Nationalist China with an Emphasis on Aviation, 1937–1941."

33. B. A. Borodin, *Pomoshch SSSR kitaiskomu narodu v antiiaponskoi voine 1937–1941*, 57–82.

34. Barbara W. Tuchman, *Stilwell and the American Experience in China, 1911–45*, 397.

35. Herbert Feis, *Churchill, Roosevelt, Stalin: The War They Waged and the Peace They Sought*, 233–34.

36. Classified.

37. Kutakov, *Istoriia*, 396.

38. Classified.

39. *Ibid.*

40. Kutakov, *Istoriia*, 395–96.

41. Henry A. Wallace with the collaboration of Andrew J. Steiger, *Soviet Asia Mission*, 36.

42. Tuchman, 464.

43. Wallace, 17, 21.

44. *Ibid.*, 48.

45. Classified.

46. *Ibid.*

47. *Oskolkov*, 430.

48. Classified.

49. IMTFE, 23, 522.

50. *Ibid.*, 23,525–23,528.

51. Classified; Kutakov, *Istoriia*, 392–93.

52. Classified.

53. *Ibid.*

54. Kutakov, *Istoriia,* 394.
55. Classified.
56. Kutakov, *Istoriia,* 394.
57. *Ibid.;* Classified.
58. Classified.
59. Japanese Archives, "Russo-Japanese Treaties," 14/9.
60. Classified.
61. *Ibid.*
62. *Ibid.*
63. *Ibid.*

4. LIQUIDATION OF THE SAKHALIN CONCESSIONS.

1. John J. Stephan, *Sakhalin,* 125–39; Classified.
2. Kutakov, *Istoriia,* 294.
3. *Ibid.;* Classified.
4. Classified; Kutakov, *Istoriia,* 399–400.
5. Classified.
6. Morishima, 69–71; Classified.
7. *Ibid.;* Kutakov, *Istoriia,* 401.
8. Classified; Kutakov, *Istoriia,* 401–402; Stephan, 140.
9. Satō, *Kaiko hachijū-nen,* 471–73; Classified.
10. Kutakov, *Istoriia,* 402.

5. EXTENSION OF THE FISHERIES PROTOCOL.

1. Classified.
2. Kutakov, *Istoriia,* 294.
3. Classified.
4. Kutakov, *Istoriia,* 291.
5. Classified.
6. Kutakov, *Istoriia,* 292.
7. Classified.
8. Kutakov, *Istoriia,* 291.
9. Classified.
10. Kutakov, *Istoriia,* 294–95.
11. *Ibid.;* Classified.
12. Kutakov, *Istoriia,* 295.
13. Classified.
14. *Ibid.;* Kutakov, *Istoriia,* 403–404.
15. Classified; Kutakov, *Istoriia,* 397–98; IMTFE, 23,577.

6. THE AGONY OF THE JAPANESE EMBASSY.

1. Morishima, 7–27.
2. *Ibid.,* 30–36.
3. *Ibid.,* 37–42.
4. *Ibid.,* 42–55.
5. *Ibid.,* 56–58.
6. *Ibid.,* 59–65.
7. *Ibid.,* 66.

7. DENUNCIATION OF THE NEUTRALITY PACT.

1. Classified; Morishima, 73–74; Kase, 162–63.
2. Classified.
3. Morishima, 74–75; Kase, 163.
4. Classified.
5. Cordell Hull, *The Memoirs of Cordell Hull,* edited by Walter Johnson, II, 968.
6. Kase, 163.
7. Shigemitsu Mamoru, *Shōwa no dōran,* II, 181–82.
8. Classified; Morishima, 75; Kase, 163–64.
9. Classified.
10. *Ibid.;* Morishima, 67–69 and 75–77.
11. Morishima, 76–79.
12. Classified; IMTFE, 23,578; Kase, 164.
13. Classified.
14. Morishima, 83–90.
15. *Ibid.,* 90–91.
16. *Ibid.*
17. *Ibid.,* 93–94.
18. *Ibid.,* 101–103.
19. *Ibid.,* 103–104; Satō, *Kaiko hachijū-nen,* 476–81.
20. Kase, 194.
21. Morishima, 103–104; Classified.
22. Morishima, 98–100.
23. IMTFE, 23,578–23,579.
24. Morishima, 100–103.
25. Classified; IMTFE, 23,579; Morishima, 105–106.
26. Morishima, 104–105.
27. Classified; Kutakov, 435; IMTFE, 23,579–23,580.
28. *Izvestiia,* April 6, 1945; *The New York Times,* April 6, 1945.
29. Kase, 155.
30. Satō, *Kaiko hachijū-nen,* 476–81.

8. ATTEMPTS AT A RAPPROCHEMENT.

1. Classified; Satō, *Kaiko hachijū-nen,* 476–81; Satō, *Futatsu no Roshia.*

2. Classified.

3. Butow, *Japan's Decision to Surrender,* 88.

4. *Ibid.,* 113–14.

5. George Alexander Lensen (comp.), *Japanese Diplomatic and Consular Officials in Russia,* 35.

6. Kutakov, *Istoriia,* 447.

7. *Ibid.,* 447–48.

8. Butow, *Japan's Decision,* 85; Kase, 170.

9. *Istoriia voiny na Tikhom okeane,* IV, 187.

10. Butow, *Japan's Decision,* 84–85, 97.

11. Classified; Butow, *Japan's Decision,* 89; John Toland, *The Rising Sun,* 746–47; Lensen, *The Russian Push Toward Japan,* 443–44 and 501–506.

12. Butow, *Japan's Decision,* 89–90.

13. Kase, 169.

14. Butow, *Japan's Decision,* 88 n. 33.

15. Kutakov, 449.

16. Classified; Hirota Kōki Denki Kankō-kai (comp.), *Hirota Kōki,* 365–68.

17. Kutakov, *Istoriia,* 449.

18. Classified.

19. Butow, *Japan's Decision,* 117–21.

20. *Ibid.,* 123, n. 35.

21. Classified; Morishima, 120–24; Butow, *Japan's Decision,* 121–22; Kase, 170–71, 187; Kutakov, *Istoriia,* 451.

22. Butow, *Japan's Decision,* 117–18.

23. Morishima, 107–11.

24. *Ibid.,* 113–16.

25. *Ibid.,* 120.

26. *Ibid.,* 117–18.

27. Confidential; Morishima, 124.

28. Toland, 754.

29. From a document found in Prince Konoe's residence after the war, IMT 34/2, Japanese Archives reel WT 9.

30. Kase, 187–88.

31. Classified; Morishima, 124–25.

32. Butow, *Japan's Decision,* 123.

33. Morishima, 125–27; IMT 34/2, p. 3, Japanese Archives reel WT 9; Butow, *Japan's Decision,* 122–23.

34. Kase, 193.
35. Butow, *Japan's Decision*, 119.
36. Kase, 188–89; IMTFE, 23,590.
37. Classified; Morishima, 127–29; IMT 34/3, Japanese Archives reel WT 9 (slightly different wording).
38. IMTFE, 23,590–23,591; Classified.
39. Kase, 189 and 193; Butow, *Japan's Decision*, 125 n. 44.
40. File No. 59/13 (Prince Konoe), IMT 34/3, Japanese Archives reel WT 9.
41. Classified; Japan, Foreign Office, *Shūsen shiroku*, I, 444–47; IMTFE, 23,594–23,595; IMT 34/4, Japanese Archives reel WT 9; Kutakov, *Istoriia*, 452–53; Kase, 194; Butow, *Japan's Decision*, 125–26.
42. Morishima, 131.
43. Tōgō Shigenori, *The Cause of Japan*, translated and edited by Tōgō Fumihiko and Ben Bruce Blakeney, 306.
44. Classified; IMTFE, 23,596–23,597.
45. Butow, *Japan's Decision*, 127 n. 50.
46. *Ibid.*, 127 n. 52.
47. IMTFE, 23,599–23,600.
48. Morishima, 133.
49. Classified; IMTFE, 23,597 and 23,606–23,607.
50. Classified; Morishima, 135–37; Satō, *Futatsu no Roshia*, 206–207; Kase, 218; IMTFE, 23,603–23,604.
51. Morishima, 136.
52. IMTFE, 23,609–23,610.
53. Kutakov, *Istoriia*, 457.
54. Classified; Morishima, 138.
55. *The New York Times*, August 9, 1945, p. 3; Satō, *Kaiko hachijū-nen*, 476–81.
56. Toland, 797.
57. Satō, *Kaiko hachijū-nen*, 476–81.
58. Classified; Morishima, 139–40.
59. Classified; Lester Brooks, *Behind Japan's Surrender*, 14.
60. Classified; *Shūsen shiroku*, II, 554–56.

9. SOVIET ENTRY INTO THE PACIFIC WAR.

1. General of the Army Sergei M. Shtemenko, *The Soviet General Staff at War, 1941–1945*, 327; Marshal K. A. Meretskov, *Na sluzhbe narodu*, 410–11; James Joseph Hagerty, Jr., "The Soviet Share in the War with Japan," 93; Raymond L. Garthoff, "The Soviet Man-

churian Campaign, August 1945," *Military Affairs,* vol. XXXIII, No. 2, p. 314.

2. Shtemenko, 332–33.

3. *Ibid.,* 337; N. Iakovlev, *3 sentiabria 1945,* 150.

4. Shtemenko, 341–42; Meretskov, 419–20.

5. *Ibid.,* 336–38.

6. *Ibid.,* 339–41; Major General V. N. Evstigneev, *Razgrom imperialisticheskoi Iaponii na Dal'nem Vostoke v 1945 godu,* 18–19; Marshal R. Ia. Malinovskii (ed.), *Final. Istoriko-memuarnyi ocherk o razgrome imperialisticheskoi Iaponii v 1945 g.,* 73–75; Hagerty, 94, 102; Garthoff, 314; L. N. Vnotchenko, *Pobeda na Dal'nem Vostoke,* 48–50.

7. *Istoriia Mongol'skoi Narodnoi Respubliki,* 378–79.

8. Hagerty, 98–99.

9. Meretskov, 433.

10. Shtemenko, 351–52; Malinovskii, 165–66 and 178; Vnotchenko, 138, 162, 166.

11. *Istoriia Mongol'skoi Respubliki,* 381; Vnotchenko, 138–46; Hagerty, 102–104.

12. Vnotchenko, 162.

13. Garthoff, 335 n. 73.

14. Vnotchenko, 146–47; Malinovskii, 166.

15. Butow, *Japan's Decision,* 173.

16. *Ibid.,* 189; Vnotchenko, 147–48.

17. Max Beloff, *Soviet Policy in the Far East 1944–1951,* 106.

18. Vnotchenko, 155.

19. Garthoff, 318.

20. Hagerty, 109; Garthoff, 318.

21. Vnotchenko, 148–51.

22. Hagerty, 113–16.

23. Vnotchenko, 151–53; Garthoff, 318.

24. Vnotchenko, 153–54; Hagerty, 107–108, 116.

25. Vnotchenko, 161–62.

26. *Velikaia otechestvennaia voina Sovetskogo Soiuza 1941–1945,* 536.

27. Vnotchenko, 162–63; Malinovskii, 178–79.

28. Lieutenant General S. P. Platonov and others (eds.), *Vtoraia mirovaia voina 1939–1945 gg.,* 803; Vnotchenko, 167–68.

29. Vnotchenko, 175–76.

30. Malinovskii, 186; Garthoff, 324.

31. Vnotchenko, 168–70; Platonov, 803.

32. Vnotchenko, 176–79.

33. Malinovskii, 181.

34. Vnotchenko, 186; Malinovskii, 186.
35. Vnotchenko, 186; Malinovskii, 186.
36. *Velikaia otechestvennaia voina,* 539.
37. Vnotchenko, 170–74; Platonov, 803; N. I. Krylov, N. I. Alekseev, and I. G. Dragan, *Navstrechu pobede. Boevoi put' 5–i Armii,* 441.
38. Vnotchenko, 186; Malinovskii, 186; Krylov, 441.
39. Malinovskii, 186.
40. Platonov, 179–80; Vnotchenko, 174; Malinovskii, 182–83.
41. *Velikaia otechestvennaia voina,* 539.
42. Malinovskii, 186; Meretskov, 438; Garthoff, 324.
43. Malinovskii, 213, 215.
44. Platonov, 803–804; Garthoff, 323–24.
45. *Velikaia otechestvennaia voina,* 536.
46. Malinovskii, 195.
47. *Velikaia otechestvennaia voina,* 540; Malinovskii, 195; Vnotchenko, 191–97.
48. Garthoff, 321.
49. Platonov, 806–807; *Velikaia otechestvennaia voina,* 540.
50. U.S. Army, Far East Command, Military History Section, "Homeland Operations Record," vol. IV, supplement: "Operations in Karafuto (Sakhalin) and Chishima (Kuriles Area)," Appendix I, pp. i–iii.
51. Stephan, 148.
52. *Ibid.,* 149–50.
53. Grigorii Mikhailovich Gel'fond, *Sovetskii flot v voine s Iaponiei,* 112–18; S. E. Zakharov, M. N. Zakharov, V. N. Bagrov and M. P. Kotykhov, *Tikhookeanskii flot,* 211–14.
54. "Homeland Operations," vi–x.
55. Stephan, 148–55.
56. "Homeland Operations," 5–7.
57. Zakharov, 225–26.
58. Gel'fond, 136–37; Zakharov, 235–36.
59. "Homeland Operations," IV, "Fifth Area Army," 44–45.
60. Platonov, 809; Shtemenko, 354.
61. Edward Norbeck, "Edokko. A Narrative of Japanese Prisoners-of-War in Russia," *Rice University Studies,* vol. 57, No. 1, p. 37.
62. Platonov, 816–17.
63. Shtemenko, 355.
64. *Ibid.,* 356; Meretskov, 439–43.
65. Garthoff, 320.
66. *Ibid.,* 331.

67. Norbeck, 46.
68. *Ibid.,* 67.

10. RECRIMINATIONS AT THE WAR CRIMES TRIAL.

1. Aisin-Gioro Pu Yi, *From Emperor to Citizen,* translated
by W. J. F. Jenner, II, 320; Malinovskii, 286–88.
2. Shtemenko, 357.
3. Pu Yi, II, 317.
4. *Ibid.,* 323.
5. *Ibid.,* 324, 328.
6. *Ibid.,* 333.
7. *Ibid.,* 472.
8. *Materialy sudebnogo protsessa po delu byvshikh voenno-sluzhashchikh iaponskoi armii, obviniaemykh v podgotovke i primenenii bakteriologicheskogo oruzhiia,* 534–36.
9. Hugh Borton, *Japan's Modern Century,* 475–76.
10. *Japan Biographical Encyclopedia & Who's Who,* 1964.
11. *Pravda,* September 3, 1945.
12. IMTFE, 7,231–7,233.
13. IMTFE, 7,269.
14. IMTFE, 7,281–7,282.
15. IMTFE, 23,358.
16. IMTFE, 7,309–7,310.
17. Richard Storry, *The Double Patriots,* 267–77.
18. IMTFE, 7,409–7,410.
19. IMTFE, 7,428–7,432.
20. IMTFE, 23,406.
21. IMTFE, 23,407.
22. IMTFE, 23,477–23,480.
23. IMTFE, 23,480–23,482.
24. IMTFE, 23,415–23,416.
25. IMTFE, 23,202; 23,392–23,393; 23,458–23,460; 23,469–23,470.
26. IMTFE, 23,085–23,086.
27. IMTFE, 23,359 and 23,278.
28. IMTFE, 23,467.
29. IMTFE, 23,557–23,560.
30. IMTFE, 23,363.
31. IMTFE, 23,375–23,377.
32. IMTFE, 23,304–23,305.
33. IMTFE, 23,298.
34. IMTFE, 23,338–23,341.

35. IMTFE, 23,192–23,193.
36. IMTFE, 23,264–23,265.
37. IMTFE, 23,305–23,306.
38. IMTFE, 23,196–23,197.
39. IMTFE, 23,428–23,432.
40. IMTFE, 7,277.
41. IMTFE, 23,447–23,449.
42. IMTFE, 23,656–23,658.
43. IMTFE, 23,508–23,509.
44. IMTFE, 23,577–23,578.
45. IMTFE, 23,580.
46. IMTFE, 23,582–23,583.
47. IMTFE, 7,281–7,282.

REFLECTIONS.

1. Hagiwara Tōru, *Taisen no Kaibō*, 234–60.
2. Johanna M. Meskill, *Hitler and Japan: The Hollow Alliance*, 16–17.
3. Alexander Werth, *Russia at War, 1941–1945*, xiii.
4. Libal, 250.
5. Hankey, 31 and 46.
6. United States, Department of State, *The Conferences at Malta and Yalta*, 385–88.
7. Lensen, *The Russian Push Toward Japan*, 61–71; Lensen, *Russia's Japan Expedition of 1852 to 1855*, 122.
8. Kase, 224–45.
9. Brooks, 16.
10. Meretskov, 449.
11. Charles Eade (comp.), *The War Speeches of the Rt. Hon. Winston S. Churchill, O. M., C. H., P. C., M. P.*, III, 516.
12. Robert Guillain, *Le Peuple Japonais et la guerre*, 265–66.
13. *Ibid.*
14. Joseph Laurence Marx, *Nagasaki. The Necessary Bomb?*
15. David I. Gol'dberg, *Vneshniaia politika Iaponii v 1941–1945 gg.*, 312–18.
16. Hankey, 47.
17. Gol'dberg, 318–24; V. Trukhanovsky, *British Foreign Policy During World War II*, 472–73.
18. Brooks, 18.
19. Major-General S. Woodburn Kirby, *et al.*, *The War Against Japan*, IV, 207–208.
20. Tōgō, *The Cause of Japan*, 316–17.

21. Kase, 217.

22. Kirby, IV, 433–34.

23. F. C. Jones, *Japan's New Order in East Asia, Its Rise and Fall, 1937–45,* 466.

24. Adam B. Ulam, *Expansion and Coexistence. The History of Soviet Foreign Policy, 1917–67,* 405.

25. *Ibid.,* 408.

26. *Ibid.,* 740.

27. *Ibid.,* 751.

28. Kutakov, *Istoriia,* 387–88.

29. *The Tehran, Yalta, & Potsdam Conferences,* 86.

30. John R. Deane, *The Strange Alliance,* 295.

31. Feis, *Churchill, Roosevelt, Stalin,* 116.

32. Deane, 281.

33. *Ibid.,* 278.

34. Harry S Truman, *Memoirs,* I, 442–43.

35. Werth, xiv.

36. John W. Dower, "Occupied Japan and the American Lake, 1945–1950," in *America's Asia,* edited by Edward Friedman and Mark Selden, 155.

37. Toland, 145.

38. *Ibid.,* 147.

39. Katherine Sansom, *Sir George Sansom and Japan,* 54.

40. James William Morley, *The Japanese Thrust into Siberia,* 309.

41. Lensen (ed.), *Revelations of a Russian Diplomat: The Memoirs of Dmitrii I. Abrikossow,* 276.

42. Lensen, *Japanese Recognition of the U.S.S.R.,* 26–30.

43. *Ibid.,* 180–83; Stephan, 107.

44. Jones, 451.

45. Sansom, 66.

46. Lensen, *The Soviet Union and the Manchurian Crises.*

47. Butow, *Japan's Decision,* 30; Toland, 680.

48. Toland, 33.

49. Butow, 88–89.

50. *Izvestiia,* August 9, 1945.

51. Werth, 1038.

52. *Ibid.,* 1039.

53. *Ibid.,* 1038.

54. Classified.

55. Raymond H. Dawson, *The Decision to Aid Russia, 1941,* 250.

56. *Ibid.,* 123–25.

57. United States, National Archives, documents FW 861.01/1913.

58. *Ibid.*, FW 861.01/1954.

59. Feis, *Contest Over Japan.*

60. Lensen, *Russia's Japan Expedition of 1852 to 1855*, 128–29.

61. Butow, *Japan's Decision,* 129.

62. Werth, 1041.

63. Gar Alperovitz, *Atomic Diplomacy,* 239–40.

64. Len Giovanniti and Fred Freed, *The Decision to Drop the Bomb,* 309–10.

65. B. H. Liddell Hart, *History of the Second World War,* 687–88.

66. Document No. 490, IMT 32, p. 4, reel WT 9.

67. Meretskov, 447.

68. Japan, Ministry of Foreign Affairs, *The Northern Territorial Issue,* 8.

69. Front page dispatch by Oka Takashi in the *New York Times,* August 4, 1971.

70. *The Japan Weekly Chronicle,* July 5, 1934.

APPENDIX

A. BORDER PROBLEMS.

1. Tanaka, 537–40; Kutakov, *Istoriia,* 256.

2. Lupke, 39.

3. Classified.

4. *Ibid.,* IMTFE, 23,151–23,152.

5. Classified.

6. *Ibid.*

7. Harriet L. Moore, *Soviet Far Eastern Policy 1931–1945,* 139; Lupke, 41.

8. Tanaka, 538–42; Lupke, 43–44.

9. Classified.

10. *Ibid.;* Lupke, 45–46.

11. Classified.

12. Kutakov, *Istoriia,* 383.

13. IMTFE, 7,745–7,746.

14. Classified.

B. COMMERCE AND THE TRANSIT OF GOODS.

1. Classified.

2. Lupke, 51; Kutakov, *Istoriia,* 292–93.

3. Classified; Lupke, 52–53; Kutakov, *Istoriia,* 295.
4. Union of Soviet Socialist Republics, Ministry of Foreign Trade, *Vneshniaia torgovlia SSSR za 1918–1940 gg. Statisticheskii obzor,* 1013–21.
5. *Ibid.,* 1028.
6. Lupke, 48.
7. Classified.
8. *Ibid.*
9. Kutakov, *Istoriia,* 295, 304.
10. Classified.

C. MISCELLANEOUS PROBLEMS.

1. Classified.
2. *Ibid.*
3. *Ibid.*
4. *Ibid.*
5. *Ibid.*
6. *Ibid.*
7. *Ibid.*
8. *Ibid.*
9. *Ibid.*
10. Kutakov, *Istoriia,* 404.
11. Classified.
12. Kutakov, *Istoriia,* 404.
13. Classified.
14. *Ibid.*
15. *Ibid.*

D. SOVIET TREATMENT OF AMERICAN FLIERS.

1. Pickler, "Features of Soviet Wartime Relations," 3.
2. Mary H. Williams (comp.), *Chronology 1941–1945,* Special Study Series, *United States Army in World War II,* 34; Ted W. Lawson, *Thirty Seconds Over Tokyo,* edited by Robert Considine, 201.
3. William H. Standley and Arthur A. Ageton, *Admiral Ambassador to Russia,* 222.
4. FRUS, 1942, III, 548.
5. Pickler, "Features of Soviet Wartime Relations," 5–6, 10.
6. Harry L. Coles, "The Aleutians Campaign," in *The Army Air Forces in World War II,* vol. IV, 390; FRUS, 1943, III, 698.
7. FRUS, 1944, IV, 983, 999, 1003, 1027, 1031.
8. Howard R. Jarrel, "I Was Forced Down in Russia," *Royal Air Force Flying Review,* XII, 28–29 and 44.
9. James Lea Cate, "The XX Bomber Command Against

Japan," in *The Army Air Forces in World War II,* vol. V, 114–15; FRUS, 1944, IV, 1026–28.

  10. Lt. Col. Robert G. Emmens, *Guests of the Kremlin;* Standley, 232–34; FRUS, 1943, III, 643, 721.

  11. Deane, 60–62.

  12. Kutakov, *Istoriia,* 397.

  13. Deane, 61–63.

E. AMERICAN REQUESTS FOR SOVIET PARTICIPATION IN THE WAR.

  1. Snell, 133; Sherwood, 748–49.

  2. "Entry of the Soviet Union," 2.

  3. *Ibid.*

  4. *Ibid.,* 6.

  5. *Ibid.,* 13–14.

  6. *Ibid.,* 18–19.

  7. *Ibid.,* 20.

  8. *Ibid.,* 21.

  9. Hull, II, 1309; Feis, *Churchill, Roosevelt, Stalin,* 234.

  10. Feis, *Churchill, Roosevelt, Stalin, 234; Deane,* 25.

  11. Deane, 41.

  12. Feis, *Churchill, Roosevelt, Stalin,* 503.

  13. Shtemenko, 323–24.

  14. "Entry of the Soviet Union," 24.

  15. Shtemenko, 323.

  16. Feis, *Churchill, Roosevelt, Stalin,* 255.

  17. "Entry of the Soviet Union," 29.

  18. Feis, *Churchill, Roosevelt, Stalin,* 406.

  19. *Ibid.,* 462–63.

  20. *Ibid.,* 463.

  21. *Ibid.,* 464–65.

  22. Deane, 241–42; 246–47.

  23. "Entry of the Soviet Union," 41.

  24. Lensen, *The Soviet Union and the Manchurian Crises,* in preparation.

  25. *The Conferences at Malta and Yalta,* 984.

  26. John A. White, *The Diplomacy of the Russo-Japanese War,* 332; Victor A. Yakhontoff, *Russia and the Soviet Union in the Far East,* 372.

  27. Snell, 152.

  28. Eugene P. Trani, *The Treaty of Portsmouth,* 164.

  29. Snell, 143.

  30. Feis, *Churchill, Roosevelt, Stalin,* 503–504.

31. "Entry of the Soviet Union," 57.
32. *Ibid.,* 70.
33. *Ibid.,* 72.
34. *Ibid.,* 74.
35. *Ibid.*
36. *Ibid.,* 79.
37. *Ibid.,* 92.
38. Admiral William D. Leahy, *I Was There,* 420.
39. Winston S. Churchill, *The Second World War,* VI, 552–54.
40. Werth, 1032–1035.

F. PREPARATIONS FOR WAR.

1. United States Army, Far East Command, Military Section, "Political Strategy Prior to the Outbreak of the War," hereafter cited as "Political Strategy," part V, 1, 11.
2. *Ibid.,* 11–12.
3. *Ibid.,* 13.
4. *Ibid.,* 71.
5. *Ibid.,* 142–43.
6. "Japanese Operational Planning," 15.
7. *Ibid.,* 16–54.
8. *Ibid.,* 139.
9. *Ibid.,* 140.
10. *Ibid.,* 148.
11. *Ibid.,* 159; IMTFE, 23, 328.
12. "Japanese Operational Planning," 160–75.
13. Shtemenko, 322–23.
14. *Ibid.,* 325–36.
15. Meretskov, 411.
16. *Velikaia otechestvennaia voina,* 534.
17. Garthoff, 314; Shtemenko, 327; Hagerty, 93.
18. Garthoff, 314.
19. Shtemenko, 339.
20. *Ibid.,* 347–48.
21. *Ibid.,* 347–49.
22. *Ibid.,* 351.
23. Garthoff, 314.
24. Malinovskii, 160.

G. DOCUMENTS.

1. TASS, April 13, 1941.
2. *Moscow News,* April 1, 1944; "Russo-Japanese Treaties," 37/50–37/52.

3. *Moscow News,* April 1, 1944; "Russo-Japanese Treaties," 37/2–37/29.

BIBLIOGRAPHY.

1. IMTFE, 22,759–22,778.
2. IMTFE, 22,845–22,846.

Bibliography

The vast collection of microfilms of the Japanese Foreign Office Archives, photographed during the Occupation for the Library of Congress, is less complete than is generally realized. The gaps, particularly in material pertaining to the Pacific War, are due to the destruction of large parts of the Foreign Office Archives during the war. Many documents had been burned in a fire that had partly destroyed the Foreign Office complex in June 1942; the bulk of the archives had perished in the Allied air raid of May 23–24, 1945, which had destroyed the remaining Foreign Office buildings and all but one of the archival vaults. The most sensitive documents that had remained (pertaining, no doubt, to a large extent to the war) had been burned by Foreign Office officials during the last week of June 1945 in expectation of an Allied invasion and the removal of the capital from Tokyo, though some important documents had been overlooked in the haste with which the destruction had been carried out.[1] The records and archives of the Japanese embassy in Moscow had been burned by the Japanese on August 8, 1945, upon the Soviet declaration of war.[2]

With the recovery of full independence and the return of the archives seized by the Americans, the Foreign Office reconstructed the record of its wartime dealings with the U.S.S.R., supplementing extant documents with the recollections of officials who had participated in the events. This monumental, unpublished source, prepared by Foreign Office officials for Foreign Office use and made available to me with the understanding that I would not cite it directly, formed the foundation for this book. It was supplemented, on the Japanese side, by the published memoirs of statesmen and diplomats, the recollections of Morishima Gorō, *Kunō suru chū So taishikan*, being most helpful.

The regular series of diplomatic correspondence published by the Ministry of Foreign Affairs of the U.S.S.R. (equivalent to the *Foreign Relations of the United States*) has reached only 1933 to date. Among special volumes the *Correspondence between the Chairman of the Council of Ministers of the U.S.S.R. and the Presidents of the U.S.A. and the Prime Ministers of Great Britain during the Great Patriotic War of 1941–1945* and *The Tehran, Yalta, & Potsdam Conferences. Documents* have provided a modicum of information. The major Soviet source which served as counterweight to the Japanese point of view was Dr. Leonid Kutakov's *Istoriia sovetsko-iaponskikh diplomaticheskikh otnoshenii*, based heavily on Soviet archival material, not accessible unfortunately to Western scholars. The memoirs of Soviet marshals and generals shed light on the Manchurian campaign.

Japanese and Soviet accounts of wartime Japanese-German relations were supplemented primarily with the aid of Bernd Martin's *Deutschland und Japan im Zweiten Weltkrieg*, based on German documents. Much material on Soviet-American dealings and attitudes was found in General John R. Deane's *The Strange Alliance*. The views of my old friend and comrade-in-arms Robert J. C. Butow on the nature of Japanese soliciting of Soviet assistance, expressed in *Japan's Decision to Surrender*, most nearly equalled my own. The mimeographed report of the United States Department of Defense on "The Entry of the Soviet Union into the War Against Japan" proved to be a major source for this topic. Monographs prepared by the Historical Section of the Far Eastern Command of the United States Army on the basis of studies made for it by former Japanese officers balanced the eye-witness accounts of Russian participants in the war. Of American works on the Soviet conflict with Japan, James J. Hagerty's doctoral dissertation, though incomplete in coverage, deserves special mention, because Raymond L. Garthoff's better known article on the same subject seems to have drawn on it heavily without giving due credit.

UNPUBLISHED SOURCES

Hagerty, James Joseph, Jr. "The Soviet Share in the War with Japan," MS, doctoral dissertation in history, Georgetown University, 1966.

International Military Tribunal of the Far East. Mimeographed transcript of proceedings, cited as IMTFE.

Japan, Foreign Office Archives. Documents photocopied during the Occupation for the Library of Congress and available on microfilm, cited as "Japanese Archives."

—————. Material compiled since the Occupation on the history of Soviet-Japanese relations during the Second World War, marked "Secret," but made available for this study with the understanding that it would not be quoted directly; cited as "Classified."

Oskolkov, Iu. N. "Aggressivnaia politika iaponskogo imperializma protiv SSSR v 1939–1941 gg" (The aggressive policy of Japanese imperialism against the U.S.S.R. in 1939–1941). MS, dissertation for the degree of Candidate of Historical Sciences, Leningrad State University, 1953.

Pickler, Colonel Gordon K. "Features of Soviet Wartime Relations in the Pacific: American Internees and Air Rights," MS, doctoral seminar paper in history, Florida State University, 1971.

—————. "Soviet Aid to Nationalist China with an Emphasis on Aviation, 1937–1941," MS, doctoral seminar paper in in history, Florida State University, 1970.

—————. "United States Aid to the Chinese Nationalist Air

Force, 1931–1949," MS, doctoral dissertation in history, Florida State University, 1971.

Thornton, Sandra Winterberger. "The Soviet Union and Japan, 1939–1941." MS, doctoral dissertation in government, Georgetown University, 1964.

United States Army, Far East Command, Military History Section. "Air Operations Record Against Russia." Japanese Monograph No. 151 (mimeographed). Tokyo, 1952.

———. "Homeland Operations Record," vol. IV. "Supplement: Operations in Karafuto (Sakhalin) and Chishima (Kuriles) Area." Japanese Monograph No. 153 (mimeographed). Tokyo, 1954 (?).

———. "Japanese Operational Planning." Japanese Special Study on Manchuria, vol. I (mimeographed). Tokyo, 1955.

———. "Naval Operations Against Soviet Russia." Japanese Monograph No. 106 (mimeographed). Tokyo, 1952.

———. "Political Strategy Prior to the Outbreak of the War." Japanese Monograph No. 152 (mimeograph). Tokyo, 1953.

———. "Record of Operations Against Soviet Russia, Eastern Front (August 1945)." Japanese Monograph No. 154 (mimeographed). Tokyo, 1954.

———. "Record of Operations Against Soviet Russia, On Northern and Western Fronts of Manchuria, and in Northern Korea (August, 1945)." Japanese Monograph No. 155 (mimeographed). Tokyo, 1954.

United States Department of Defense. "The Entry of the Soviet Union into the War Against Japan: Military Plans, 1941–1945." Mimeographed report released on October 19, 1955.

United States National Archives. Unpublished diplomatic correspondence.

PUBLISHED SOURCES

Acheson, Dean. *Present at the Creation. My Years in the State Department.* New York: W. W. Norton, 1969.

Alperovitz, Gar. *Atomic Diplomacy: Hiroshima and Potsdam. The Use of the Atomic Bomb and the American Confrontation with Soviet Power.* New York: Simon and Schuster, 1965.

Ashida Hitoshi. *Dainiji sekaitaisen gaikō-shi* (History of diplomacy in World War II). Tokyo, 1965.

Beloff, Max. *Soviet Policy in the Far East 1944–1951.* London: Oxford University Press, 1953.

Borodin, B. A. *Pomoshch' SSSR kitaiskomu narodu v antiiaponskoi voine 1937–1941* (Aid of the U.S.S.R. to the Chinese people in the anti-Japanese war 1937–1941). Moscow: Mysl', 1965.

Borton, Hugh. *Japan's Modern Century.* Second edition. New York: Ronald Press, 1970.

Brooks, Lester. *Behind Japan's Surrender. The Secret Struggle That Ended an Empire.* New York: McGraw-Hill, 1968.

Budkevich, S. L. *"Delo Zorge." Sledstvie i sudebnyi protsess* ("The Sorge case." The inquest and the trial). Moscow: Glavnaia redaktsiia vostochnoi literatury, 1969.

Butow, Robert J. C. *Japan's Decision to Surrender.* Stanford: Stanford University Press, 1954.

————. *Tojo and the Coming of the War.* Princeton: Princeton University Press, 1961.

Cales, Harry L. "The Aleutians Campaign," in *The Army Air Forces in World War II,* vol. IV, edited by Wesley Frank Craven and James Lea Cate. Chicago: Chicago University Press, 1950.

Cate, James Lea. "The XX Bomber Command Against Japan," in *The Army Air Forces in World War II,* vol. V, edited by Wesley Frank Craven and James Lea Cate. Chicago: Chicago University Press, 1953.

Churchill, Winston S. *The Second World War,* vol. VI (*Triumph and Tragedy*). Boston: Houghton Mifflin, 1953.

Clubb, O. Edmund. *China & Russia. The Great Game.* New York: Columbia University Press, 1971.

Coox, Alvin D. *Japan: The Final Agony.* New York: Ballantine Books, 1970.

Dawson, Raymond H. *The Decision to Aid Russia, 1941.* Chapel Hill: University of North Carolina Press, 1959.

Deakin, F. W. and G. R. Storry. *The Case of Richard Sorge.* London: Chatto and Windus, 1966.

Deane, John R. *The Strange Alliance; The Story of Our Efforts at Wartime Co-Operation with Russia.* New York: The Viking Press, 1947.

Diplomaticheskii Slovar' (Diplomatic Dictionary). Moscow: Gosudarstvennoe Izdatel'stvo politicheskoi literatury, 1960–64. 3 vols.

Dower, John W. "Occupied Japan and the American Lake, 1945–1950," in *America's Asia: Dissenting Essays on Asian-American Relations,* edited by Edward Friedman and Mark Selden. New York: Vintage Books, 1971.

Eade, Charles (comp.). *The War Speeches of the Rt. Hon. Winston S. Churchill, O. M., C. H., P. C., M. P.* vol. III. London: Cassel, 1952.

Emmens, Lt. Col. Robert G. *Guests of the Kremlin.* New York: Macmillan, 1949.

Evstigneev, Major General V. N. *Razgrom imperialisticheskoi Iaponii na Dal'nem Vostoke v 1945 godu* (The crushing of imperialist Japan in the Far East in 1945). Moscow: Vsesoiuznoe obshchestvo po rasprostraneniiu politicheskikh i nauchnykh znanii, 1951.

Feis, Herbert. *Churchill, Roosevelt, Stalin: The War They Waged and the Peace They Sought.* Princeton: Princeton University Press, 1957.

———. *Contest Over Japan.* New York: W. W. Norton, 1967.

———. *Japan Subdued. The Atomic Bomb and the End of the War in the Pacific.* Princeton: Princeton University Press, 1961.

Forrestal, James. *The Forrestal Diaries.* Edited by Walter Millis. New York: Viking, 1951.

Gaimushō Hyakunen-shi Hensan I-inkai (comp.). *Gaimushō no hyakunen* (A century of the Foreign Office). Tokyo, 1969. 2 vols.

Gardner, Lloyd C. *Architects of Illusion. Men and Ideas in American Foreign Policy 1941–1949*. Chicago: Quadrangle Books, 1970.

Garthoff, Raymond L. "The Soviet Manchurian Campaign, August 1945," *Military Affairs,* vol. XXXIII, No. 2 (October 1969), pp. 312–36.

Gel'fond, Grigorii Mikhailovich. *Sovetskii flot v voine s Iaponiei* (The Soviet navy in the war with Japan). Moscow: Voennoe izdatel'stvo Ministerstva oborony soiuza SSR, 1958.

Giovannitti, Len and Fred Freed. *The Decision to Drop the Bomb*. New York: Coward-McCann, 1965.

Gol'dberg, David Isakovich. *Vneshniaia politika Iaponii (Sentiabr' 1939 g. – dekabr' 1941 g.)* (The foreign policy of Japan [September 1939–December 1941]). Moscow: Izdatel'stvo vostochnoi literatury, 1969.

———. *Vneshniaia politika Iaponii v 1941–1945 gg.* (The foreign policy of Japan in 1941–1945). Moscow: Izdatel'stvo sotsial'no-ekonomicheskoi literatury, 1962.

Guillain, Robert. *Le Peuple Japonais et la guerre. Choses vues 1936–1946* (The Japanese people and the war. Things seen 1936–1946). Paris: R. Juillard, 1947.

Hagiwara, Tōru. *Taisen no Kaibō* (Post-mortem of the great war). Tokyo, 1950.

Hankey, Lord Maurice. *Politics, Trials and Errors*. Chicago: Henry Regnery, 1950.

Hayashi, Saburō, in collaboration with Alvin D. Coox. *Kōgun. The Japanese Army in the Pacific War*. Quantico, Va.: The Marine Corps Association, 1959.

Heinrichs, Waldo H. Jr. *American Ambassador. Joseph C. Grew and the Development of the United States Diplomatic Tradition*. Boston: Little, Brown, 1966.

Hirota Kōki Denki Kankō-kai (comp.). *Hirota Kōki*. Tokyo, 1966.

Hull, Cordell. *The Memoirs of Cordell Hull*. Edited by Walter Johnson. New York: Macmillan, 1948. 2 vols.

Iakovlev, N. *3 sentiabria 1945* (The Third of September, 1945). Moscow: Molodaia gvardiia, 1971.

Ike, Nobutaka (transl. and ed.). *Japan's Decision for War. Records of the 1941 Policy Conferences.* Stanford: Stanford University Press, 1967.

Iklé, Frank William. *German-Japanese Relations 1936–1940.* New York: Bookman Associates, 1956.

Institut Marksizma-Leninizma pri TsK KPSS (comp.). *Istoriia Velikoi Otechestvennoi voiny Sovetskogo Soiuza 1941–1945* (History of the Great Patriotic War of the Soviet Union 1941–1945). Moscow: Voennoe izdatel'stvo Ministerstva oborony Soiuza SSR, 1963–1965). 6 vols.

Issraeljan, Victor, and Leonid Kutakov. *Diplomacy of Aggression. Berlin-Rome-Tokyo Axis, Its Rise and Fall.* Moscow: Progress Publishers, 1970.

Istoriia Mongol'skoi Narodnoi Respubliki (History of the Mongolian People's Republic). Second edition, revised. Moscow: Nauka, 1967.

Istoriia voiny na Tikhom okeane (History of the Pacific War; translation of *Taihei-yō sensō-shi*). Moscow: Izdatel'stvo inostrannoi literatury, 1957–58. 5 vols.

Izvestiia. 1941–1945.

Japan, Foreign Office (comp.). *Nihon gaikō nempyō narabi ni shuyō bunsho* (Chronology and main documents of Japanese foreign relations). Toyko, 1965. 2 vols.

――――. *The Northern Territorial Issue. Japan's Position on Unsettled Question between Japan and the Soviet Union.* Tokyo, 1968.

――――. *Shūsen shiroku* (Historical record of the ending of the war). Tokyo, 1952. 2 vols.

Japan Biographical Encyclopedia & Who's Who. Tokyo: Rengo Press, 1958.

Japan Weekly Chronicle. 1940.

Jarrel, Howard R. "I Was Forced Down in Russia," *Royal Air Force Flying Review,* XII (June 1957).

Jones, F. C. *Japan's New Order in East Asia, Its Rise and*

Fall, 1931–45. New York: Oxford University Press, 1954.

Kase, Toshikazu. *Journey to the Missouri.* Edited by David Nelson Rowe. New Haven: Yale University Press, 1950.

Kirby, Major-General S. Woodburn, *et al. The War Against Japan.* London: Her Majesty's Stationery Office, 1959. 4 vols.

Kiyosawa, Kiyoshi. *Nihon gaikō-shi* (History of Japanese diplomacy). Tokyo, 1943. 2 vols.

Kokuritsu Kokkai Toshokan. Chōsa oyobi rippō kōsa-kyoku (comp.). *Nisso kokkō chōsei mondai kiso shiryō-shu* (Collection of basic material on the problem of the rectification of Japanese-Soviet diplomatic relations). Tokyo, 1955.

Konoe Fumimaro. *Heiwa e no doryoku* (My efforts toward peace). Toyko: Nippon Dempo Tsushinsha, 1946.

Krylov, N. I., N. I. Alekseev, and I. G. Dragan. *Navstrechu pobede. Boevoi put' 5-i Armii* (Toward victory. The operations of the Fifth Army). Moscow: Nauka, 1970.

Kusachi Sadago. *Sono hi, kantō-gun wa* (That day, as for the Kwantung Army. . . .). Tokyo, 1967.

Kutakov, Leonid Nikolaevich. *Istoriia sovetsko-iaponskikh diplomatischeskikh otnoshenii* (History of Soviet-Japanese diplomatic relations). Moscow: Izdatel'stvo Instituta mezhdunarodnykh otnoshenii, 1962.

————. *Japanese Foreign Policy on the Eve of the Second World War.* Edited with a foreword by George Alexander Lensen. Tallahassee: Diplomatic Press, 1972.

————. *Vneshniaia politika i diplomatiia Iaponii* (The foreign policy and diplomacy of Japan). Moscow: Mezhdunarodnye otnosheniia, 1964.

Lawson, Ted W. *Thirty Seconds Over Tokyo.* Edited by Robert Considine. New York: Random House, 1943.

Leahy, Fleet Admiral William D. *I Was There. The Personal Story of the Chief of Staff to Presidents Roosevelt and Truman Based on His Notes and Diaries Made at the Time.* New York: Whittlesey House, 1950.

Lensen, George Alexander (comp.). *Japanese Diplomatic and Consular Officials in Russia. A Handbook*. Tokyo: Sophia University in cooperation with the Diplomatic Press, Tallahassee, 1968.

―――. *Japanese Recognition of the U.S.S.R.; Soviet-Japanese Relations, 1921–1930*. Tokyo: Sophia University in cooperation with the Diplomatic Press, Tallahassee, 1968.

―――. (ed.). *Revelations of a Russian Diplomat. The Memoirs of Dmitrii I. Abrikossow*. Seattle: University of Washington Press, 1964.

―――. (comp.). *Russian Diplomatic and Consular Officials in East Asia. A Handbook*. Tokyo: Sophia University in cooperation with the Diplomatic Press, Tallahassee, 1968.

―――. *The Russian Push Toward Japan; Russo-Japanese Relations, 1697–1875*. Princeton: Princeton University Press, 1959; reprinted New York: Octagon Press, 1971.

―――. *Russia's Japan Expedition of 1852 to 1855*. Gainesville: University of Florida Press, 1955.

―――. *The Soviet Union and the Manchurian Crises, 1929–1937*. Tallahassee: Diplomatic Press, 1973.

Libal, Michael. *Japans Weg in den Krieg. Die Auszenpolitik der Kabinette Konoye 1940/41* (Japan's road to war. The foreign policy of the Konoye cabinets 1940/41). Düsseldorf: Droste, 1971.

Liddell Hart, B. H. *History of the Second World War*. London: Caddell, 1970.

Lukas, Richard C. *Eagles East. The Army Air Forces and the Soviet Union, 1941–1945*. Tallahassee: Florida State University Press, 1971.

Lupke, Hubertus. *Japans Ruszlandpolitik von 1939 bis 1941* (Japan's Russia policy from 1939 to 1941). Frankfurt am Main: Alfred Metzner, 1962.

Malinovskii, Marshal R. Ia. (ed.). *Final. Istoriko-memuarnyi ocherk o razgrome imperialisticheskoi Iaponii v 1945 g.* (Finale. A historical memoir account of the crushing of imperialist Japan in 1945). Moscow: Nauka, 1966.

Martin, Bernd. *Deutschland und Japan im 2. Weltkrieg. Von Pearl Harbor bis zur deutschen Kapitulation* (Germany and Japan in the Second World War. From Pearl Harbor to the German capitulation). Göttingen: Musterschmidt-Verlag, 1969.

Marx, Joseph Laurence. *Nagasaki. The Necessary Bomb?* New York: Macmillan, 1971.

Materialy sudebnogo protsessa po delu byvshikh voennosluzhaschikh iaponskoi armii, obviniaemykh v podgotovke i primenenii bakteriologicheskogo oruzhiia (Materials pertaining to the court proceedings in the case of the former servicemen of the Japanese army, charged with the preparation and use of biological weapons). Moscow: Gosudarstvennoc izdatel'stvo politicheskoi literatury, 1950.

Meretskov, Marshal K. A. *Na sluzhbe narodu. Stranitsy vospominanii* (In the service of the people. Pages of memoirs). Moscow: Izdatel'stvo politicheskoi literatury, 1970.

Meskill, Johanna Menzel. *Hitler & Japan: The Hollow Alliance*. New York: Atherton Press, 1966.

Morishima Gorō. *Kunō suru chū So taishikan* (The embassy in the Soviet Union in agony). Tokyo: Minato Shuppan Gassakusha, 1953.

Morley, James William. *The Japanese Thrust into Siberia.* New York: Columbia University Press, 1957.

Morozov, Col. D. A. *O nikh ne upominalos' v svodkakh* (No mention was made of them in the communiqués). Moscow: Voennoe izdatel'stvo Ministerstva oborony SSSR, 1965.

Moore, Harriet L. *Soviet Far Eastern Policy 1931–1945.* Princeton: Princeton University Press, 1945.

Nanpō Dōhō Gokai (comp.). *Hoppō ryōdo chii. Chishima, Karafuto wo meguru shomondai* (Status of the northern Territories. Various questions concerning the Kuril Islands and Sakhalin). Tokyo, 1962.

————. *Hoppō ryōdo mondai shiryō shu* (Collection of material on the northern territories problem). Revised edition. Tokyo, 1968.

318   THE STRANGE NEUTRALITY

The New York Herald Tribune.

The New York Times.

Nihon Kokusai Seiji Gakkai (comp.). *Nichiro-Nisso kankei no tenkai* (The development of Japanese-Russian-Soviet relations). Tokyo, 1966.

Norbeck, Edward. "Edokko. A Narrative of Japanese Prisoners-of-War in Russia," *Rice University Studies,* vol. 57, No. 1 (Winter 1971).

Platonov, Lieutenant General S. P. and others (eds.). *Vtoraia mirovaia voina 1939–1945 gg. Voenno-istoricheskii ocherk* (The Second World War 1939–1945. A military history). Moscow: Voennoe izdatel'stvo Ministerstva oborony Soiuza SSR, 1958.

Ponomaryov, B., A. Gromyko and V. Khvostov (eds.). *History of Soviet Foreign Policy 1917–1945.* Moscow: Progress Publishers, 1969.

Presseisen, Ernst L. *Germany and Japan. A Study in Totalitarian Diplomacy 1933–1941.* The Hague: Nijhoff, 1958.

Pu Yi, Aison Gioro. *From Emperor to Citizen. The Autobiography of Aisin-Gioro Pu Yi.* Translated by W. J. F. Jenner. Peking: Foreign Language Press, 1964–65. 2 vols.

Rytov, Colonel General of Aviation A. G. *Rytsari piatogo okeana* (Knights of the fifth ocean). Second revised edition. Moscow: Voennoe izdatel'stvo Ministerstva oborony SSSR, 1970.

Sansom, Lady Katharine. *Sir George Sansom and Japan. A Memoir.* Tallahassee: Diplomatic Press, 1972.

Satō Naotake. *Futatsu no Roshia* (The two Russias). Tokyo, 1948.

———. *Kaiko hachijū-nen* (Recollections of eighty years). Tokyo, 1963.

Sherwood, Robert E. *Roosevelt and Hopkins: An Intimate History.* New York: Harper and Brothers, 1948.

Schmidt, Dr. Paul. *Statist auf diplomatischer Bühne 1923–45. Erlebnisse des Chefdolmetschers im Auswärtigen Amt mit den Staatsmännern Europas* (Supernumerary on the diplomatic stage 1923–45. Experiences of the chief interpreter in the Foreign Office with the statesmen of Europe). Bonn: Athenäum, 1950.

Schroeder, Paul W. *The Axis Alliance and Japanese-American Relations 1941.* Ithaca, N.Y.: Cornell University Press, 1958.

Shigemitsu, Mamoru. *Shōwa no dōran* (The Shōwa upheavals). Tokyo, 1952. 2 vols.

Shtemenko, General of the Army Sergei M. *The Soviet Staff at War, 1941–1945.* Moscow: Progress Publishers, 1970.

Snell, John L. (ed.). *The Meaning of Yalta. Big Three Diplomacy and the New Balance of Power.* Baton Rouge: Louisiana State University Press, 1956.

Sommer, Theo. *Deutschland und Japan Zwischen den Mächten 1935–1940. Vom Antikominternpakt zum Dreimächtepakt* (Germany and Japan between the powers 1935–1940. From the Anti-Comintern Pact to the Tripartite Pact). Tübingen: J. C. B. Mohr (Paul Siebeck), 1962.

Stahmer, H. G. *Japans Niederlage—Asiens Sieg. Aufstieg eines Gröszeren Ostasiens* (Japan's defeat—Asia's victory. The rise of a Greater East Asia). Bielefeld: Deutscher Heimat-Verlag, 1952.

Standley, William H. and Arthur A. Ageton. *Admiral Ambassador to Russia.* Chicago: Henry Regnery, 1955.

Stephan, John J. *Sakhalin: A History.* Oxford: Clarendon Press, 1971.

Stimson, Henry L. and Mc George Bundy. *On Active Service in Peace and War.* New York: Harper, 1948.

Storry, Richard. *The Double Patriots.* London: Chatto and Windus, 1957.

Takakura, Shinichiro, *Ocherk istorii Kuril'skikh ostrovov* (Sketch of the history of the Kuril Islands). Tokyo, 1961.

Tamura, Kōsaku. *Sovieto gaikō-shi kenkyū* (Study of the history of Soviet diplomacy). Tokyo, 1965.

Tanaka, Bunichirō. *Nisso koshō-shi* (History of negotiations between Japan and the Soviet Union). Tokyo: Foreign

Office, Europe and Asia Bureau, 1942, "Secret"; declassified and reprinted in 1969.

The Tehran, Yalta & Potsdam Conferences. Documents. Moscow: Progress Publishers, 1969.

Tōgō, Shigenori. *The Cause of Japan.* Translated and edited by Tōgō Fumihiko and Ben Bruce Blakeney. New York: Simon & Schuster, 1956.

————. *Jidai no ichimen* (An aspect of the times). Tokyo, 1952.

Toland, John. *The Rising Sun.* New York: Random House, 1970.

Tolischus, Otto D. *Tokyo Record.* New York: Reynal & Hitchcock, 1943.

Tompkins, Pauline. *American-Russian Relations in the Far East.* New York: Macmillan, 1949.

Trani, Eugene P. *The Treaty of Portsmouth. An Adventure in American Diplomacy.* Lexington: University of Kentucky Press, 1969.

Trukhanovsky, V. G. *British Foreign Policy During World War II 1939–1945.* Moscow: Progress Publishers, 1970.

————. (ed.). *Istoriia mezhdunarodnykh otnoshenii i vneshnei politiki SSSR* (History of the international relations and foreign policy of the U.S.S.R..), vol II (1939–1945). Moscow: Institut mezhdunarodnykh otnoshenii, 1962.

Truman, Harry S. *Memoirs.* Vol I: *Year of Decisions.* Garden City: Doubleday, 1955.

Tuchman, Barbara W. *Stilwell and the American Experience in China, 1911–45.* New York: Macmillan, 1971.

Ulam, Adam B. *Expansion and Coexistence. The History of Soviet Foreign Policy, 1917–67.* New York: Frederick A. Praeger, 1968.

Union of Soviet Socialist Republics, Ministry of Foreign Affairs, *Correspondence between the Chairman of the Council of Ministers of the U.S.S.R. and the Presidents of the U.S.A. and the Prime Ministers of Great Britain during the Great Patriotic War of 1941–1945.* Moscow: Foreign Languages Publishing House, 1957.

————. Ministry of Foreign Trade. *Vneshniaia torgovlia SSSR za 1918–1940 gg. Statisticheskii obzor* (The foreign trade of the U.S.S.R. for the years 1918–1940. A statistical survey). Moscow: Vneshtorgizdat, 1960.

United States, Department of State. *The Conferences at Malta and Yalta.* Washington: U.S. Government Printing Office, 1955.

————. *Foreign Relations of the United States. Diplomatic Papers.* 1941–1945. Washington: U.S. Government Printing Office, 1958–1969.

United States Strategic Bombing Survey. *Japan's Struggle to End the War.* Washington, 1946.

Velikaia otechestvennaia voina Sovetskogo Soiuza 1941–1945 (The Great Patriotic War of the Soviet Union 1941–1945). Edited by P. N. Pospelov and others. Moscow: Voennoe izdatel'stvo Ministerstva oborony SSSR, 1965.

Vishwanathan, Savitri. *Japan's Relations with the U.S.S.R. since 1945. An Indian View.* Tallahassee: Diplomatic Press, 1973.

Vnotchenko, Leonid Nikolaevich. *Pobeda na Dal'nem Vostoke* (Victory in the Far East). Moscow: Voennoe izdatel'stvo Ministerstva oborony SSSR, 1966.

Vorontsov, Vladlen Borisovich. *Tikhookeanskaia politika SShA 1941–1950* (The Pacific policy of the U.S.A. 1941–1950). Moscow: Nauka, 1967.

Wallace, Henry A. with the collaboration of Andrew J. Steiger. *Soviet Asia Mission.* New York: Reynal & Hitchcock, 1946.

Werth, Alexander. *Russia at War, 1941–1945.* New York: Dutton, 1964.

White, John A. *The Diplomacy of the Russo-Japanese War.* Princeton: Princeton University Press, 1964.

Williams, Mary H. (comp.). *Chronology 1941–1945.* Special Study Series, United States Army in World War II. Washington: Department of the Army, 1960.

Yakhontoff, Victor A. *Russia and the Soviet Union in the Far East.* London: George Allen & Unwin, 1932.

Yoshida, Shien. *Hoppō ryōdo* (The northern territories). Tokyo, 1968.

Zakharov, S. E., M. N. Zakharov, V. N. Bagrov, and M. P. Kotykhov. *Tikhookeanskii flot* (The Pacific Fleet). Moscow: Voennoe izdatel'stvo Ministerstva oborony SSSR, 1966.

Index

323